Sadlier

# WE·BELIEVE™

# We Meet Jesus in the Sacraments

## Grade Five

**Sadlier**
A Division of William H. Sadlier, Inc.

*Nihil Obstat*
Reverend John G. Stillmank, S.T.L.
*Censor Librorum*

*Imprimatur*
✠ Most Reverend William H. Bullock
Bishop of Madison
March 6, 2003

The *Nihil Obstat* and *Imprimatur* are official declarations that a book or pamphlet is free of doctrinal or moral error. No implication is contained therein that those who have granted the *Nihil Obstat* and *Imprimatur* agree with the contents, opinions, or statements expressed.

**Acknowledgments**

Excerpts from the English translation of the *Catechism of the Catholic Church* for the United States of America, copyright © 1994, United States Catholic Conference, Inc.—Libreria Editrice Vaticana. English translation of the *Catechism of the Catholic Church: Modifications from the Editio Typica* copyright © 1997, United States Catholic Conference, Inc.—Libreria Editrice Vaticana. Used with permission.

Scripture excerpts are taken from the *New American Bible with Revised New Testament and Psalms* Copyright © 1991, 1986, 1970, Confraternity of Christian Doctrine, Inc., Washington, D.C. Used with permission. All rights reserved. No part of the *New American Bible* may be reproduced by any means without permission in writing from the copyright owner.

Excerpts from the English translation of *Rite of Marriage* © 1969, International Committee on English in the Liturgy, Inc. (ICEL); excerpts from the English translation of *Rite of Baptism for Children* © 1969, ICEL; excerpts from the English translation of *Rite of Holy Week* © 1972, ICEL; excerpts from the English translation of *The Roman Missal* © 1973, ICEL; excerpts from the English translation of *The Liturgy of the Hours* © 1974, ICEL; excerpts from the English translation of *Holy Communion and Worship of the Eucharist Outside Mass* © 1974, ICEL; excerpts from the English translation of *Rite of Penance* © 1974, ICEL; excerpts from the English translation of *Rite of Confirmation* (2nd Edition) © 1975, ICEL; excerpts from the English translation of *Pastoral Care of the Sick* © 1982, ICEL; excerpts from the English translation of *A Book of Prayers* © 1982, ICEL; excerpts from the English translation of *Order of Christian Funerals* © 1985, ICEL; excerpts from the English translation of *Book of Blessings* © 1988, ICEL; excerpt from the *Presidential Prayers for Experimental Use at Mass* © 1986, ICEL. All rights reserved.

Excerpts from *Catholic Household Blessings and Prayers* Copyright © 1988 United States Catholic Conference, Inc. Washington, D.C. Used with permission. All rights reserved. No part of this document may be reproduced in any way without permission in writing from the copyright holder.

English translation of the Glory to the Father, Apostles' Creed, Nicene Creed, Lord's Prayer and *Gloria in Excelsis* by the International Consultation on English Texts. (ICET)

Elena Larsen, *CyberFaith: How Americans Pursue Religious Life Online*, Pew Internet & American Life Project, December 2001.

Excerpt from Internet Family Values poll reprinted with the permission of FamilyEducation.com.

The seven themes of Catholic Social Teaching are taken from *Sharing Catholic Social Teaching, Challenges and Directions: Reflections of the U.S. Catholic Bishops*, USCC, Washington, D.C. © 1998.

"We Believe, We Believe in God," © 1979, North American Liturgy Resources (NALR), 5536 NE Hassalo, Portland, OR 97213. All rights reserved. Used with permission. "Jesus Is with Us," © 1990, OCP Publications, 5536 NE Hassalo, Portland, OR 97213. All rights reserved. Used with permission. "We Are the Body of Christ (Somos el Cuerpo de Cristo)," © 1994, Jaime Cortez. Published by OCP Publications, 5536 NE Hassalo, Portland, OR 97213. All rights reserved. Used with permission. "We Belong to God's Family," © 1992, OCP Publications, 5536 NE Hassalo, Portland, OR 97213. All rights reserved. Used with permission. "Saints of God," (Enter the Journey Collection). © 2000, Mark Friedman and Janet Vogt. Published by OCP Publications, 5536 NE Hassalo, Portland, OR 97213. All rights reserved. Used with permission. "Envía Tu Espíritu," © 1988, Bob Hurd. Published by OCP Publications, 5536 NE Hassalo, Portland, OR 97213. All rights reserved. Used with permission. "I Am the Bread of Life," Suzanne Toolan, RSM, © 1970, G.I.A. Publications, Inc. All rights reserved. Used with permission. "Calling the Children," © 1991, Christopher Walker and Matthew Wooten. Published by OCP Publications, 5536 NE Hassalo, Portland, OR 97213. All rights reserved. Used with permission. "With Open Hands," © 1999, Robert F. O'Connor, S.J. Published by OCP Publications, 5536 NE Hassalo, Portland, OR 97213. All rights reserved. Used with permission. "Psalm 23: The Lord Is My Shepherd," © 2000, Carey Landry. Published by OCP Publications, 5536 NE Hassalo, Portland, OR 97213. All rights reserved. Used with permission. The English translation of the psalm response for Psalm 23 from *Lectionary for Mass* © 1969, 1981, 1997, International Committee on English in the Liturgy, Inc. (ICEL) All rights reserved. "Canticle of Mary," © 1993, Owen Alstott and Bernadette Farrell. Published by OCP Publications, 5536 NE Hassalo, Portland, OR 97213. All rights reserved. Used with permission. "Sign Us with Ashes," (Enter the Journey Collection). © 2000, Mark Friedman and Janet Vogt. Published by OCP Publications, 5536 NE Hassalo, Portland, OR 97213. All rights reserved. Used with permission. "God's Greatest Gift," © 1999, Owen Alstott. Published by OCP Publications, 5536 NE Hassalo, Portland, OR 97213. All rights reserved. Used with permission. "Come, Follow Me," © 1992, Barbara Bridge. Published by OCP Publications, 5536 NE Hassalo, Portland, OR 97213. All rights reserved. Used with permission. "Holy Mary," (Enter the Journey Collection). © 2000, Mark Friedman and Janet Vogt. Published by OCP Publications, 5536 NE Hassalo, Portland, OR 97213. All rights reserved. Used with permission.

William H. Sadlier, Inc.
9 Pine Street
New York, NY 10005-1002

ISBN: 0-8215-5505-7
23456789/07 06 05 04 03

The Ad Hoc Committee to Oversee the Use of the Catechism,
United States Conference of Catholic Bishops,
has found this catechetical text, copyright 2004,
to be in conformity with the *Catechism of the Catholic Church*.

The Sadlier *We Believe* Program was developed by nationally recognized experts in catechesis, curriculum, and child development. These teachers of the faith and practitioners helped us to frame every lesson to be age-appropriate and appealing. In addition, a team including respected catechetical, liturgical, pastoral, and theological experts shared their insights and inspired the development of the program.

The Program is truly based on the wisdom of the community, including:

Gerard F. Baumbach, Ed.D.
Executive Vice President and Publisher

Carole M. Eipers, D.Min.
Director of Catechetics

## Catechetical and Liturgical Consultants

Reverend Monsignor John F. Barry
Pastor, American Martyrs Parish
Manhattan Beach, CA

Sister Linda Gaupin, CDP, Ph.D.
Director of Religious Education
Diocese of Orlando

Mary Jo Tully
Chancellor, Archdiocese of Portland

Reverend Monsignor John M. Unger
Assoc. Superintendent for Religious Education
Archdiocese of St. Louis

## Curriculum and Child Development Consultants

Brother Robert R. Bimonte, FSC
Former Superintendent of Catholic Education
Diocese of Buffalo

Gini Shimabukuro, Ed.D.
Associate Director/Associate Professor
Institute for Catholic Educational Leadership
School of Education, University of
San Francisco

## Catholic Social Teaching Consultants

John Carr
Secretary, Department of Social Development
and World Peace, USCCB

Joan Rosenhauer
Coordinator, Special Projects
Department of Social Development and
World Peace, USCCB

## Inculturation Consultants

Reverend Allan Figueroa Deck, SJ, Ph.D.
Executive Director, Loyola Institute for
Spirituality, Orange, CA

Kirk Gaddy
Principal, St. Katharine School
Baltimore, MD

Reverend Nguyễn Việt Hưng
Vietnamese Catechetical Committee

Dulce M. Jiménez-Abreu
Director of Spanish Programs
William H. Sadlier, Inc.

# Contents

# UNIT 2 Confirmation and Eucharist Complete Our Initiation

# We·Believe

The *We Believe* program will help us to

**learn     share** and **live our**
**celebrate           Catholic faith.**

Throughout the year we will hear about many saints and holy people.

Saint Alexius

Saint Andrew Kim Taegon

Saint Anthony Claret

Saint Barbara

Saint Dominic

Saint Elizabeth Ann Seton

Saint John Bosco

Saint Joseph

Saint Josephine Bakhita

Blessed Kateri Tekakwitha

Martyrs of Vietnam

Saint Margaret of Scotland

Mary, Mother of God

Our Lady of Guadalupe

Saint Padre Pio

Pope Gregory XIII

Blessed Pope Pius IX

Pope John Paul II

Together, let us grow as a community of faith.

# Welcome!

## WE GATHER

✝ **Leader:** Welcome, everyone, to Grade 5 *We Believe*. As we begin each chapter, we gather in prayer. We pray to God together. Sometimes, we will read from Scripture; other times we will say the prayers of the Church or sing a song of thanks and praise to God.

Today, let us sing the *We Believe* song!

## 🎵 We Believe, We Believe in God

Refrain:

We believe in God;
We believe, we believe in Jesus;
We believe in the Spirit who gives us life.
We believe, we believe in God.

We believe in the Holy Spirit,
Who renews the face of the earth.
We believe we are part of a living Church,
And forever we will live with God.

(Refrain)

We also focus on life.

 means it's time to

think about
talk about
act out
draw about
write about

**Life**

at school
at home
in our parish
in our world
in our neighborhood

Talk about your life right now. What groups, teams, or clubs do you belong to?

Why do you like being a part of these groups?

What does belonging to these groups tell other people about you?

When we see **We Believe** we learn more about our Catholic faith.

## Each day we learn more about God.

In each chapter, we find four main faith statements. They focus us on what we will be learning.

### WE BELIEVE

We learn about:

- the Blessed Trinity—God the Father, God the Son, and God the Holy Spirit
- Jesus, the Son of God, who became one of us
- the Church and its history and teachings
- the Mass and the sacraments
- our call to be a disciple of Jesus.

**UNIT 1** **Jesus Christ Shares His Life with Us**
"As the Father loves me, so I also love you."
(John 15:9)

 **UNIT 2** **Confirmation and Eucharist Complete Our Initiation**
"Do this in memory of me." (Luke 22:19)

 **UNIT 3** **The Sacraments of Healing Restore Us**
"Is anyone among you suffering? He should pray. Is anyone in good spirits? He should sing praise." (James 5:13)

 **UNIT 4** **We Love and Serve as Jesus Did**
"So faith, hope, love remain, these three; but the greatest of these is love." (1 Corinthians 13:13)

> A major theme in your *We Believe* textbook this year is learning more about the seven sacraments of the Catholic Church. Your book is divided into four units.

## Watch for these special signs:

Whenever we see ✝ we make the sign of the cross. We pray and begin our day's lesson.

📖 is an open Bible. When we see it, or a reference like this (John 13:34), we hear the word of God. We hear about God and his people. We hear about Jesus and the Holy Spirit.

When we see 🏃 we do an activity. We might:

- talk together
- write a story
- draw a picture
- act out a story or situation
- imagine ourselves doing something
- sing a song together, or make up one
- work together on a special project.

There are all kinds of activities! We might see 🏃 in any part of our day's lesson. Be on the lookout!

Can you guess what 🎵 means? That's right, it means it is time to sing, or listen to music. We sing songs we know, make up our own, and sing along with those in our *We Believe* music program.

When we see  we review the meanings of important words we have learned in the day's lesson.

### As Catholics...

Here we discover something special about our faith. We reflect on what we have discovered and try to make it a part of our life. Don't forget to read it!

## WE RESPOND

We can respond by:

- thinking about ways our faith affects the things we say and do

- sharing our thoughts and feelings

- praying to God.

Then in our home, neighborhood, school, parish, and world, we say and do the things that show love for God and others.

When we see **We Respond** we reflect and act on what we have learned about God and our Catholic faith.

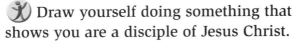 Draw yourself doing something that shows you are a disciple of Jesus Christ.

We are so happy you are with us!

14

## Review

Here we check to see what we have learned in this chapter.

## Reflect & Pray

We take a few moments to think about our faith and to pray.

## Key Words

We review the meanings of important words from the chapter.

---

Grade 5
Chapter 23

## Review

**Circle the letter of the correct answer.**

1. _____ are baptized members of the Church who share in the mission to bring the good news of Christ to the world.

   a. Laypeople   b. Vows   c. Vocations

2. _____ are men and women who belong to communities in which they dedicate their lives to the service of God and the Church.

   a. Christian faithful   b. Laity   c. Religious

3. _____ are an important part of finding out what it means to be faithful to Christ and one another.

   a. Vocations   b. Laity   c. Friendships

4. The _____ is Christ's priestly mission in which all those who are baptized share.

   a. Laypeople   b. ordained priesthood   c. priesthood of the faithful

**Short Answers**

5. Name three things that help us to live out the priesthood of the faithful.

6. As Christians, what is our common vocation?

7. Name three ways that laypeople can be active and serve in their parish community.

8. What are the three vows, or promises, that religious sisters, brothers, and priests might make to God?

**Write a sentence to answer the question.**

9–10. How do friendships prepare us for future vocations?

**ASSESSMENT** How do the Christian faithful, religious, and ordained ministers serve God and the Church? Design a brochure that illustrates ways the Christian faithful, religious, and ordained ministers serve God and the Church.

200

---

## We Respond in Faith

### Reflect & Pray

Jesus, you said that your kingdom is already here and that it is growing. To help spread your kingdom, we ask that you

**Key Words**
priesthood of the faithful (p. 269)
laypeople (p. 268)
religious (p. 269)

### Remember

- Jesus calls the baptized to serve him in the priesthood of the faithful.
- The laity share in the mission to bring the good news of Christ to the world.
- Women and men in religious life serve Christ, their communities, and the whole Church.
- Friendships prepare us for future vocations.

### OUR CATHOLIC LIFE

**Pastoral Administrators**

Some religious sisters and brothers as well as laypeople serve as pastoral administrators. When a parish does not have a priest to serve the people, the bishop of the diocese appoints a pastoral administrator to serve the parish. This person is responsible for parish life and business. She or he makes sure the parish community is being offered religious education, worship, and social outreach programs. The administrator often leads the faith community in prayer services and community outreach. The bishop assigns a priest to celebrate the Mass and other sacraments with the parish, or the community joins with another parish for the celebration of the sacraments.

---

**ASSESSMENT** We do a chapter activity in which we show that we have discovered more about our Catholic faith.

## OUR CATHOLIC LIFE

Here we read an interesting story about the ways people make the world better by living out their Catholic faith.

## Remember

We recall the four main faith statements of the chapter.

15

# SHARING FAITH
## with My Family

At the end of each chapter, you will bring a page like this home to your family. It will offer fun activities that the whole family can enjoy!

## Sharing What I Learned

Discuss the following with your family.

**WE GATHER**

**WE BELIEVE**

**WE RESPOND**

## A Family Prayer

Lead your family in prayer.

People who love us make love grow. Thank you, God, for our family.

People who love us make love grow. Thank you, God, for all the friends of our family.

Most of all, thank you, God, for loving us!

### We Believe
#### Family Contract

As a **We Believe** family, this year we promise to

_____

_____

Names

_____

_____

_____

WE MEET JESUS IN THE SACRAMENTS

Look here for connections to the Web and to the Catechism.

Visit Sadlier's

**www.WeBelieveweb.com**

**Connect to the Catechism of the Catholic Church**
For adult background and reflection, Catechism paragraph references are given here.

# Jesus Christ Shares His Life with Us

# SHARING FAITH as a Family

## Note the Quote

"The family that prays together stays together."

**Servant of God Father Patrick Peyton, CSC**
*(Slogan for Family Rosary)*

## Where Does God Fit in Your Family?

How would you assess the presence of God in your home? When was the last time you, or someone in your family, stopped to marvel at something? It might be the beauty of the sunlight spilling across the breakfast table or the smile of a small child. It isn't necessary to travel to exotic places to experience the wonders of God's creation.

Our busy lives can dull our ability to be thankful. In family life, it is common to take those around us for granted. Yet everyone has good qualities and specific skills. Concentrating on the positive traits of our family members helps us to be more thankful for them. Becoming mindful of all of our blessings helps us to be aware of God's continual presence in our lives.

Prayer is our lifeline to God's continual presence in our lives. Prayer does not need to be lengthy or formalized. It can become a part of each day, especially as we become more attentive to those glimpses of grace that happen all the time.

## From the Catechism

**"Jesus gives us the example of holiness in the daily life of family and work."**
*(Catechism of the Catholic Church, 564)*

## What Your Child Will Learn in Unit 1

Grade 5 of the *We Believe* program focuses on the seven sacraments of the Catholic Church. Unit 1 begins with Jesus Christ. The children will recognize Jesus as the Son of God who shows us God's love. The children will become more aware that they proclaim the good news of Christ by what they say and do. The liturgy is presented as a way we celebrate Christ's Paschal Mystery—his passion, death, Resurrection from the dead, and Ascension into heaven. It is by his Paschal Mystery that Jesus saves us from sin and gives us new life. The children recognize Jesus' presence in the Church, and their call to give witness and serve as Jesus did is explained. Unit 1 also focuses on the sacrament of Baptism. As the foundation of Christian life, this sacrament initiates us into the Church, the Body of Christ, the people of God. The unit concludes with a presentation of the Rite of Baptism and includes the roles of parents and godparents in Baptism.

## Plan & Preview

▶ Pieces of cardboard or stiff paper could be used for the *We Believe* Sacrament Trading Cards. The front and back of the cards can be glued to the board to form a sturdy trading card.

▶ Your child will be asking you to help him or her assemble some scrapbook items that focus on the sacrament of Baptism. You might want to obtain a scrapbook for use in this Sacraments Scrapbook activity (*Chapter 4*).

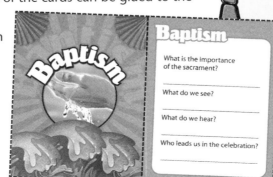

## Meditation Exercise

Find a quiet place in your home, preferably a favorite sofa or chair. Rest comfortably. Begin to relax by closing your eyes. Now take a few deep breaths. Breathe in and hold for three seconds, then slowly breathe out. As you are breathing, take in the positive spirit of God's love and breathe out all the negatives in your life.

End with your body relaxed and your eyes closed. Say this prayer quietly to yourself.

> Glory to the Father,
> and to the Son,
> and to the Holy Spirit:
> as it was in the beginning,
> is now, and will be for
> ever.
>
> Amen.

# Jesus Shares God's Life with Us

## WE GATHER

✝ **Leader:** Blessed are you, Lord, God of tenderness and compassion, rich in kindness and faithfulness.

(Cf. Exodus 34:6)

**All:** Now and for ever.

**Leader:** Father, you sent your Son to us so that we could know your love and feel your mercy. May all who follow Christ be a sign of your love.

**Reader:** A reading from the holy Gospel according to Matthew

"Jesus went around to all the towns and villages, teaching in their synagogues, proclaiming the gospel of the kingdom, and curing every disease and illness."

(Matthew 9:35)

The Gospel of the Lord.

**All:** Praise to you, Lord Jesus Christ.

♫ **Jesus Is with Us**

Refrain:

Jesus is with us today,
beside us to guide us today.
Jesus teaches us, Jesus heals us,
for we are his Church;
we are his chosen;
we are the children of God.

Jesus teaches us to love one another,
to care for our brothers and
sisters in need.
For when we show kindness
to others,
we are God's children indeed.

(Refrain)

☀ How do you show people what is important to you?

## WE BELIEVE
### Jesus is the Son of God.

In the New Testament we read about John the Baptist. John was Jesus' cousin. John talked to people about repentance and asked them to change their lives. He was preparing the people for the Messiah, the Anointed One. *Messiah* is another word for "Christ." Jesus Christ is the Anointed One who would bring new life.

John baptized people as a sign of their desire to change. John said, "I am baptizing you with water, for repentance, but the one who is coming after me is mightier than I. I am not worthy to carry his sandals. He will baptize you with the holy Spirit and fire" (Matthew 3:11).

Jesus had grown up in Nazareth with Mary, his mother, Joseph, his foster father and many relatives and friends. When Jesus was about thirty, he went to the Jordan River and asked John to baptize

him. But John said to Jesus, "I need to be baptized by you, and yet you are coming to me?" (Matthew 3:14). However, Jesus convinced John to baptize him. As Jesus came up from the water, the heavens opened. The Holy Spirit in the form of a dove descended upon Jesus, and a voice from the heavens said, "This is my beloved Son, with whom I am well pleased" (Matthew 3:17).

Jesus Christ is the Son of God. He is the second Person of the Blessed Trinity who became man. The **Blessed Trinity** is the three Persons in one God: God the Father, God the Son, and God the Holy Spirit.

After his baptism Jesus returned to Nazareth. In the synagogue he read the following passage from the prophet Isaiah:

**Blessed Trinity** (p. 266)

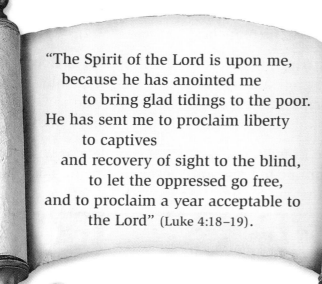

"The Spirit of the Lord is upon me,
    because he has anointed me
        to bring glad tidings to the poor.
He has sent me to proclaim liberty
        to captives
    and recovery of sight to the blind,
        to let the oppressed go free,
and to proclaim a year acceptable to
        the Lord" (Luke 4:18–19).

What can you do today to follow Jesus' example and live a life acceptable to the Lord?

_____

_____

## Jesus shows us God's love.

In his ministry Jesus brought people closer to God his Father. Jesus:

- taught about the love of God his Father

- welcomed all people into his life

- fed the hungry and shared meals with people whom others ignored

- forgave the sins of those who were truly sorry

- healed those who were sick.

In the gospels we read that Jesus traveled from town to town. Once a crowd was following Jesus while he taught. He said, "My heart is moved with pity for the crowd, because they have been with me now for three days and have nothing to eat" (Mark 8:2). Jesus then fed the people. Jesus' concern for them shows us that God cares for us.

Jesus was fair to sinners, strangers, those who were ignored, and those who were poor. Jesus' treatment of people shows that God is just.

A religious leader once criticized Jesus for forgiving a sinner. Jesus told the leader that the one who is forgiven more loves more.

Jesus' actions also show us that God is merciful.

Luke 18:35–43

Once a blind beggar was trying to get Jesus' attention. People told the man to be quiet, but he would not. Jesus stopped to talk to him, the man said, "Lord, please let me see." Jesus then said to the man, "Have sight; your faith has saved you" (Luke 18:41, 42). Immediately the man could see.

In all these ways Jesus showed others God's love. In Jesus we see a God who cares for us, has mercy on us, and is just to everyone.

Read the following situation. In groups role-play what you could do as followers of Jesus.

You need a passing grade on the math final exam or you will go to summer school. Your friend Roberto is an "A" student. He is sitting next to you during the test.

## Jesus invites people to follow him.

Jesus invited people to follow him. These people became his disciples. Jesus wanted them to live as he did. He taught them to obey God's law and to rely on God, not money, power, or possessions. He invited all people to trust in God and seek God's forgiveness. This was **Jesus' mission**, to share the life of God with all people and to save them from sin.

Jesus called people to change the way they lived and to love God and others. He told them, "The kingdom of God is at hand. Repent, and believe in the gospel" (Mark 1:15). The **Kingdom of God** is the power of God's love active in our lives and in the world. The Kingdom of God is here among us through the life and love of Jesus.

In his teaching Jesus used parables, short stories about everyday life. In his parables, he used examples from nature, farming, feasts, and everyday work to describe the Kingdom of God.

Matthew 13:31–32

Jesus compared the Kingdom of God to a mustard seed. "It is the smallest of all the seeds, yet when full-grown it is the largest of plants. It becomes a large bush, and the 'birds of the sky come and dwell in its branches'" (Matthew 13:32).

Like the mustard seed, the Kingdom of God can grow and spread. Jesus encouraged his disciples to respond to God's love and to spread the message of the Kingdom of God.

The Kingdom of God is not complete. It will continue to grow until Jesus returns in glory at the end of time.

If you were to explain God's Kingdom, what image would you use? The Kingdom of God is like

### Jesus' disciples continue his work.

From among his disciples Jesus chose twelve men to be his apostles. The **apostles** shared in Jesus' mission in a special way. They would continue Jesus' saving work when Jesus returned to his Father. Jesus told the apostles that the Holy Spirit would come to them and help them remember all that he had said and done.

After his Resurrection, Jesus told his apostles, "All power in heaven and on earth has been given to me. Go, therefore, and make disciples of all nations, baptizing them in the name of the Father, and of the Son, and of the holy Spirit, teaching them to observe all that I have commanded you" (Matthew 28:18–20).

When the Holy Spirit came at Pentecost, the apostles were strengthened. They went out to share the good news of Jesus Christ.

This was the beginning of the Church. The word *church* means "a group that is called together." The **Church** is all those who believe in Jesus Christ, have been baptized in him, and follow his teachings.

With Christ as its head, the Church is the seed of the Kingdom of God on earth. Through the Church, the power of God's life in the world increases. The Kingdom of God grows when we:

- have faith in Jesus Christ and share our belief

- live as Jesus did and follow God's will for us

- seek to build a better community, a more just nation, and a peaceful world.

### WE RESPOND

With a partner discuss some signs of God's Kingdom. Then act out one way you can help God's Kingdom to grow.

### As Catholics...

"The names of the twelve apostles are these: first, Simon called Peter, and his brother Andrew; James, the son of Zebedee, and his brother John; Philip and Bartholomew, Thomas and Matthew the tax collector; James, the son of Alphaeus, and Thaddeus; Simon the Cananean, and Judas Iscariot who betrayed him." (Matthew 10:2–4)

How can you find out about the apostles?

**Key Words**

Jesus' mission (p. 267)

Kingdom of God (p. 267)

apostles (p. 266)

Church (p. 266)

**Write True or False for the following sentences.**
**Then change the false sentences to make them true.**

1. _____ The Blessed Trinity is the three Persons in one God: God the Father, God the Son, and God the Holy Spirit.

_____

_____

2. _____ Jesus encouraged his followers to respond to God's love and to spread the message of the Kingdom of God.

_____

_____

3. _____ In Jesus, we see a God who cares for us, has mercy on us, and is just to everyone.

_____

_____

4. _____ Jesus was baptized by Joseph in the Jordan River.

_____

_____

**Write the letter of the definition that matches each term.**

5. _____ Jesus' mission

6. _____ apostles

7. _____ Kingdom of God

8. _____ Church

a. all those who believe in Jesus Christ, have been baptized in him, and follow his teachings

b. the power of God's love active in our lives and in the world

c. short stories about everyday life

d. to share the life of God with all people and to save them from sin

e. men chosen by Jesus to share in his mission in a special way

**Write a sentence to answer the question.**

**9–10.** What are some ways we can help to spread the Kingdom of God?

_____

_____

**ASSESSMENT**

Use newspapers, magazines, television, or the Internet to gather information about people who are continuing Jesus' ministry. Write a summary of your findings and present it to the class.

# We Respond in Faith

## Reflect & Pray

Jesus said, "Come to me, all you who labor and are burdened, and I will give you rest" (Matthew 11:28).

Dear Jesus, sometimes I really need your help, especially when

_____

Give me the courage to _____

_____

Amen.

**Key Words**

Blessed Trinity (p. 267)
Jesus' mission (p. 268)
Kingdom of God (p. 268)
apostles (p. 267)
Church (p. 267)

## Remember

- Jesus is the Son of God.
- Jesus shows us God's love.
- Jesus invites people to follow him.
- Jesus' disciples continue his work.

## OUR CATHOLIC LIFE

### Saint Elizabeth Ann Seton

Saint Elizabeth Ann Seton was born in New York in 1775. Elizabeth loved to read. She especially enjoyed reading the Bible and learning about God's great love for his people. She married, had children, and was very happy.

After Elizabeth's husband died, she became a member of the Catholic Church and began educating children about the gospel. She established the Sisters of Charity in the United States. This community of religious women worked throughout the country to operate schools and homes for children without families.

Saint Elizabeth Ann Seton is the first American-born person to be named a saint, or canonized. We celebrate her feast day on January 4.

# SHARING FAITH
## with My Family

## Sharing What I Learned

Discuss the following with your family:

- John the Baptist and Jesus at the Jordan River
- Jesus' disciples and apostles
- Jesus' mission
- the Kingdom of God.

## Family Faith Checklist

Ask your family to complete the Family Faith Checklist. Share your experiences.

### Our Family

Jesus lived his life by being compassionate, merciful, and just to all people. How can you live as Jesus did?

☐ At home:

_____

☐ At school/work:

_____

☐ In the parish:

_____

☐ In the community:

_____

"This is my beloved Son, with whom I am well pleased."
(Matthew 3:17)

Visit Sadlier's

**www.WeBelieveweb.com**

**Connect to the Catechism**
For adult background and reflection, see paragraphs 535, 543, 546, and 737.

# Jesus Shares His Mission with the Church

## WE GATHER

✝ **Leader:** Jesus is with us. He said, "For where two or three are gathered together in my name, there am I in the midst of them" (Matthew 18:20).

**All:** Jesus be with us as we pray in your name.

**Reader:** A reading from the holy Gospel according to Matthew

**All:** Glory to you, Lord.

**Reader 1:** "Go, therefore, and make disciples of all nations, baptizing them in the name of the Father, and of the Son, and of the holy Spirit, teaching them to observe all that I have commanded you. And behold, I am with you always, until the end of the age." (Matthew 28:19–20)

The Gospel of the Lord.

**All:** Praise to you, Lord Jesus Christ.

**Leader:** Jesus, we are gathered today in your name. Help us share your love and be with us now and forever.

**All:** Amen.

☀ Think of a family member or friend with whom you are very close. How would you describe that relationship?

BE A VOLUNTEER!

CATHOLIC RELIEF SERVICES

27

## WE BELIEVE

### We are joined to Jesus Christ and to one another.

Jesus often spoke of his relationship with God his Father. He once said that he was the vine and his Father was the vine grower. Jesus also told his disciples "Just as a branch cannot bear fruit on its own unless it remains on the vine, so neither can you unless you remain in me. I am the vine, you are the branches. Whoever remains in me and I in him will bear much fruit, because without me you can do nothing" (John 15:4–5).

Jesus Christ is the vine; we are the branches. We are joined to Jesus and to one another. As members of the Church, we need Jesus so that we can grow in faith and love.

The work, or mission, of the Church is to share the good news of Christ and to spread the Kingdom of God. We are the Church. This is the good news that we share:

- God loves and cares for all people because we are created in his image and likeness.

- God so loved the world that he sent his only Son to show us how to live and to save us from sin.

- Jesus shares the life of God with us and gives us the hope of life forever with God.

- All people are invited to believe in Jesus and to be baptized in the faith of the Church.

Write one way that you see the Church sharing the good news of Christ.

_____

_____

_____

### We proclaim the good news of Christ by what we say and do.

We all share in the mission of the Church. We are called to proclaim the good news of Christ by what we say and do. This is known as **evangelization**. Evangelization takes place in our everyday lives. We evangelize those who have not yet heard the message of Jesus Christ. We also evangelize those who have heard the message but need encouragement to live out the gift of faith.

Proclaiming the good news is very important. People need to hear the message of Jesus Christ in order to believe it. So we tell others about the wonderful things that Christ has done. We encourage them to find out more about his great love.

We also proclaim the good news of Jesus Christ through personal and communal prayer. We pray by listening and talking to God with our minds and hearts. The **liturgy** is the official public prayer of the Church. In the liturgy we gather as a community joined to Christ to celebrate what we believe.

Teaching the history and beliefs of the Church is an important part of evangelization. We are involved in this right now as we learn more about Jesus and the Church. As we learn, we grow in faith and can share what we believe. We can tell others what it means to be a disciple of Jesus.

People from all parts of the world can work together to spread the message of Jesus Christ. Each of us has something to share and bring to the Church and to the world.

We can proclaim the good news by giving witness to Christ. We give witness when we speak and act based upon the good news. We give witness when we follow Jesus' example of loving God and others. We give witness when we work for justice and peace. We can help others to see God's love active in their lives and in the world.

Name some people you know who proclaim the good news of Jesus Christ. In what ways do they do this? How can you proclaim the good news this week?

Key Word
**evangelization** (p. 268)
**liturgy** (p. 332)

## In the liturgy we celebrate Christ's Paschal Mystery.

In the liturgy we gather to praise and worship God, Father, Son, and Holy Spirit. We proclaim the good news of Jesus Christ and celebrate his Paschal Mystery. The **Paschal Mystery** is Christ's passion, death, Resurrection from the dead, and Ascension into heaven. By his Paschal Mystery Jesus saves us from sin and gives us life.

The liturgy includes the celebration of the Eucharist, also called the Mass, and the other sacraments. It includes prayers called the Liturgy of the Hours. The Church prays the Liturgy of the Hours at different times during the day. In these prayers we celebrate God's work in creation and in our lives.

The community of faith gathers on Sundays for the celebration of the Mass. In this gathering our relationship with Christ and one another is strengthened.

We read in the New Testament that "we, though many, are one body in Christ and individually parts of one another" (Romans 12:5). We are joined to Christ who "is the head of the body, the church" (Colossians 1:18).

So we call the Church the Body of Christ. The Body of Christ is all the members of the Church, with Christ as its head. The whole Body of Christ celebrates the liturgy.

## As Catholics...

Catholic social teaching reminds us to love and care for others as Jesus did. This teaching is the Church's way of putting the good news of Christ into action.

Catholic social teaching is based on the belief that every person has human dignity. Human dignity is the value and worth that come from being created in God's image and likeness. The seven themes of Catholic social teaching are found on page 265.

How does your parish promote justice and peace

 **Somos el Cuerpo de Cristo/ We Are the Body of Christ**

Somos el cuerpo de Cristo.
*We are the body of Christ.*
Traemos su santo mensaje.
*We come to bring the good news to the world.*

## When we serve others we give witness to Christ.

When we serve others we show our love and care for them. Jesus is our greatest example of service. He cared for the needs of others, especially those who were neglected. He welcomed them and made sure that they had what they needed. Jesus prayed for those in need, visited those who were sick, and provided food for the hungry.

Matthew 25:31–40

Jesus tells us that when we care for others, we are serving him, too. He tells us that when he comes again in glory at the end of time, we will be judged by the way we have treated others. Jesus Christ coming at the end of time to judge all people is called the last judgment. At that time all people will be brought before him. He will say to those who acted justly, "For I was hungry and you gave me food, I was thirsty and you gave me drink, a stranger and you welcomed me, naked and you clothed me, ill and you cared for me, in prison and you visited me" (Matthew 25:35–36).

Then those who were just will ask him when they had cared for him. And he will say, "Amen, I say to you, whatever you did for one of these least brothers of mine, you did for me" (Matthew 25:40).

We give witness to Jesus when we perform the Works of Mercy. The Works of Mercy are acts of love that help us care for the needs of others. The Corporal Works of Mercy deal with the physical and material needs of others. The Spiritual Works of Mercy deal with the needs of people's hearts, minds, and souls. The Works of Mercy are listed on page 264.

**Key Words**

Paschal Mystery (p. 269)

last judgment (p. 268)

Corporal Works of Mercy (p. 267)

Spiritual Works of Mercy (p. 269)

## WE RESPOND

Design a thirty-second TV commercial to get people interested in the good news of Jesus Christ. Use this storyboard to plan your commercial.

00:10          00:20          00:30

What work of mercy can you ask your family to perform this week?

**Circle the letter of the correct answer.**

1. We are joined to Jesus Christ and one another. He is the vine, and we are the _____.

   **a.** vine grower   **b.** fruit   **c.** branches

2. Forgiving those who hurt us is an example of a _____ Work of Mercy.

   **a.** Corporal   **b.** Spiritual   **c.** Personal

3. The _____ of the Church is to share the good news of Christ and to spread the Kingdom of God.

   **a.** mission   **b.** kingdom   **c.** liturgy

4. When we _____ others, we give witness to Christ.

   **a.** serve   **b.** celebrate   **c.** liturgy

**Choose a word(s) from the box to complete each sentence.**

| Spiritual | liturgy | Paschal Mystery | Corporal | evangelization |
|---|---|---|---|---|

5. The _____ Works of Mercy deal with the physical and material needs of others.

6. The _____ refers to Christ's passion, death, Resurrection from the dead, and Ascension into heaven.

7. _____ is proclaiming the good news of Jesus Christ by what we say and do.

8. The _____ is the official public prayer of the Church.

**Write a sentence to answer the question.**

9–10. How does the Church continue Jesus' mission?

_____

_____

ASSESSMENT

Design a screen saver for your school or parish Web site that promotes evangelization. Use images of things that people can say and do to proclaim the good news and spread the Kingdom of God. Include a caption for each image. Share your screen saver idea with your class or family.

# We Respond in Faith

## Reflect & Pray

Dear Father, I am your child. Give me the strength and courage to live my life as Jesus lived his.

Help me this week to _____

_____

**Key Words**

evangelization (p. 268)
liturgy (p. 268)
Paschal Mystery (p. 269)
last judgment (p. 268)
Corporal Works
of Mercy (p. 267)
Spiritual Works
of Mercy (p. 269)

## Remember

- We are joined to Jesus Christ and to one another.

- We proclaim the good news of Christ by what we say and do.

- In the liturgy we celebrate Christ's Paschal Mystery.

- When we serve others we give witness to Christ.

## OUR CATHOLIC LIFE

### Jesuit Volunteer Corps

The Jesuit Volunteer Corps (JVC) are young people who volunteer their time to help people in need. JVC volunteers often delay their college education or possible job offers to serve others. Since 1956, more than 7,000 volunteers have served the homeless, the unemployed, refugees, people with AIDS, the elderly, and other people who need help. In fact, JVC has become the largest Catholic lay volunteer program in the United States.

These volunteers will tell you that living out this commitment to Catholic social teaching can be a most rewarding experience.

# SHARING FAITH
## with My Family

## Sharing What I Learned

Discuss the following with your family:

- the vine and the branches
- evangelization
- the Paschal Mystery and the liturgy
- the Works of Mercy.

## Family Faith Checklist

Ask your family to complete the Family Faith Checklist. Share your experiences.

### Our Family

Through service to others, the Church continues Jesus' mission. How can you serve others?

☐ At home:

_____

☐ At school/work:

_____

☐ In the parish:

_____

☐ In the community:

_____

"Worship the LORD with cries of gladness;
come before him with joyful song."
(Psalm 100:2)

Visit Sadlier's

www.WeBelieveweb.com

**Connect to the Catechism**
For adult background and reflection,
see paragraphs 787, 863, 1067, and 2449.

## WE GATHER

✝ **Leader:** Let us remember that Jesus is present in our lives.

**Reader:** A reading from the holy Gospel according to John

"As the Father loves me, so I also love you. Remain in my love. If you keep my commandments, you will remain in my love, just as I have kept my Father's commandments and remain in his love.

I have told you this so that my joy might be in you and your joy might be complete. This is my commandment: love one another as I love you."
(John 15:9–12)

The Gospel of the Lord.

**All:** Praise to you, Lord Jesus Christ.

**Leader:** As we pray together, let us praise and thank Jesus Christ who is with us always.

**All:** Jesus, Good Shepherd,
thanks and praise to you.

Jesus, Lamb of God,
thanks and praise to you.

Jesus, Bread of life and love,
thanks and praise to you.

Jesus, Source of strength and joy,
thanks and praise to you.

Thank you, Jesus, for your life in mine. Help me live your good news of love and peace.

Amen.

☀ What are some signs that you see every day? Why are they important to you?

## Jesus gave the Church seven sacraments.

A sign stands for or tells us about something. A sign can be something that we see, such as a stop sign. A sign can be something that we do, such as shaking hands or hugging someone. An event or a person can also be a sign. The world is filled with signs of God's love. But Jesus Christ is the greatest sign of God's love. Everything that Jesus said or did pointed to God's love for us. Jesus treated all people fairly. He welcomed people whom others neglected. He fed those who were hungry and he forgave sinners. Jesus is the greatest sign of God the Father's love because he is the Son of God.

Talk about some of the signs of God's love and presence in the world.

The Holy Spirit helps us to be signs of Jesus. By continuing Jesus' work, the Church itself is a sign of God's love and care.

The Church has seven celebrations that are special signs of God's love and presence. We call these special signs sacraments. Jesus instituted, or began, the sacraments so that his saving work would continue for all time.

**THE SEVEN SACRAMENTS**

Baptism

Confirmation

Eucharist

Penance and Reconciliation

Anointing of the Sick

Holy Orders

Matrimony

The sacraments are different from all other signs. Sacraments truly bring about what they represent. For example, in Baptism we not only celebrate being children of God, we actually become children of God. This is why we say that a **sacrament** is an effective sign given to us by Jesus through which we share in God's life.

The gift of sharing in God's life that we receive in the sacraments is **sanctifying grace**. This grace helps us to trust and believe in God. It strengthens us to live as Jesus did.

The sacraments are the most important celebrations of the Church. The sacraments join Catholics all over the world with Jesus and with one another. They unite us as the Body of Christ.

**Baptism** In Baptism we are united to Christ and become part of the Body of Christ and the people of God. The celebration of this first sacrament of initiation is very important. It is our welcome into the Church.

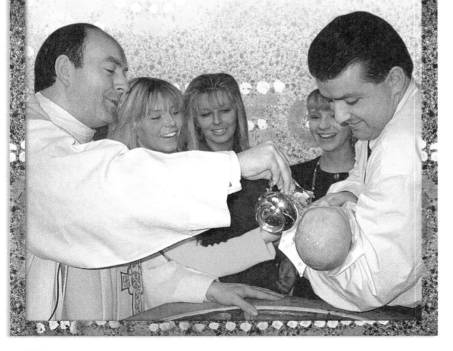

**Confirmation** In Confirmation we are sealed with the Gift of the Holy Spirit. Confirmation continues what Baptism has begun. We are strengthened to live as Christ's followers.

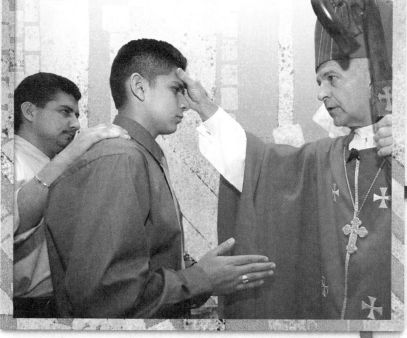

### The sacraments of Christian initiation are Baptism, Confirmation, and Eucharist.

**Christian initiation** is the process of becoming a member of the Church. The sacraments of Baptism, Confirmation, and Eucharist initiate us into the Church.

All those who receive the sacraments of Christian initiation share a **common vocation**, a call to holiness and evangelization. God calls each of us:

- to proclaim the good news of Christ
- to share and give witness to our faith
- to grow in holiness.

God alone is holy, but he shares his holiness with us. **Holiness** is sharing in God's goodness and responding to his love by the way we live. Our holiness comes through grace.

To grow in holiness we have to respond to the grace we receive in the sacraments. The Holy Spirit helps us to do this. We try to follow Jesus' example and his commandment to love others.

Write one way you will respond to God's love today.

_____

_____

_____

**The Eucharist** The Eucharist is the sacrament of the Body and Blood of Christ. The Eucharist is connected to our Baptism, too. Each time we receive Holy Communion, our bonds as the Body of Christ are made stronger. Our community of faith is nourished by God's life.

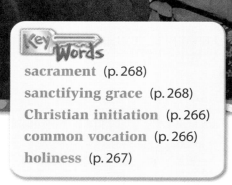

**Key Words**

sacrament (p. 268)

sanctifying grace (p. 268)

Christian initiation (p. 266)

common vocation (p. 266)

holiness (p. 267)

their relationship with God and the entire Church is made whole again.

The Church offers the sacrament of the Anointing of the Sick to those who are very sick. It is also for those who are near death. In this sacrament the priest anoints the person who is sick and all gathered pray for his or her health. Those who receive the sacrament are given the grace to respond to their illness with hope. Their faith in a loving God can be strengthened.

Pray for someone you know who is in need of reconciliation or healing.

### The sacraments of healing are Reconciliation and Anointing of the Sick.

We learn from the gospels that Jesus often forgave and healed those who believed. Jesus was showing that God has power over sickness and sin. Jesus gave the apostles the authority to forgive and to heal. This authority continues in the Church. The sacraments of Reconciliation and Anointing of the Sick are two ways that we celebrate Jesus' healing power.

In the sacrament of Reconciliation members of the Church are reconciled with God and with the Church. Those who are truly sorry confess their sins to a priest and are forgiven. For those who receive the sacrament of Reconciliation,

### Holy Orders and Matrimony are sacraments of service to others.

Those who receive the sacraments of Holy Orders and Matrimony are strengthened to serve God and the Church through a particular vocation. In the sacrament of Holy Orders, God calls some men to serve him as ordained ministers in the Church. They are ordained as bishops, priests, or deacons. They have different roles and duties in serving the Church.

## As Catholics...

A vocation is a calling to a way of life. God calls each of us to serve him in a particular way. We can follow our vocation in the single life, marriage, the religious life, and the priesthood.

Discovering our vocation is an exciting part of our lives. The Holy Spirit guides us as we pray. Family, friends, and teachers also help us to know the ways that God is calling us.

Pray that you will know how God is calling you to live.

The bishops are the successors of the apostles. They are the leaders and official teachers of the Church. The bishops are called to help Jesus' followers grow in holiness. They do this through prayer, preaching, and the celebration of the sacraments.

Priests are coworkers with the bishops. They are called to preach the good news, celebrate the sacraments with and for us, and guide the members of the Church.

Deacons assist the bishops in works of service for the whole Church. They baptize, witness marriages, preside at funerals, proclaim the good news, and preach.

In the sacrament of Matrimony, a man and a woman pledge to love each other as God loves them. They promise to remain faithful to each other and to live lives of service to each other and to their children.

The sacrament of Matrimony strengthens the couple to build a family rooted in a strong faith in God and each other. It enables them to share their faith with their family and to serve the Church and the community.

## WE RESPOND

List the sacraments you have received. Discuss ways each has helped you grow closer to God and the Church.

_____

_____

**Write True or False for the following sentences.**
**Then change the false sentences to make them true.**

1. _____ Saint Paul instituted the sacraments so that his saving work would continue.

_____

_____

2. _____ The Church celebrates Holy Orders and Matrimony as sacraments of service to others.

_____

_____

3. _____ Reconciliation and Anointing of the Sick are two ways that the Church celebrates Jesus' healing power.

_____

_____

4. _____ The sacraments of Christian initiation are Baptism, Eucharist, and Matrimony.

_____

_____

**Write the letter of the definition that matches each term.**

5. _____ holiness

6. _____ sanctifying grace

7. _____ common vocation

8. _____ sacrament

a. the gift of sharing in God's life that we receive in the sacraments

b. sharing God's goodness and responding to his love by the way we live; this comes through grace

c. the process of being a member of the Church through the sacraments of Baptism, Confirmation, and Eucharist

d. an effective sign given to us by Jesus through which we share God's life

e. the call to holiness and evangelization that all Christians share

**Write a sentence to answer the question.**

9–10. What is the purpose of the sacraments?

_____

ASSESSMENT

Discuss the sacraments with your family. Which sacraments have they celebrated? Make a poster that illustrates this information.

# We Respond in Faith

## Reflect & Pray

Jesus, you are my model of holiness because _____

_____

_____

## Remember

- Jesus gave the Church seven sacraments.

- The sacraments of Christian initiation are Baptism, Confirmation, and Eucharist.

- The sacraments of healing are Reconciliation and Anointing of the Sick.

- Holy Orders and Matrimony are sacraments of service to others.

### Key Words

sacrament (p. 269)
sanctifying grace (p. 269)
Christian initiation (p. 267)
common vocation (p. 267)
holiness (p. 268)

## OUR CATHOLIC LIFE

### The Claretians

The Claretian Missionaries are a religious community of priests and brothers. They are dedicated to evangelization. They bring the gospel message to those who are poor or in need throughout the world. The Claretians are involved in a variety of ministries devoted to social concerns and issues of justice, peace, and the environment. They pay special attention to the needs of immigrants, young people, and families.

The Claretians were founded by Saint Anthony Claret in 1849. Today, more than 3,000 Claretian priests and brothers are in fifty-eight counties on five continents. Visit their Web site at www.claretians.org.

# SHARING FAITH
## with My Family

## Sharing What I Learned

Discuss the following with your family:

- sanctifying grace
- sacraments of Christian initiation
- sacraments of healing
- sacraments of service to others.

## Family Faith Checklist

Ask your family to complete the Family Faith Checklist. Share your experiences.

### Our Family

Jesus Christ is the greatest sign of God's love. How are you a sign of God's love?

☐ At home:

_____

☐ At school/work:

_____

☐ In the parish:

_____

☐ In the community:

_____

"[Jesus] is the image of the invisible God."
(Colossians 1:15)

Visit Sadlier's

**www.WeBelieveweb.com**

**Connect to the Catechism**
For adult background and reflection,
see paragraphs 1210, 1212, 1421, and 1534.

# New Life in Christ

## WE GATHER

✝ **Leader:** Let us pray to God as one family.

**Reader:** A reading from the Book of the Prophet Isaiah

"Hear then, O Jacob, my servant,
Israel, whom I have chosen.
I will pour out water upon the thirsty ground,
and streams upon the dry land;
I will pour out my spirit upon your offspring,
and my blessing upon your descendants."
(Isaiah 44:1, 3)

The word of the Lord.

**All:** Thanks be to God.

🎵 **We Belong to God's Family**

Refrain:
We belong to God's family.
Brothers and sisters are we,
singing together in unity about
one Lord and one faith, one family.

We are one in the water,
the fountain of rebirth.
We are God's new creation
and our song will cover the earth.
(Refrain)

☀ What are some things that unite you with members of your family? your classmates? people in your neighborhood?

## WE BELIEVE
### Baptism is the foundation of Christian life.

Jesus wanted everyone to know him and to share his life and love. Before he returned to his Father in heaven, Jesus asked his disciples to tell others about him. He sent his apostles out to all nations to baptize believers.

With the coming of the Holy Spirit on Pentecost, Jesus' disciples were strengthened to do as he asked. They told the crowds that Jesus Christ had died and risen to new life. They shared their belief that Christ is the Son of God. Peter told them, "Repent and be baptized, every one of you, in the name of Jesus Christ for the forgiveness of your sins; and you will receive the gift of the holy Spirit" (Acts of the Apostles 2:38).

Many people who heard the good news of Christ were baptized and became disciples.

Baptism is the foundation of Christian life. It is upon Baptism that we build our lives as followers of Christ. **Baptism** is the sacrament in which we are freed from sin, become children of God, and are welcomed into the Church. Through this sacrament we:

- are joined to Christ and rise to new life in him

- become members of the Church, the Body of Christ and the people of God

- are united with all others who have been baptized.

Baptism is the very first sacrament that we celebrate. In fact, we are unable to receive any other sacrament until we first have been baptized. Baptism leads us to the other two sacraments of initiation, Confirmation and Eucharist.

What are some ways that you can show that you are united to other members of the Church?

_____

_____

_____

_____

_____

_____

_____

_____

## In Baptism we are freed from sin and become children of God

God created human beings to know him, to be close to him, to share in his love forever. However, the first human beings turned away from God and disobeyed him. Because of their sin, called original sin, they lost their closeness with God.

Because of original sin, human beings suffer. We all are born with original sin and are affected by it throughout our lives. We are tempted to turn away from God and commit personal sin.

But God did not turn away from his people. He promised to save us. Out of love, God sent his Son to restore our relationship with God. The truth that the Son of God became man is called the **Incarnation**.

By his death and Resurrection, Jesus Christ—the Son of God—saves us from sin. His victory over sin and death offers us salvation. **Salvation** is the forgiveness of sins and the restoring of friendship with God.

Like faith, Baptism is necessary for salvation. Baptism draws us into a community of believers led by the Holy Spirit. It frees us from original sin and all of our personal sins are forgiven.

When we are baptized we become children of God. We become sisters and brothers with all who have been baptized. Baptism makes us members of one family led by the Holy Spirit. In this family, there are no boundaries or preferences. God sees us all as his children. He loves each of us.

What will you do this week to live as a member of God's family?

## As Catholics...

The Body of Christ unites us to all who have been baptized. The union of the baptized members of the Church on earth with those who are in heaven and in purgatory is called the communion of saints. We pray that those who have died may know God's love and mercy and may one day share in eternal life.

When are some times that your parish prays for those who have died?

**Key Words**

**Baptism** (p. 267)

**Incarnation** (p. 268)

**salvation** (p. 269)

## We are a priestly, prophetic, and royal people.

At Jesus' baptism at the Jordan River the Holy Spirit came upon him. This anointing by the Holy Spirit established Jesus as priest, prophet, and king. We call Jesus a priest because he gave the sacrifice that no one else could. Jesus offered himself to save us. Jesus was a prophet because he delivered God's message of love and forgiveness. He spoke out for truth and justice. Jesus showed himself to be a king by the care he gave to all his people.

In Baptism we are anointed, blessed with holy oil. This seal of Baptism marks us as belonging to Christ, and thus we receive Baptism only once. We share in Jesus' role of priest, prophet, and king.

We know that Jesus is the only one, true priest. However, he calls all the baptized to share in his priesthood. This is the priesthood of the faithful. We can live out our priesthood in many ways. We can pray daily. We can participate in the liturgy, especially the Eucharist. We can offer our lives to God.

St.Joseph

St.Dominic

Blessed Kateri Tekakwitha

St.Francis of Assisi

St.Frances Cabrini

A **prophet** is someone who speaks on behalf of God, defends the truth, and works for justice. We are called to be prophets like the men and women in the Old Testament, like John the Baptist and like Christ. We are prophets when we speak truthfully about Christ and live as we should. We can be prophets in our schools, communities, and families.

As the Anointed King and Messiah, Jesus came to serve not to be served. He leads his people as a servant-king. Jesus' reign makes God's love present and active in the world.

Jesus calls us to be servants. He wants us to care for others, especially those who are poor or suffering. He asks us to encourage others to respond to God's love in their lives.

> You share in Jesus' role of priest, prophet, and king. What tasks would you assign yourself as a priest, as a prophet, and as a servant-king?
>
> Priest
>
> Prophet
>
> Servant-King

## Because of our Baptism, we have hope of eternal life.

As part of the Body of Christ, we follow Christ's teachings and try to live as he did. People who have responded to God's grace and have remained in his friendship will have eternal life when they die. **Eternal life** is living in happiness with God forever. Those who have lived lives of holiness on earth will immediately share in the joy of heaven and eternal life. Others who need to grow in holiness will prepare for heaven in purgatory. These people will eventually enjoy the happiness of heaven, too.

Unfortunately, there are those who have chosen to completely break their friendship with God. They have continually turned away from God's mercy and refused his forgiveness. They remain forever separated from God and do not share in eternal life.

However, God wants all of his children to respond to his grace in their lives. God gives each of us the grace to grow in holiness. This makes it possible for us to respond to his love. We show our love by the way we live our lives.

**Saints** are followers of Christ who lived lives of holiness on earth and now share in eternal life with God in heaven. Because the saints are closely united to Christ, they help the Church to grow in holiness. Their lives teach us about true discipleship. Their love and prayers for the Church are constant. We ask the saints to pray to God for us and for those who have died.

### WE RESPOND

The sacrament of Baptism is the foundation of Christian life. Trace the pattern using a separate sheet of paper. Follow the directions on the pattern to create a "baptismal building block." On each side write or illustrate an example that shows you are a baptized follower of Jesus Christ.

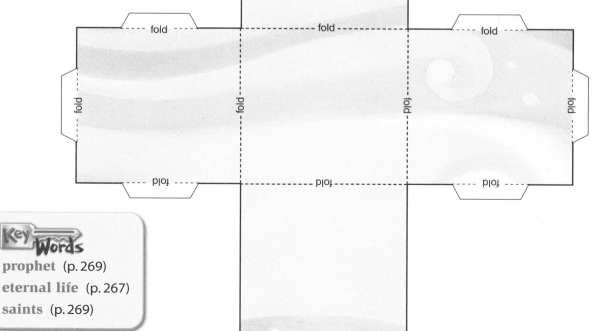

**Key Words**

prophet (p. 269)

eternal life (p. 267)

saints (p. 269)

**Choose a word(s) from the box to complete each sentence.**

| | | | | |
|---|---|---|---|---|
| salvation | eternal life | Incarnation | prophet | saint |

1. The truth that the Son of God became man is known as the

   _____ .

2. A _____ is a follower of Christ who lived a life of holiness on earth and now shares in eternal life with God in heaven.

3. The forgiveness of sins and the restoring of friendship with God is

   known as _____ .

4. A _____ is someone who speaks on behalf of God, defends the truth, and works for justice.

**Short Answers**

5. Which sacrament is considered the foundation of Christian life?

   _____

6. How does the gift of grace that we receive at Baptism help us?

   _____

7. What is one way we can live out the priesthood of the faithful?

   _____

8. What is eternal life? _____

**Write a sentence to answer the question.**

9–10. What happens to us in the sacrament of Baptism?

   _____

   _____

ASSESSMENT

Make a pamphlet that illustrates the importance of Baptism. Use the chapter to gather your information. Share your pamphlet with your class, family, or parish.

# We Respond in Faith

## Reflect & Pray

God our Father, help me to use your gift of grace and grow in

holiness by _____

_____

Amen.

**Key Words**

Baptism (p. 267)
Incarnation (p. 268)
salvation (p. 269)
prophet (p. 269)
eternal life (p. 267)
saints (p. 269)

## Remember

- Baptism is the foundation of Christian life.

- In Baptism we are freed from sin and become children of God.

- We are a priestly, prophetic, and royal people.

- Because of our Baptism, we have the hope of eternal life.

## OUR CATHOLIC LIFE

### Patron Saints

A patron is a person who encourages and takes care of someone or something. For example, "a patron of the arts" is someone who may collect art and contribute time and money to art museums.

At Baptism many people are given the name of a saint. That saint is known as the person's patron saint. Patron saints can care for their namesakes and encourage them in following Jesus.

Many parishes have patron saints, too. For example, your parish patron may be Saint Frances Cabrini or Saint Patrick. Hospitals and Catholic groups may also be named for patron saints. Even occupations have patron saints. For example, Saint Barbara is the patron of architects.

# SHARING FAITH
## with My Family

## Sharing What I Learned

Discuss the following with your family:

- the importance of Baptism
- salvation
- eternal life
- a priestly, prophetic, and royal people.

## A Sacraments Scrapbook

Work with your family to collect prayers, poems, songs, Scripture, pictures, photographs, and so on, that reflect the sacrament of Baptism. Place your findings on sheets of paper to include in your Sacraments Scrapbook.

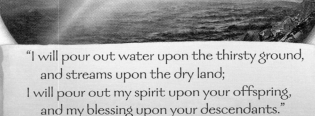

"I will pour out water upon the thirsty ground,
and streams upon the dry land;
I will pour out my spirit upon your offspring,
and my blessing upon your descendants."

(Isaiah 44:3)

Visit Sadlier's

www.WeBelieveweb.com

**Connect to the Catechism**
For adult background and reflection,
see paragraphs 1213, 1265, 783, and 1274.

# The Celebration of Baptism

## WE GATHER

✝ **Leader:** Do you believe in God, the Father almighty, creator of heaven and earth?

**All:** I do.

**Leader:** Do you believe in Jesus Christ, his only Son, our Lord, who was born of the Virgin Mary, was crucified, died, and was buried, rose from the dead, and is now seated at the right hand of the Father?

**All:** I do.

**Leader:** Do you believe in the Holy Spirit, the holy catholic Church, the communion of saints, the forgiveness of sins, the resurrection of the body, and the life everlasting?

**All:** I do.

**Leader:** This is our faith. This is the faith of the Church. We are proud to profess it, in Christ Jesus our Lord.

**All:** Amen.

☀ How does your family welcome people who come to your home? Why is it important to make them feel welcome?

## WE BELIEVE
### The Church welcomes all to be baptized.

Not everyone begins or completes Christian initiation at the same time. Many people are baptized as infants or young children. They celebrate the remaining sacraments of initiation when they are older. Other people are baptized as older children or adults. These adults and older children participate in the Rite of Christian Initiation of Adults (RCIA) and enter the catechumenate.

Key Word

**catechumenate** (p. 267)

The **catechumenate** is a period of formation for Christian initiation. It includes prayer and liturgy, religious instruction, and service to others. Those who enter this formation are called catechumens. They celebrate the three sacraments of initiation in one celebration, usually at the Easter Vigil.

The entire parish takes part in the formation of the catechumens. Some parish members serve as sponsors. Others teach the catechumens about the Catholic faith. The catechumens participate in prayer celebrations that introduce them to the symbols of the sacraments. They usually join the assembly for part of the Sunday celebration of the Eucharist.

When infants or young children are baptized in the faith of the Church, the parents choose godparents for the child. The godparents are to be a Christian example, and along with the parents and parish community agree to help the child grow in faith.

An ideal day to celebrate Baptism is on Sunday, the Lord's Day and the day of Jesus' Resurrection. The celebration of Baptism on Sunday highlights the fact that we rise to new life like Jesus did. It also allows the parish to welcome the newly baptized.

Imagine that you have been asked to be a godparent. What do you think you will have to do as a godparent?

Write a short letter to your future godchild.

_____
_____
_____
_____
_____
_____
_____

## The parish community participates in the celebration of Baptism.

Here is the way the Church celebrates the Baptism of infants and young children.

A celebrant is the bishop, priest, or deacon who celebrates the sacrament for and with the community. At Baptism the celebrant greets the family, and the parents and godparents present the child to the Church for Baptism. The celebrant traces the sign of the cross on the child's forehead. He invites the parents and godparents to do the same. This tracing is a sign of the new life Christ has won for us on the cross.

Two or three readings from the Bible are proclaimed. A psalm or song is often sung between the readings. Then the celebrant gives a homily to explain the readings and the meaning of the sacrament.

Intercessions, or the prayer of the faithful, are offered by the people. The community prays for the child about to be baptized, for the whole Church, and for the world.

The celebrant then prays asking God to free the child from original sin. He asks God to send the Holy Spirit to dwell in the child's heart. He then anoints the child on the chest with the oil of catechumens. This cleanses and strengthens the child about to be baptized.

What are some times that you make the sign of the cross? Why?

## As Catholics...

Did you know that in an emergency, anyone can baptize? The person baptizes by pouring water over the head of the one to be baptized while saying, "N., I baptize you in the name of the Father, and of the Son, and of the Holy Spirit."

Who do you think might need to baptize in an emergency?

## Water is an important sign of Baptism.

In the sacrament of Baptism the water is blessed with a prayer. In this prayer we hear about the power of water at the time of creation, during the great flood, and in the Israelites' escape from slavery in Egypt. We recall that water has been a source of holiness, freedom, and new life. Because of Jesus' dying and rising to new life, each of us can have eternal life.

The celebrant continues to pray, calling upon God for help and support. He touches the water with his right hand and says,

"We ask you, Father, with your Son
to send the Holy Spirit upon the waters of this font.
May all who are buried with Christ in the death of baptism
rise also with him to newness of life.

We ask this through Christ our Lord."

"Amen."

Next the celebrant asks the parents and godparents some questions. The parents and godparents reject, or say no to, sin. Then they state what they believe. This is called a profession of faith.

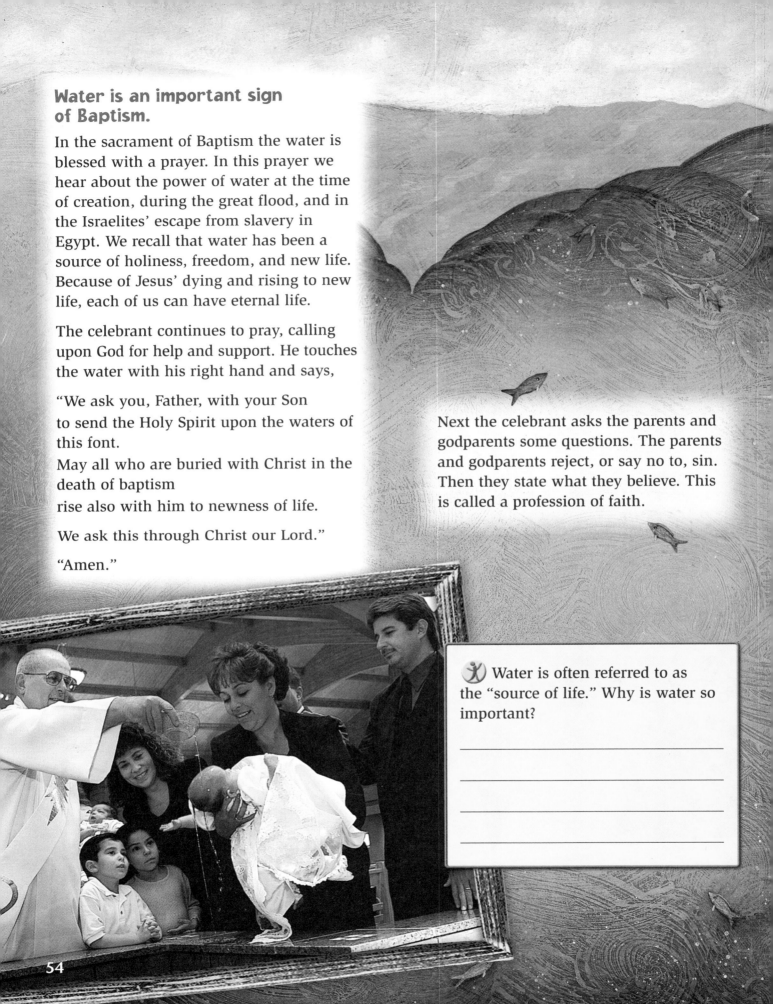

Water is often referred to as the "source of life." Why is water so important?

_____

_____

_____

_____

## The baptized begin their new life as children of God.

We have now arrived at the heart of the sacrament. The actual Baptism can take place in two ways. The celebrant can immerse, or plunge, the child in water three times. Or the celebrant can pour water over the child three times. While immersing or pouring, the celebrant says,

"N., I baptize you in the name of the Father, and of the Son, and of the Holy Spirit.

The celebrant anoints the child on the crown of the head with **chrism**, perfumed oil blessed by the bishop. This anointing is a sign of the gift of the Holy Spirit. It shows that the newly baptized child shares in Christ's mission as priest, prophet, and king.

A white garment is placed on the newly baptized child. This symbolizes the child's new life in Christ. One of the parents or godparents then lights the child's candle from the Easter candle. The lit candle symbolizes that Christ has enlightened the newly baptized child. He or she is to be a child of light.

Everyone gathers by the altar to pray the Our Father. This connects Baptism to the Eucharist. The celebrant then offers a final blessing, and those gathered are dismissed.

## WE RESPOND

Fill in this road map for the journey of faith begun in Baptism. Include in this map the starting point, the challenges, who might be traveling with you, the people who help you on the journey, the things that you are called to do on this journey, and the destination.

Take a moment to thank God for the people who help you on your journey of faith.

Key Word
**chrism** (p. 267)

**Review**

**Write the letter that best defines each term.**

1. _____ chrism

2. _____ water

3. _____ celebrant

4. _____ catechumenate

a. a period of formation for Christian initiation that includes prayer and liturgy, religious instruction, and service to others

b. an important sign in the sacrament of Baptism

c. profession of faith

d. the bishop, priest, or deacon who celebrates the sacrament for and with the community

e. perfumed oil blessed by the bishop

**Circle the correct answer.**

5. The anointing with chrism is a sign of the Gift of the _____.

    **a.** grace          **b.** Holy Spirit

            **c.** godparents

6. During Baptism, a person is baptized in the name of _____.

    **a.** the Father and the Son

    **b.** the Son and the Holy Spirit

    **c.** the Father, the Son, and the Holy Spirit

7. The white garment of the newly baptized is a symbol of _____.

    **a.** the celebrant     **b.** light

            **c.** new life in Christ

8. The _____ symbolizes that Christ enlightens the newly baptized.

    **a.** chrism         **b.** lighted candle

            **c.** white garment

**Write a sentence to answer the question.**

**9–10.** Why is water so important in the sacrament of Baptism?

_____

_____

**ASSESSMENT**

Design a storyboard that describes the celebration of the sacrament of Baptism. Include and explain the symbols that are used in the Rite of Baptism. Share your storyboard with the class.

# We Respond in Faith

## Reflect & Pray

How can I remind myself that I am a baptized Christian? How can I be the light of Christ today?

Christ, help me to share your light by _____

_____

**Key Words**
catechumenate (p. 267)
chrism (p. 267)

## Remember

- The Church welcomes all to be baptized.
- The parish community participates in the celebration of Baptism.
- Water is an important sign of Baptism.
- The baptized begin their new life as children of God.

## OUR CATHOLIC LIFE

### The Sign of the Cross

The cross of Jesus Christ is part of everyday Catholic life. When we go into church, a holy water font or baptismal font is near the entrance. We dip our hands into the holy water. This is the same water used for Baptism. As we bless ourselves with the sign of the cross we remember that we belong to Jesus and are children of God. We can bless one another with the sign of the cross, too. This is something that parents can do for children before they leave for school each day, or before they go to sleep.

# SHARING FAITH
## with My Family

## Sharing What I Learned

Discuss the following with your family:

- those celebrating Baptism
- the role of the community in this celebration
- the importance of water in Baptism
- the anointing with chrism.

## Sacrament Trading Cards

Design a trading card for the sacrament of Baptism using the pattern below. Use your knowledge about this sacrament to write "sacrament facts" on the back of the card. Collect all seven!

"Receive the light of Christ."
(*Rite of Baptism for Children*, 64)

**Baptism**

What is the importance of the sacrament?

_____

What do we see?

_____

What do we hear?

_____

Who leads us in the celebration?

_____

Visit Sadlier's

**www.WeBelieveweb.com**

**Connect to the Catechism**
For adult background and reflection, see paragraphs 1226, 1248, 1217–1222, and 1254.

# The Liturgical Year

*"All things are of your making,*
*all times and seasons obey your laws."*
Preface for Sunday in Ordinary Time V

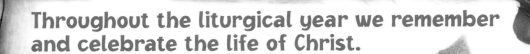

# Throughout the liturgical year we remember and celebrate the life of Christ.

## WE GATHER

✝ *Lord, you create all things to give you glory.*

How do you keep track of the day, the month, the year, or the season? How does knowing these things help you?

## WE BELIEVE

The Church year is based on the life of Christ and the celebration of his life in the liturgy. So, the Church's year is called the liturgical year. The Church has its own way of marking the passing of time and the liturgical seasons of the year. In one liturgical year we recall and celebrate the whole life of Jesus Christ. We celebrate his birth, younger years, his later years of teaching and ministry, and most especially his Paschal Mystery— his suffering, death, Resurrection, and Ascension into heaven. During the year we also venerate, or show devotion to, Mary the Mother of God, and all the saints.

The liturgical year begins with the season of Advent in late November or early December. The Easter Triduum is the center of our year, and the dates of all the other liturgical seasons are based upon the dates of the Easter Triduum. This is why the seasons begin and end at slightly different times each year.

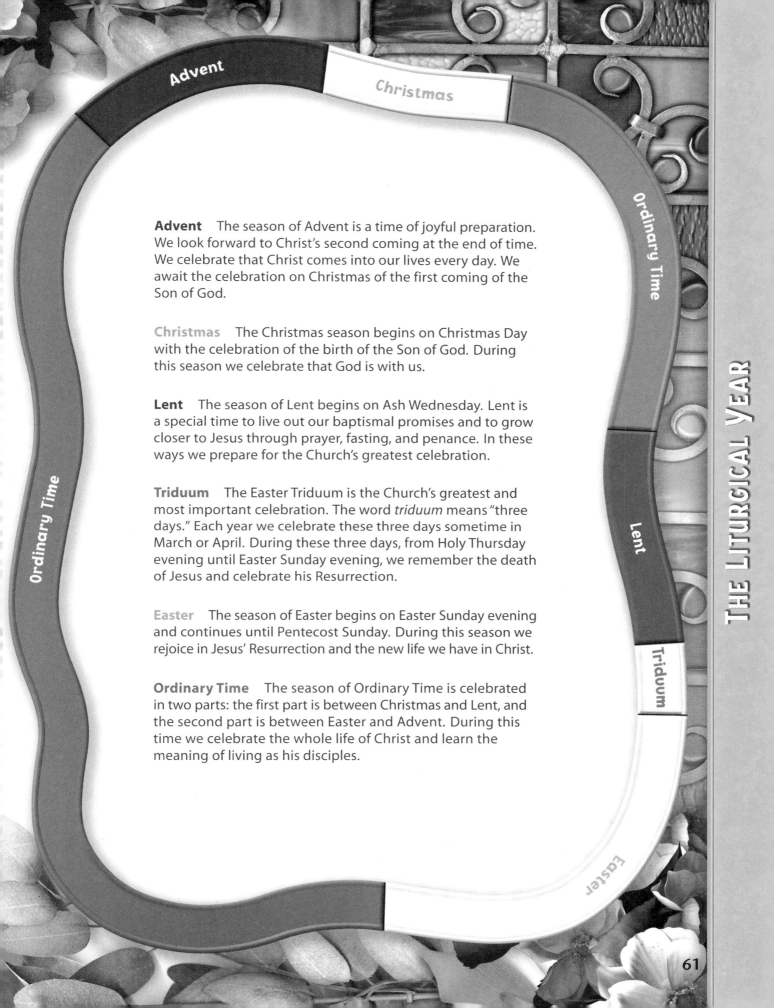

**Advent**   The season of Advent is a time of joyful preparation. We look forward to Christ's second coming at the end of time. We celebrate that Christ comes into our lives every day. We await the celebration on Christmas of the first coming of the Son of God.

**Christmas**   The Christmas season begins on Christmas Day with the celebration of the birth of the Son of God. During this season we celebrate that God is with us.

**Lent**   The season of Lent begins on Ash Wednesday. Lent is a special time to live out our baptismal promises and to grow closer to Jesus through prayer, fasting, and penance. In these ways we prepare for the Church's greatest celebration.

**Triduum**   The Easter Triduum is the Church's greatest and most important celebration. The word *triduum* means "three days." Each year we celebrate these three days sometime in March or April. During these three days, from Holy Thursday evening until Easter Sunday evening, we remember the death of Jesus and celebrate his Resurrection.

**Easter**   The season of Easter begins on Easter Sunday evening and continues until Pentecost Sunday. During this season we rejoice in Jesus' Resurrection and the new life we have in Christ.

**Ordinary Time**   The season of Ordinary Time is celebrated in two parts: the first part is between Christmas and Lent, and the second part is between Easter and Advent. During this time we celebrate the whole life of Christ and learn the meaning of living as his disciples.

THE LITURGICAL YEAR

Do you know this rhyme?

*Thirty days hath September,*
*April, June, and November.*
*All the rest have thirty-one,*
*Save February, which has twenty-eight,*
*And in leap-year, twenty-nine.*

This rhyme helps us to remember how many days there are in each month. The calendar of the year was once very different from what it is today. It did not always begin in January. The early Greeks and Romans began their year in the spring, when they planted their crops. Later, the Romans, for military reasons, ordered the year and the calendar so that it began in January.

However, the calendar often did not match the season. People would look at a calendar that said it was spring, then look outside to see that it was really still winter! The Roman calendar constantly had to be revised.

In 1582, Pope Gregory XIII formed a group to revise the calendar. He even founded the Vatican Observatory so that astronomers could check their calculations against the movement of the sun and the stars.

These experts gave some months thirty days, others thirty-one. They made February a month of twenty-eight days, with an extra day every four years. This is the system we still have today. It is called the Gregorian calendar. It was named after Pope Gregory XIII who started the revision.

## WE RESPOND

Parishes prepare for each season and each celebration of the liturgy. In groups list some ways that your parish helps you to know which liturgical season you are celebrating. What are some signs of that season? Make plans to prepare your prayer space for each of the seasons in the liturgical year.

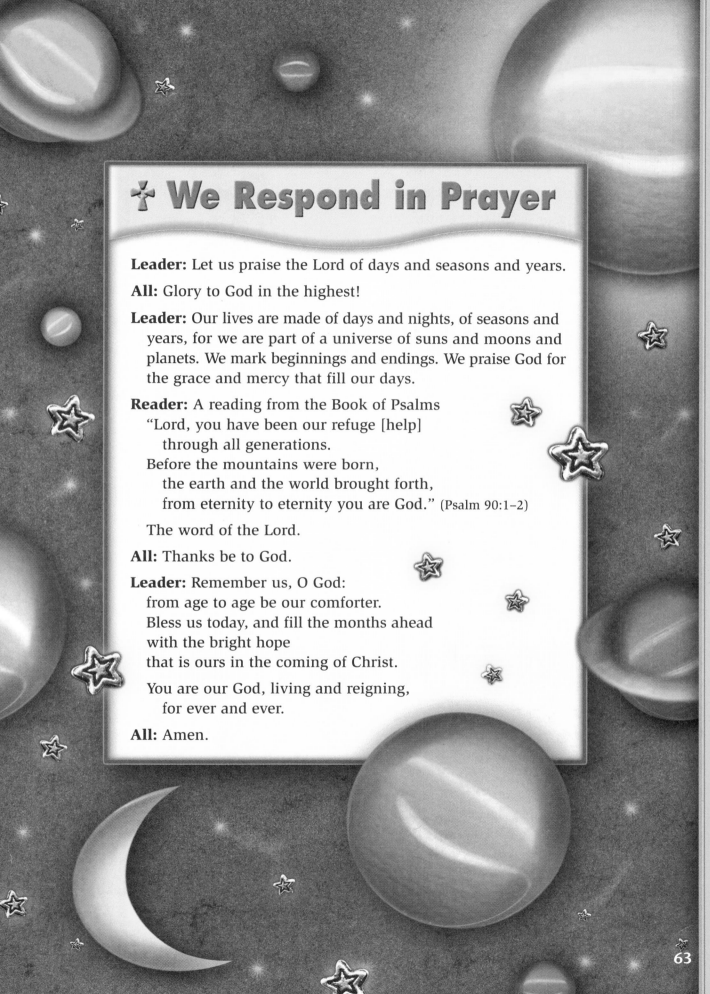

# ✝ We Respond in Prayer

**Leader:** Let us praise the Lord of days and seasons and years.

**All:** Glory to God in the highest!

**Leader:** Our lives are made of days and nights, of seasons and years, for we are part of a universe of suns and moons and planets. We mark beginnings and endings. We praise God for the grace and mercy that fill our days.

**Reader:** A reading from the Book of Psalms
"Lord, you have been our refuge [help]
    through all generations.
Before the mountains were born,
    the earth and the world brought forth,
        from eternity to eternity you are God." (Psalm 90:1–2)

The word of the Lord.

**All:** Thanks be to God.

**Leader:** Remember us, O God:
from age to age be our comforter.
Bless us today, and fill the months ahead
with the bright hope
that is ours in the coming of Christ.

You are our God, living and reigning,
    for ever and ever.

**All:** Amen.

THE LITURGICAL YEAR

# SHARING FAITH
## with My Family

## Sharing What I Learned

Discuss the following with your family:

• the Church year is called the liturgical year

• the reasons we celebrate the different seasons of the liturgical year

• the Gregorian calendar.

## Around the Table

Share some things your family does at home and in church to celebrate each season of the liturgical year.

Advent _____

Christmas _____

Lent _____

Triduum _____

Easter _____

Ordinary Time _____

## Family Prayer

A special time for family prayer is right before we go to sleep. Begin this prayer with the Sign of the Cross. You may want to follow it with a Hail Mary.

Protect us, Lord, as we stay awake; watch over us as we sleep, that awake we may keep watch with Christ, and asleep, rest in his peace.

Visit Sadlier's

**www.WeBelieveweb.com**

**Connect to the Catechism**
For adult background and reflection, see paragraph 1168.

# Ordinary Time

## 7

Advent  Christmas  Ordinary Time  Lent  Triduum  Easter  Ordinary Time

"Every day I will bless you;
I will praise your name forever."

Psalm 145:2

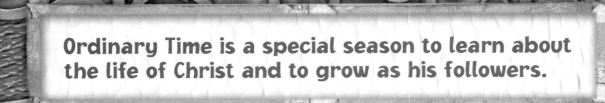

# Ordinary Time is a special season to learn about the life of Christ and to grow as his followers.

## WE GATHER

✝ *Jesus, be with us all the days of our lives.*

If someone asked you to describe an ordinary day, what would you say? In groups discuss what might make a day ordinary.

## WE BELIEVE

We often use the word *ordinary* when we want to describe something as "normal," "common," or "average." In some ways we could describe the season of Ordinary Time in these ways. As the longest season of the liturgical year, Ordinary Time is a time to learn and follow the teachings of Christ in our daily lives. It is a time to grow as his followers and to become better able to give witness to his good news in our "normal" or everyday lives.

However, in the name of this season, the word *ordinary* means "in number order." The season is called Ordinary Time because the weeks are "ordered." This means they are named in number order. For example, the First Sunday in Ordinary Time is followed by the Second Sunday in Ordinary Time, and so on.

The season of Ordinary Time lasts thirty-three to thirty-four weeks, and it is celebrated twice during the liturgical year. The first part is short. It takes place between the seasons of Christmas and Lent. The second part lasts for several months between the seasons of Easter and Advent. This part begins in late May or June and ends in late November or early December. Ordinary Time is a season of life and hope. We use the color green during its many weeks to remind us of the life and hope that come from Christ.

Other seasons during the liturgical year focus on a particular event or period in Jesus' life. During the season of Ordinary Time, we remember all of the events and teachings of the life of Jesus Christ. We celebrate all that he gave us through his birth, life, death, Resurrection, and Ascension.

During the season of Ordinary Time, we can concentrate in a special way on the word of God. On the Sundays and weekdays of Ordinary Time, we read from one of the gospels of the New Testament in number order, chapter by chapter. In this way we learn about the whole life of Jesus Christ. We hear his teachings on God his Father, love and forgiveness, and the meaning of being his disciples. Jesus is our great teacher, and during this season we say, "Teach me, O Lord, and I will follow your way."

**The witness of the saints**
This season is a time to grow as followers of Christ. It is a time to look to the example of the holy women and men who have given witness to Christ in their daily lives. The Church has special days in memory of Mary and the saints. These days are special because they help us to thank God for the lives of the saints and to ask the saints to remember and pray for us. The Church celebrates these days all year long, but it is especially during the many weeks of Ordinary Time that we honor the saints.

These special days to celebrate the lives of Mary, the saints, and events in the life of Jesus, are divided into three categories: memorials, feasts, and solemnities.

Memorials are usually celebrated in honor of the saints. A memorial for a saint is usually celebrated on or near the day he or she died. On these days we rejoice because the saint now lives in happiness with God forever.

Feasts are celebrations that recall some of the events in the lives of Jesus and Mary. On feasts we celebrate the apostles, angels, and great martyrs, the followers of Christ who died for their faith.

Solemnities are the most important celebrations of all. Solemnity comes from the word *solemn*, and these feasts are great celebrations for the Church.

**Some solemnities we celebrate are:**

Christmas Day (December 25)
Mary, the Mother of God (January 1)
Easter Sunday (changes every year)
Pentecost Sunday (changes every year)
Body and Blood of Christ (changes every year)
Saints Peter and Paul, Apostles (June 29)
All Saints' Day (November 1)
Immaculate Conception (December 8)

What practices or devotions to the saints are you most familiar with? Do you have a saint that you remember in a special way?

What are some ways your family, parish, and school remember and celebrate the lives of the saints? Work in groups to list some of these ways.

Family _____

Parish _____

School _____

An important solemnity during Ordinary Time is All Saints' Day, November 1. On this day we remember and honor all those who were faithful followers of Christ and now share in eternal life. We know the stories of the lives of some of the saints. Other saints are known only to God. On this day we celebrate all of the saints. We are especially mindful of our patron saints—the saints whose names we share, the saints for whom our schools and parishes are named, and the saints that our families honor.

On November 2 the Church celebrates All Souls' Day. On this day we remember all those who have died, especially those in our own families and parishes. This day is usually a day for visiting the graves of family members and friends.

We pray that they may know God's love and share in his life forever.

**All Souls' Day in Mexico** All Souls' Day is one of the great celebrations in Mexico. There are different prayer practices and celebrations to celebrate "El Día de los Muertos," or Day of the Dead. In some parts of Mexico the celebration actually starts on October 31 with the welcoming of the souls of children who have died and ends on November 2 with the farewell of the souls of adults.

Besides the celebration of the Masses in honor of all souls, many people in Mexico set up a prayer altar in their homes for family members who have died. Another tradition is to visit the graves of their loved ones. They clean and decorate the area with flowers and candles, and sometimes even bring the favorite foods of those who have died and spend time there celebrating their lives.

Families gather in a cemetery on the Day of the Dead in Acatlan, Mexico

### WE RESPOND

What are some ways families in your parish, school, and neighborhood remember those who have died?

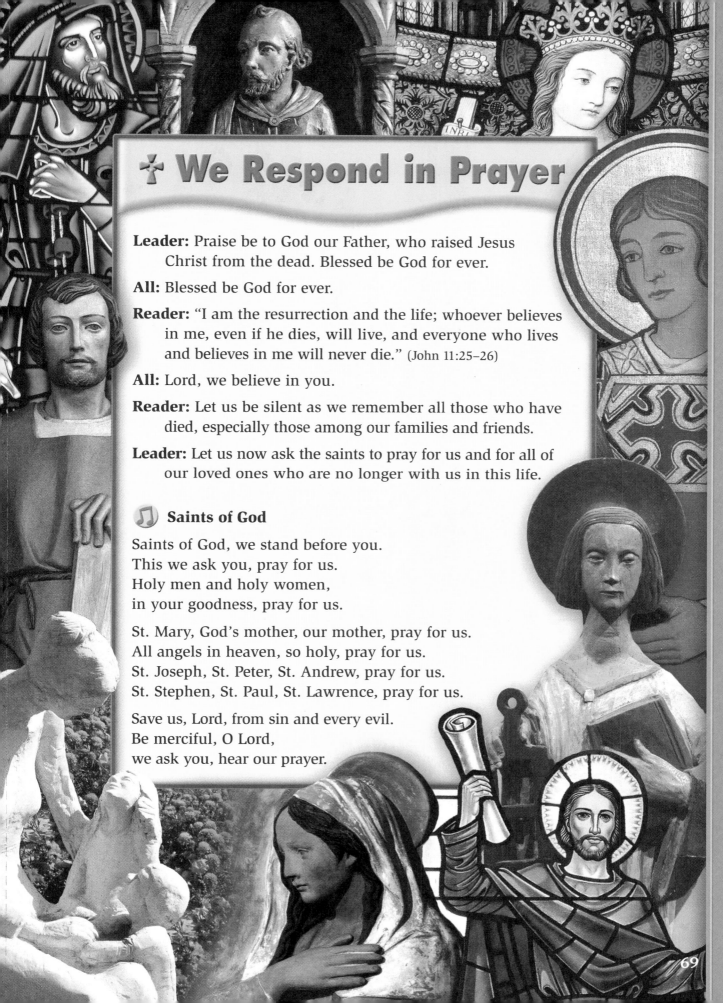

# ✝ We Respond in Prayer

**Leader:** Praise be to God our Father, who raised Jesus Christ from the dead. Blessed be God for ever.

**All:** Blessed be God for ever.

**Reader:** "I am the resurrection and the life; whoever believes in me, even if he dies, will live, and everyone who lives and believes in me will never die." (John 11:25–26)

**All:** Lord, we believe in you.

**Reader:** Let us be silent as we remember all those who have died, especially those among our families and friends.

**Leader:** Let us now ask the saints to pray for us and for all of our loved ones who are no longer with us in this life.

## 🎵 Saints of God

Saints of God, we stand before you.
This we ask you, pray for us.
Holy men and holy women,
in your goodness, pray for us.

St. Mary, God's mother, our mother, pray for us.
All angels in heaven, so holy, pray for us.
St. Joseph, St. Peter, St. Andrew, pray for us.
St. Stephen, St. Paul, St. Lawrence, pray for us.

Save us, Lord, from sin and every evil.
Be merciful, O Lord,
we ask you, hear our prayer.

# SHARING FAITH
## with My Family

## Sharing What I Learned

Discuss the following with your family:

- the season of Ordinary Time
- memorials, feasts, solemnities
- All Saints' Day and All Souls' Day.

## Around the Table

With your family focus on the life and teachings of Jesus during this Ordinary Time by sharing these questions:
How does our family celebrate Sunday?
Has it become another day of chores and errands?
How can we make Sunday more special in our family?
How can we make it a day of celebration and of rest?

## Family Prayer

During Ordinary Time, we try to follow Jesus in thought, word, and action. Pray this prayer of Saint Patrick with your family.

Christ be with me, Christ within me,
Christ behind me, Christ before me,
Christ beside me, Christ to win me,
Christ to comfort and restore me.
Christ beneath me, Christ above me,
Christ in quiet, Christ in danger,
Christ in hearts of all that love me,
Christ in mouth of friend or stranger.

*Saint Patrick's Breastplate*

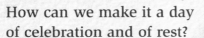

Visit Sadlier's

**www.WeBelieveweb.com**

**Connect to the Catechism**
For adult background and reflection, see paragraph 1163.

Assessment

**Fill in the circle beside the correct answer.**

1. The _____ is the power of God's love active in our lives and in the world.

   ○ Kingdom of God    ○ liturgy    ○ Incarnation

2. The _____ is all those who believe in Jesus Christ, have been baptized in him, and follow his teachings.

   ○ common vocation    ○ Church    ○ catechumenate

3. The gift of sharing in God's life that we receive in the sacraments is _____.

   ○ chrism    ○ Christian initiation    ○ sanctifying grace

4. All Christians share _____, a call to holiness and evangelization.

   ○ the catechumenate    ○ a common vocation    ○ original sin

5. Acts of love that help us care for the needs of people's hearts, minds, and souls are _____.

   ○ sacraments    ○ Corporal Works of Mercy    ○ Spiritual Works of Mercy

6. The _____ is the three persons in one God: God the Father, God the Son, and God the Holy Spirit.

   ○ Kingdom of God    ○ Blessed Trinity    ○ Christian initiation

7. Christ's passion, death, Resurrection from the dead, and Ascension into heaven is _____.

   ○ Jesus' mission    ○ the Incarnation    ○ the Paschal Mystery

8. _____ is the forgiveness of sins and the restoring of friendship with God.

   ○ Salvation    ○ Evangelization    ○ Eternal life

**Choose a word from the box to complete each sentence.**

| | | | | | |
|---|---|---|---|---|---|
| liturgy | Baptism | chrism | vocation | Incarnation | holiness |
| sacrament | | evangelization | | Eucharist | catechumenate |

9. Proclaming the good news of Christ by what we say and do

  is _____ .

10. Sharing in God's goodness and responding to his love by the way we

  live is _____ .

11. The period of formation for Christian initiation, that includes prayer and liturgy, religious instruction, and service to others is the _____ .

12. The official public prayer of the Church is the _____ .

13. The truth that the Son of God became man is the _____ .

14. An effective sign given to us by Jesus through which we share God's

  life is a _____ .

15. _____ is perfumed oil blessed by the bishop

16. _____ is the sacrament in which we are freed from sin, become children of God, and are welcomed into the Church.


**Answer the questions.**

17–18. How can a fifth grader proclaim the good news to those who have not yet heard Jesus' message, or help those who have heard but who need encouragement to live out their gift of faith?

19–20. How would you explain to a young child the importance of water, the significance of chrism, the wearing of a white garment, and the lighting of a candle at Baptism?

# Confirmation and Eucharist Complete Our Initiation

# UNIT 2 SHARING FAITH as a Family

## Three Reasons Families Need Rituals

A ritual is defined as a patterned way of doing something that includes symbols, movement, and words and is rooted in a common history. It is characterized by repetition and regularity. Families *need* rituals for the following reasons.

1. **Rituals** *teach.* Every ritual has a story attached to it, one that tells something about who we are, where we have come from, and what is important to us.

2. **Rituals** *connect.* Participating in a family ritual signifies belonging. It tells us that we are part of something bigger than ourselves. Cherished family traditions link us with our past and present as members of a family.

3. **Rituals** *heal.* Rituals can provide comfort and stability. It is a relief when routines are reestablished after a trauma or loss. At such times, "getting back to normal" also conveys a sense of hope that all is—or will be—well.

Your fifth grader will be learning about the sacraments. A way for him or her to understand the sacraments as sacred rituals is by taking part in the everyday rituals that are integral to your family.

## What Your Child Will Learn in Unit 2

Unit 2 concentrates on the sacrament of Confirmation and the sacrament of the Eucharist as completing our Christian initiation begun at our Baptism. The children first will understand the origin of sacrament of Confirmation in Scripture with the story of Pentecost and the sign of the laying on of hands. Next, the children will become aware of the rite, or celebration, of the sacrament of Confirmation. The Eucharist is seen as a memorial, a meal, and a sacrifice with emphasis placed on the real presence of Christ in the sacrament. An entire chapter is devoted to full explanations of the celebration of the Eucharist: the Introductory Rites, the Liturgy of the Word, the Liturgy of the Eucharist, and the Concluding Rite. The children will feel that when we celebrate the Eucharist we are strengthened to answer our call to discipleship. The last chapter of Unit 2 concentrates on the importance of prayer in the Christian life.

## Plan & Preview

▶ Have markers, pencils, cardboard, or pens available for the various activities on the family pages.

▶ Your child will be asking you to help him or her assemble some scrapbook items that focus on the sacraments of Confirmation and the Eucharist (*Chapters 8 & 10*).

## From the Catechism

"The Christian family is a communion of persons, a sign and image of the communion of the Father and the Son in the Holy Spirit."

(*Catechism of the Catholic Church*, 2205)

## Bible Q & A

**Q:** My child is learning about the sacraments of the Eucharist and Confirmation. What can we read in the Bible to learn about the origins of these sacraments?

—*Chapel Hill, North Carolina*

**A:** For the Eucharist, read about the Lord's Supper in Mark 14:22–25. For Confirmation, read the Acts of the Apostles 2:1–4.

## Family Prayer Corner

Set aside a space in your home for a Family Prayer Corner. A sturdy table covered with a pretty tablecloth sets the tone. Place your family Bible on a stand, if possible. Prayer cards and pictures add to the theme of prayer and reflection.

A *We Believe* parent sent us a letter. She suggests placing a "Being Thankful" notebook on the table. Anytime a family member wishes to thank God for something, he or she writes about it in the notebook. At the end of the year, the family reads what they have written all year long. This parent says, "You can't imagine how this adds to our joyful celebration of the new year. It's become a family tradition, and I've even got my sister's family doing it!"

74

# The Coming of the Holy Spirit

## WE GATHER

✝ **Leader:** Let us pray as one family filled with the Holy Spirit.

**Reader:** A reading from the Book of Ezekiel

"I will put my spirit in you that you may live, and I will settle you upon your land; thus you shall know that I am the Lord. I have promised, and I will do it, says the Lord." (Ezekiel 37:14)

The word of the Lord.

**All:** Thanks be to God.

🎵 **We Belong to God's Family**

Refrain:
We belong to God's family.
Brothers and sisters are we,
singing together in unity about
one Lord and one faith, one family.

We are one in the Spirit,
the gift from God above.
We are sent to proclaim God's word
and live together in love. (Refrain)

☀ Think of a time someone helped you to change something about yourself. Who helped you and how did you change?

75

## WE BELIEVE

### On Pentecost the Holy Spirit came upon the first disciples.

After his Resurrection, Jesus sent his apostles to preach in his name and to baptize those who believed in him. He promised to send the Holy Spirit to guide and help them.

The Holy Spirit would change their lives. Jesus promised, "you will receive power when the holy Spirit comes upon you, and you will be my witnesses in Jerusalem, throughout Judea and Samaria, and to the ends of the earth" (Acts of the Apostles 1:8).

After Christ ascended to his Father, the apostles returned to Jerusalem. Mary, the mother of Jesus, and some other disciples were there, too. It was during this time that the Holy Spirit came as Jesus had promised.

 Acts of the Apostles 2:1–47

They were all in one place together. And suddenly there came from the sky a noise like a strong driving wind, and it filled the entire house in which they were. Then there appeared to them tongues as of fire, which parted and came to rest on each one of them. And they were all filled with the holy Spirit and began to speak in different tongues, as the Spirit enabled them to proclaim." (Acts of the Apostles 2:1–4)

The apostles went outside. Peter told the people that God the Father had indeed raised Jesus. He said that what they had just heard had been the coming of the Holy Spirit.

Each person heard this good news in his or her own language, and they were amazed. Peter told them to be sorry for their sins and to repent. He told them to be baptized and receive the gift of the Holy Spirit. About three thousand people believed and became disciples that day.

Each year on Pentecost we celebrate in a special way the coming of the Holy Spirit. Strengthened by the Holy Spirit, we are all God's workers in the world.

In groups role-play the story of Pentecost as if it were happening today.

## As Catholics...

We can find two symbols of the Holy Spirit in the Pentecost story: wind and fire. The word *spirit* comes from a Hebrew word that means "wind," "air," and "breath." Wind travels everywhere. It surrounds us. The Holy Spirit does the same.

The symbol of fire suggests warmth, energy, power, and change. Fire changes whatever it touches. So does the Holy Spirit. We are changed by the power of the Holy Spirit.

Talk about other symbols or images of the Holy Spirit.

## Laying on of hands and anointing are signs of the Holy Spirit's presence.

After Pentecost the Holy Spirit strengthened and guided the apostles. They gave witness to Christ and baptized many believers. The newly baptized received the strengthening power of the Holy Spirit when the apostles placed their hands on them. The laying on of hands was a sign of God's blessing. By this action, authority and grace were given in God's name.

The laying on of hands by the apostles was the beginning of the sacrament of Confirmation. As the Church grew, an anointing was joined to the laying on of hands. The word *anoint* means to apply oil to someone as a sign that God has chosen that person for a special mission. Like the laying on of hands, anointing is an ancient practice. Anointing was an important part of Jewish life during Jesus' time.

The anointing that took place with the laying on of hands was a sign of the Holy Spirit's presence and of the receiving of the Holy Spirit. In time the anointing became the essential sign of the Gift of the Holy Spirit. Chrism, oil blessed by a bishop, was used in this anointing. Today in the sacrament of Confirmation, the anointing with oil is done as the celebrant lays his hand on the head of the one being confirmed.

With a partner talk about the actions that are part of our worship. Illustrate one.

## In Confirmation we become more like Christ and are strengthened to be his witnesses.

God the Holy Spirit is always with the Church. We can turn to the Holy Spirit for comfort, guidance, and strength. In the sacrament of **Confirmation** we receive the Gift of the Holy Spirit in a special way. We become more like Christ and are strengthened to be his witnesses.

Confirmation is a sacrament of Christian initiation. The first sacrament of Christian initiation is Baptism. All baptized members of the Church are called to receive the sacrament of Confirmation. Confirmation completes Baptism and along with the Eucharist fully initiates us into the Church.

The sacrament of Confirmation deepens the grace we first received at Baptism. In Confirmation:

• we are sealed with the Gift of God the Holy Spirit

• we become more like Jesus the Son of God and are strengthened to be active witnesses of Jesus

• our friendship with God the Father is deepened

• our relationship with the Church is strengthened

• we are sent forth to live our faith in the world.

Confirmation takes place in the parish community. The bishop usually visits parishes throughout the year and confirms all those who have prepared to receive the sacrament. Adults and older children who are catechumens receive Baptism, Confirmation, and Eucharist at one celebration.

Discuss the way your parish celebrates the sacrament of confirmation.

**Key Word**
Confirmation (p. 267)

## Preparation is an important part of Confirmation.

Those preparing for Confirmation are called candidates. With the help of their parish communities, they pray and reflect on the life of Jesus Christ and on the mission of the Church. Candidates discover what it means to be anointed with chrism and how this anointing will change their lives.

During this preparation candidates grow closer to Christ. They begin to feel a greater sense of belonging to the Church. They learn to share more completely in the mission of the Church.

If we were baptized as infants, our parents selected a name for us. Our name is often that of a saint or someone whom our parents admire. At Confirmation we choose a name, usually that of a saint whose example we can follow. We are encouraged to take our baptismal name to show the connection between Baptism and Confirmation.

If we were baptized as infants, our parents also chose godparents for us. When we are preparing for Confirmation, we choose a sponsor to help us grow in our faith.

A sponsor needs to be a Catholic who has received the sacraments of initiation and is someone we respect and trust. Our sponsor should be an example of Christian living so that he or she can encourage us to follow Jesus. Our sponsor can be one of our godparents, a family member, a friend, or someone from our parish.

Sponsors can help us prepare for Confirmation by sharing their experiences and answering our questions. At the celebration of Confirmation, sponsors present us to the bishop for anointing.

### WE RESPOND

Think of people who are examples of Christian living. In what ways do they encourage others to follow Jesus?

_____

_____

How can the way you live encourage others to follow Jesus?

_____

_____

# Review

**Circle the letter of the correct answer.**

1. Confirmation deepens the gift of grace we first received at _____.

   **a.** Mass    **b.** Baptism    **c.** Eucharist

2. To _____ is to apply oil to someone as a sign that God has chosen that person for a special mission.

   **a.** anoint    **b.** bless    **c.** pray

3. A _____ is a Catholic who helps prepare a candidate for Confirmation.

   **a.** godparent    **b.** disciple    **c.** sponsor

4. There are _____ sacraments of Christian initiation.

   **a.** two    **b.** three    **c.** seven

**Write True or False for the following sentences.**
**Then change the false sentences to make them true.**

5. _____ The Holy Spirit came upon the first disciples at Pentecost.

   _____

   _____

6. _____ In Confirmation we become more like Christ and are strengthened to be his witnesses.

   _____

   _____

7. _____ Laying on of hands and anointing are signs of our sponsor's presence.

   _____

   _____

8. _____ During preparation for Confirmation, godparents learn about the Gift of the Holy Spirit.

   _____

   _____

**Write a sentence to answer the question.**

9–10. What is the importance of the sacrament of Confirmation?

   _____

   _____

ASSESSMENT

Use Scripture, interviews with family or friends, parish sources, periodicals, and the Internet to make a booklet about the meaning of Confirmation. Share your booklet with your classmates or family.

# We Respond in Faith

## Reflect & Pray

Holy Spirit, help the Church to grow. Holy Spirit, help us all to follow Jesus Christ. Help me to

_____

_____

**Key Word**

**Confirmation** (p. 267)

## Remember

- On Pentecost the Holy Spirit came upon the first disciples.

- Laying on of hands and anointing are signs of the Holy Spirit's presence.

- In Confirmation we become more like Christ and are strengthened to be his witnesses.

- Preparation is an important part of Confirmation.

## OUR CATHOLIC LIFE

### Saint John Bosco

John Bosco was born into a poor family near Turin, Italy. He learned about Jesus and the gospel from his mother. He loved to share these teachings with the other children in his neighborhood. Even as a young boy, he witnessed to Christ. He learned ventriloquism so that he could put on puppet shows. He learned to juggle and to walk a tightrope. Before he began his shows, he first led the crowd in prayers and hymns. Only then would he perform for them his latest tricks!

John later became a priest who dedicated himself to helping poor children. He founded a religious order called the Salesians to help children. He also was the first to publish religious education materials for children. Saint John Bosco's feast day is January 31.

# SHARING FAITH
## with My Family

## Sharing What I Learned

Discuss the following with your family:

- Pentecost
- the meaning of Confirmation
- Confirmation as a sacrament of initiation
- preparation for Confirmation.

## A Sacraments Scrapbook

Work with your family to collect prayers, poems, songs, Scripture, pictures, photographs, and so on, that reflect the sacrament of Confirmation. Place your findings on sheets of paper to include in your Sacraments Scapbook.

## A Family Prayer

God of power and mercy,
send your Holy Spirit
to live in our hearts
and make us temples of his glory.

We ask this through our Lord Jesus Christ,
    your Son,
who lives and reigns with you and the
    Holy Spirit, one God, for ever and ever.
Amen.

*from the Rite of Confirmation*

Visit Sadlier's

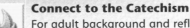
www.WEBELIEVEweb.com

**Connect to the Catechism**
For adult background and reflection, see paragraphs 1287, 1288–1289, 1303, and 1309.

# The Celebration of Confirmation

Right Judgment

Knowledge

Understanding

Reverence

Wonder & Awe

Wisdom

Courage

## WE GATHER

**Leader:** Lord, send out your Spirit.

**All:** And renew the face of the earth!

### ♫ Envía Tu Espíritu

Refrain:
Envía tu Espíritu,
envía tu Espíritu,
envía tu Espíritu, sea renovada
la faz de la tierra.
Sea renovada la faz de la tierra.

**Leader:** Come, Holy Spirit, fill the hearts of your faithful.

**All:** And kindle in them the fire of your love.

**Leader:** Send forth your Spirit and they shall be created.

**All:** And you will renew the face of the earth.

**Leader:** Let us pray.
Lord,
by the light of the Holy Spirit
you have taught the hearts of your faithful.
In the same Spirit
help us to relish what is right
and always rejoice in your consolation.

We ask this through Christ our Lord.

**All:** Amen.

If you could change something in your city or town what would it be? Why?

## WE BELIEVE
### Confirmation leads us from Baptism to the Eucharist.

In the celebration of Confirmation, we gather with our parish community and express our belief in Jesus Christ. Because Confirmation leads us to the Eucharist and full initiation into the Church, we usually celebrate Confirmation within Mass.

As in all the other sacraments, the word of God is proclaimed. The first reading is usually from the Old Testament, and the second is usually from the New Testament. The third reading is always from one of the gospels.

GIFT

After the readings the pastor or a parish leader presents those to be confirmed. These candidates may be called by name as they stand with their sponsors. After the presentation, the bishop gives a brief homily to help everyone understand the readings. He reminds us of our gift of faith, and of the power of the Holy Spirit in our lives. The bishop may ask the candidates about their faith.

The candidates then stand and renew their baptismal promises. They answer each of the questions about their belief in the Blessed Trinity and the Church with the words "I do".

The renewal of the baptismal promises at Confirmation is very important. This is a good time for those who were baptized as infants to profess their faith for themselves.

As Catholics we share the same beliefs. What do you believe as a Catholic? Work in groups and list some of these beliefs.

_____

_____

_____

_____

_____

_____

_____

_____

_____

How can living these beliefs make the world different?

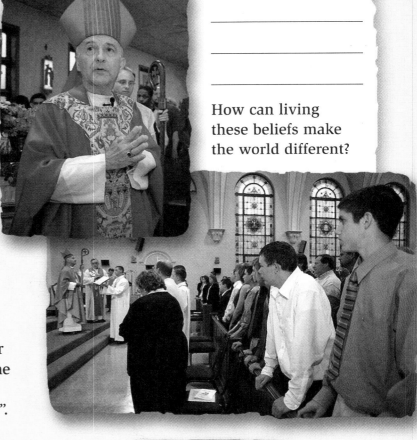

GUIDE

84

# Helper

**In the sacrament of Confirmation, we are sealed with the Gift of the Holy Spirit.**

The bishop reminds all assembled of their Baptism. He invites everyone to pray for the outpouring of the Holy Spirit on those to be confirmed. In the liturgy of Confirmation, the whole Church prays for all these candidates.

The bishop and priests celebrating with him extend their hands over the whole group of candidates. The bishop prays that the Holy Spirit will come and that the candidates will receive the gifts of the Holy Spirit.

Next, the sponsor stands near the candidate and places a hand on the candidate's shoulder. This shows the support and guidance of the sponsor and the ongoing care of the whole parish for those who are being confirmed.

Holy Spirit

The bishop confirms each candidate by the anointing with chrism on the forehead, which is done by the laying on of the hand, and through the words, "N., be sealed with the Gift of the Holy Spirit." The one confirmed responds, "Amen."

The candidates are marked as people who share fully in Jesus' mission. This anointing confirms and completes the baptismal anointing. It is the seal of the Holy Spirit which identifies us as belonging to Jesus Christ. Like the seal of Baptism, it is with us always. Because of this we receive Confirmation only once.

The bishop then shares a sign of peace with the newly confirmed. This action reminds us of the union of the whole Church with the bishop. In the general intercessions we remember the newly confirmed, their families and sponsors, and the whole Church. After each prayer those gathered offer their responses.

The newly confirmed now join with all assembled to continue to worship God by sharing in the gift of Jesus in the Eucharist.

For what would you pray for the Confirmation candidates? Why?

## The gifts of the Holy Spirit help those who are confirmed.

The different titles for the Holy Spirit describe who the Holy Spirit is and the Holy Spirit's role and power in our lives. Jesus once told his apostles, "The Advocate, the holy Spirit that the Father will send in my name—he will teach you everything and remind you of all that [I] told you" (John 14:26). An advocate is someone who intercedes on our behalf, speaks for us, or even defends us. An advocate comforts and teaches.

Jesus also called the Holy Spirit "the Spirit of truth." (John 16:13). The Holy Spirit guides us as we learn the truths of our faith, the truths that Jesus and the Church teach us.

The Holy Spirit is with us to strengthen us to share in the mission of Jesus Christ and to be his witnesses to others. When we receive the sacrament of Confirmation, the Holy Spirit strengthens us with special gifts. The **gifts of the Holy Spirit** are wisdom, understanding, right judgment, courage, knowledge, reverence, and wonder and awe. These seven gifts help us to live as faithful followers of Jesus Christ.

## As Catholics...

The Eastern Catholic Churches celebrate the sacrament of Chrismation. Chrismation is another name for Confirmation. Chrismation and the first celebration of the Eucharist take place right after Baptism. So all three sacraments of initiation are celebrated in one ceremony.

Find out if there is an Eastern Catholic Church in your city or town.

### How the Gifts of the Holy Spirit Help Us

**Wisdom**
helps us to see and follow God's will in our lives.

**Understanding**
helps us to love others as Jesus calls us to do.

**Right Judgment**
aids us in making good choices.

**Courage**
strengthens us to give witness to our faith in Jesus Christ.

**Knowledge**
brings us to learn more about God and his plan, and leads us to wisdom and understanding.

**Reverence**
makes it possible for us to love and respect all that God has created.

**Wonder and Awe**
help us to see God's presence and love filling all creation.

How can these gifts of the Holy Spirit help you as a disciple of Jesus? Role-play some ways you can respond to the gifts of the Holy Spirit in your lives.

## Confirmation calls those anointed to live out their Baptism as witnesses of Jesus Christ.

When we respond to the gifts of the Holy Spirit, our lives are filled with the fruits of the Holy Spirit. "The fruit of the Spirit is love, joy, peace, patience, kindness, generosity, faithfulness, gentleness, self-control." (Galatians 5:22–23) Each day as we grow in faith, we are strengthened by the Holy Spirit to follow God's call to holiness.

As a Church we gather each week with our parish to celebrate that God is with us and to receive the great gift of Jesus Christ himself in the Eucharist. With the help and guidance of the Holy Spirit, we commit ourselves to the work of Jesus. We continue Jesus' work of building up the reign of God, a kingdom of justice and peace. We become witnesses of Jesus Christ. We can do this by becoming people who:

- show kindness to those who are poor
- help a new person in our class feel welcome
- share with others the joy of our Catholic faith
- stand up against injustice and hatred
- work for a better community and world.

Add some other ways that we can be witnesses of Jesus Christ.

- _____
- _____
- _____

## WE RESPOND

Which fruits of the Holy Spirit do you see in the people around you? What fruits can others see in the way you live as a disciple?

**Key Word**

**gifts of the Holy Spirit** (p.268)

**Underline the correct answer.**

1. The Holy Spirit strengthens us with **(six/seven)** special gifts at Confirmation.

2. In Confirmation the anointing with **(chrism/holy water)** is a sign of the Holy Spirit's presence.

3. In **(Confirmation/the Eucharist)** we are sealed with the Gift of the Holy Spirit.

4. At Confirmation, candidates stand and renew **(sponsor's/baptismal)** promises.

**Write the letter that best defines each term.**

5. _____ gifts of the Holy Spirit

6. _____ Advocate and Spirit of truth

7. _____ fruits of the Holy Spirit

8. _____ Confirmation

a. sacrament of healing

b. love, joy, peace, patience, kindness, generosity, faithfulness, gentleness, self-control

c. usually celebrated within the Mass

d. wisdom, understanding, right judgment, courage, knowledge, reverence, wonder and awe

e. titles of the Holy Spirit

**Write a sentence to answer the question.**

**9–10.** How can we give witness to Jesus Christ?

_____

_____

ASSESSMENT

Interview a candidate for Confirmation or someone who has celebrated the sacraments of initiation. Ask him or her to describe the experience. Share your findings with the class.

# We Respond in Faith

## Reflect & Pray

Jesus, you show us how to live. You show us the way to your Father. Help me to reach out to everyone I meet with love and

kindness, especially _____

Holy Spirit, strengthen and guide me as I _____

_____

**Key Word**

**gifts of the Holy Spirit**
(p. 268)

## Remember

- Confirmation leads us from Baptism to the Eucharist.
- In the sacrament of Confirmation, we are sealed with the Gift of the Holy Spirit.
- The gifts of the Holy Spirit help those who are confirmed.
- Confirmation calls those anointed to live out their Baptism as witnesses of Jesus Christ.

## OUR CATHOLIC LIFE

### World Youth Day

World Youth Day is an event that the Catholic Church celebrates every two years. It is an opportunity for Catholic youth all over the world to meet with one another and with our Holy Father, the pope. This event is a wonderful chance to renew faith, to be strengthened as part of the Body of Christ, and to give witness to the good news of Christ throughout the world.

The first World Youth Day was held in Rome in 1985. It has also been held in other cities and countries. Pope John Paul II traveled to Argentina, Spain, Poland, France, the Philippines, Canada, and the United States for World Youth Day.

# SHARING FAITH
## with My Family

## Sharing What I Learned

Discuss the following with your family:

- celebrating the sacrament of Confirmation
- receiving the gifts of the Holy Spirit
- anointing with chrism accompanied by the laying on of hands
- becoming a witness of Jesus Christ.

### A Family Prayer

Lord,
fulfill your promise:
send your Holy Spirit to make us witnesses
before the world
to the Good News proclaimed by Jesus
Christ, our Lord.
Amen.

*from the Rite of Confirmation*

## Sacrament Trading Cards

Design a trading card for the sacrament of Confirmation using the pattern below. Use your knowledge about this sacrament to write "sacrament facts" on the back of the card. Collect all seven!

### Confirmation

What is the importance of the sacrament?

_____

What do we see?

_____

What do we hear?

_____

Who leads us in the celebration?

_____

Visit Sadlier's

**www.WeBelieveweb.com**

**Connect to the Catechism**
For adult background and reflection, see paragraphs 1298, 1300, 1299, and 1305.

# Jesus Christ, the Bread of Life

## 10

## WE GATHER

✝ **Leader:** Jesus said, "Do not work for food that perishes but for the food that endures for eternal life, which the Son of Man will give you" (John 6:27).

**All:** Give us life today and forever.

**Leader:** Jesus said, "I am the bread of life; whoever comes to me will never hunger, and whoever believes in me will never thirst" (John 6:35).

**All:** Give us life today and forever.

**Leader:** Jesus said, "I am the living bread that came down from heaven; whoever eats this bread will live forever; and the bread that I will give is my flesh for the life of the world" (John 6:51).

**All:** Give us life today and forever.

**Leader:** Jesus said, "Whoever eats my flesh and drinks my blood remains in me and I in him" (John 6:56).

**All:** Give us life today and forever.

**Leader:** Jesus, help us stay close to you always. May the food you give strengthen us always.

**All:** Amen.

☀ Name some ways that people we love remain close to us even when they are not with us.

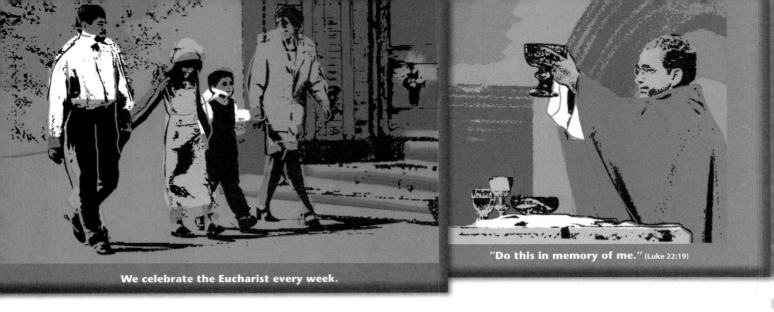

We celebrate the Eucharist every week.

"Do this in memory of me." (Luke 22:19)

## WE BELIEVE

### In the Eucharist we celebrate and receive Jesus Christ.

Every year the Jewish people gather to celebrate a feast called **Passover**. They remember the miraculous way that God saved them from slavery in ancient Egypt. God "passed over" the houses of his people, protecting them from the suffering that came to the Egyptians.

On the night before he was to die, Jesus and the apostles celebrated Passover in Jerusalem. During this meal, which we call the Last Supper, Jesus gave his disciples a special way to remember him and to be with him.

Jesus took his place among the apostles. "Then he took the bread, said the blessing, broke it, and gave it to them, saying, 'This is my body, which will be given for you; do this in memory of me.' And likewise the cup after they had eaten, saying, 'This cup is the new covenant in my blood, which will be shed for you.'" (Luke 22:19–20)

At the Last Supper Jesus gave us the gift of himself and instituted the Eucharist. Through the Eucharist Jesus remains with us forever. The **Eucharist** is the sacrament of the Body and Blood of Christ. Jesus is truly present under the appearances of bread and wine. In the sacrament of the Eucharist

- we are nourished by the word of God and receive Jesus Christ in Holy Communion

- we are joined more closely to Christ and one another

- the grace received in Baptism grows in us

- we are strengthened to love and serve others.

Why is the Eucharist important to Catholics?

## As Catholics...

A covenant is an agreement made between God and his people. God made a covenant with Moses and his people after their escape from Egypt. God promised to be their God and to protect and provide for them. The people promised to be his people. They would worship the one true God and live by his laws. Jewish people today still live by this covenant.

Christians believe that a new covenant was made by Jesus' death and Resurrection. Through this new covenant we are saved, and it is possible for us to share in God's life again. As we celebrate the Eucharist this week remember that we are celebrating the new covenant.

The Eucharist is a meal.

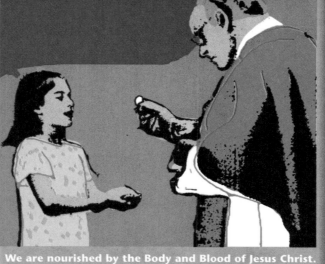

We are nourished by the Body and Blood of Jesus Christ.

The Eucharist is a sacrifice.

### The Eucharist is a memorial, a meal, and a sacrifice.

The Eucharist is the only sacrament of initiation that we receive again and again. In the Eucharist, we honor Jesus by remembering what he did for us, share in a meal, and participate in a sacrifice.

Jesus told his apostles to "do this in memory of me" (Luke 22:19). By gathering and breaking bread, we are remembering the new life we have because of Jesus' death and Resurrection. In this way the Eucharist is a memorial, but is much more than just remembering past events. In the Eucharist, Christ is really present. By the power of the Holy Spirit, the Paschal Mystery of Christ's suffering, death, Resurrection, and Ascension is made present to us.

When Jesus gave us the Eucharist, he and his friends were eating and celebrating. In the Eucharist we share in a meal. We are nourished by the Body and Blood of Christ. When we receive Holy Communion, Jesus lives in us and we live in him.

During the celebration of the Eucharist, Jesus acts through the priest. A **sacrifice** is a gift offered to God by a priest in the name of all the people. At each celebration of the Eucharist, Jesus' sacrifice on the cross,

his Resurrection, and his Ascension into heaven are made present again.

In the Eucharist Jesus also offers his Father the gifts of praise and thanksgiving. The whole Church also offers thanks and praise. We join Jesus in offering ourselves to God the Father. We offer our joys, concerns, and willingness to live as Jesus' disciples.

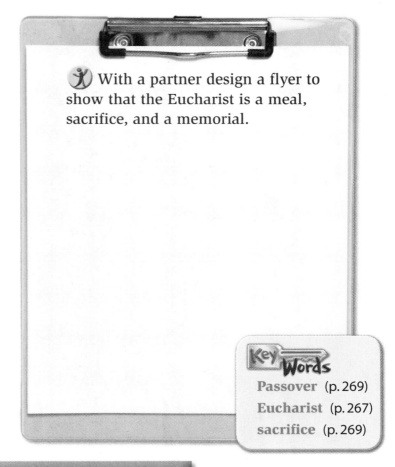

With a partner design a flyer to show that the Eucharist is a meal, sacrifice, and a memorial.

**Key Words**

Passover (p. 269)

Eucharist (p. 267)

sacrifice (p. 269)

## We recognize Jesus in the breaking of the bread.

📖 Luke 24:13–35

On the day of Jesus' Resurrection, two disciples were walking to the village of Emmaus. They were very sad about Jesus' death. They had heard about the empty tomb and were concerned. As the disciples were talking, a man joined them. It was the risen Jesus, but the disciples did not recognize him.

Jesus asked them what they had been discussing. The disciples told him about

Master of Santo Domingo de Silos (late 11th–mid 12th Century), *Journey to Emmaus*

the death of Jesus and the empty tomb, and they were amazed that this stranger had not heard about this.

As they walked Jesus taught them about Scripture. When they got to Emmaus, the disciples invited Jesus to have dinner. At this meal Jesus took bread and blessed it. He then broke the bread and gave it to them. Suddenly, the disciples recognized the risen Jesus. Then instantly, Jesus was gone.

The two disciples returned to Jerusalem. They told the others what had happened and how Jesus ". . . was made known to them in the breaking of the bread" (Luke 24:35).

🏃 Imagine that you are one of the disciples from Emmaus. Write two words that describe your feelings when you recognize Jesus.

_____

_____

**Key Word**
**real presence**
(p. 269)

The first Christians "devoted themselves to the teaching of the apostles and to the communal life, to the breaking of the bread and to the prayers" (Acts of the Apostles 2:42). They used the words "breaking of the bread" to describe their celebrations of the Eucharist.

Like the early Christians, we gather for the breaking of the bread. In the Eucharist, the Body and Blood of Christ are actually present under the appearances of bread and wine. Jesus is really and truly present in the Eucharist. This is called the **real presence**.

## Jesus is the Bread of Life.

Before Jesus died he performed a miracle to feed his hungry disciples. He fed about five thousand people with only five loaves of bread and two fish. The next day people asked Jesus about what he had done. He told them, "I am the bread of life; whoever comes to me will never hunger, and whoever believes in me will never thirst" (John 6:35).

Jesus' followers knew that they needed bread to live. But he wanted them to know that belief in him is needed to have life with God. Jesus continued, "I am the living bread that came down from heaven" (John 6:51).

By calling himself the Bread of Life and the Living Bread, Jesus helped his disciples to understand that he was the Son of God sent to bring God's life to them. Jesus brings life with God forever. Whoever truly believes that Jesus is the Son of God and lives as his disciple will have eternal life.

Jesus wants us to be nourished by his life so that we can help others in his name. He wants us to have life with God forever. So he gives

himself to us in the Eucharist. He is our Bread of Life. When we receive the Eucharist, we share in God's own life.

When we receive the Body and Blood of Christ in Holy Communion, our relationship with Christ and one another is strengthened. We become the Body of Christ, the Church. We are better able to live our faith in the world as children of God. We can do this by protecting life, respecting the rights of others, and helping people to meet their needs.

## WE RESPOND

 **I Am the Bread of Life**

I am the Bread of life.
You who come to me shall not hunger;
and who believe in me shall not thirst.
No one can come to me unless the
    Father beckons.

Pray quietly to thank Jesus for nourishing us with the Eucharist.

**Circle the letter of the correct answer.**

1. _____ is the sacrament by which Jesus truly becomes present to us.

   **a.** Baptism          **b.** Confirmation

   **c.** Eucharist

2. In the Eucharist, we receive _____ in Holy Communion.

   **a.** the priest          **b.** the disciples

   **c.** Jesus Christ

3. The Eucharist is a meal, a sacrifice, and _____.

   **a.** a memorial          **b.** an invitation

   **c.** a Passover

4. Jesus called himself the _____.

   **a.** Life of Bread          **b.** Bread of Life

   **c.** Flesh of Bread

**Write True or False for the following sentences.
Then change the false sentences to make them true.**

5. _____ Eucharist is the only sacrament of initiation that we receive again and again.

   _____

   _____

6. _____ At the Last Supper, Jesus instituted the Passover.

   _____

   _____

7. _____ While walking to Emmaus, two disciples instantly recognized the risen Jesus.

   _____

   _____

8. _____ When we receive the Eucharist, the life of grace in us grows.

   _____

   _____

**Write a sentence to answer the question.**

**9–10.** Why do we celebrate the sacrament of the Eucharist?

_____

_____

ASSESSMENT

List some important words and phrases about the Eucharist. Use them in a short presentation on the history and meaning of the Eucharist.

# We Respond in Faith

## Reflect & Pray

Close your eyes and feel Jesus' presence.

Jesus, sometimes life is _____

Stay close to me. Keep me faithful to you in the Eucharist.

Help me _____

_____

Amen.

**Key Words**

Passover (p. 269)
Eucharist (p. 267)
sacrifice (p. 269)
real presence (p. 269)

## Remember

- In the Eucharist, we celebrate and receive Jesus Christ.
- The Eucharist is a memorial, a meal, and a sacrifice.
- We recognize Jesus in the breaking of the bread.
- Jesus is the Bread of Life.

## OUR CATHOLIC LIFE

### The Feast of the Body and Blood of Christ

Each year we celebrate this feast on the second Sunday after Pentecost. It is sometimes called "Corpus Christi Sunday" because the term Body of Christ comes from the Latin words *Corpus Christi*.

On this day we celebrate in a special way the presence of Jesus Christ with us in the Eucharist. Many parishes celebrate with a Mass and procession in honor of the Blessed Sacrament, the Eucharist. People carry banners and flowers. The priest carries the Blessed Sacrament in a special holder called a monstrance, so that it can be easily seen by all. We celebrate the life that Jesus brings us in the Eucharist.

# SHARING FAITH
## with My Family

## Sharing What I Learned

Discuss the following with your family:

- Last Supper and the Eucharist
- the Eucharist as a meal, a memorial, and a sacrifice
- the real presence
- the Bread of Life.

## A Sacraments Scrapbook

Work with your family to collect prayers, poems, songs, Scripture, pictures, photographs, and so on, that reflect the sacrament of the Eucharist. Place your findings on sheets of paper to include in your Sacraments Scrapbook.

## A Family Prayer

Lord, our God,
you have given us the true bread from
   heaven.
In the strength of this food
may we live always by your life
and rise in glory on the last day.

We ask this through Christ our Lord.
Amen.

*from the Rite of the Eucharist*

Visit Sadlier's
**www.WeBelieveweb.com**

**Connect to the Catechism**
For adult background and reflection, see paragraphs 1324, 1328, 1329, 1330, and 1338.

# The Celebration of the Eucharist

## 11

## WE GATHER

✝ **Leader:** Let us listen to the story of Jesus and his apostles as they gathered for the Last Supper.

**Reader 1:** Jesus said to the apostles,

"'I have eagerly desired to eat this Passover with you before I suffer, for, I tell you, I shall not eat it [again] until there is fulfillment in the kingdom of God.' Then he took a cup, gave thanks, and said, 'Take this and share it among yourselves; for I tell you [that] from this time on I shall not drink of the fruit of the vine until the kingdom of God comes.'"
(Luke 22:15–18)

**All:** Jesus, you have given your life for us.

**Reader 2:** "Then he took the bread, said the blessing, broke it, and gave it to them, saying, 'This is my body, which will be given for you; do this in memory of me.' And likewise the cup after they had eaten, saying, 'This cup is the new covenant in my blood, which will be shed for you.'" (Luke 22:19–20)

**All:** Jesus, you have given your life for us.

🎵 **We Belong to God's Family**

Refrain:

We belong to God's family.
Brothers and sisters are we,
singing together in unity
about one Lord and one faith,
one family.
We are one in the body of
Jesus Christ the Lord.
We are one in the blood of him
whom earth and heaven adore.
(Refrain)

☀ Name a time when everyone in your school gathers together as one community. Why is this an important time?

## WE BELIEVE
### The Introductory Rites bring us together as a community.

The Mass is another name for the celebration of the Eucharist. In the Mass the Church gathers as the Body of Christ. The assembly, or community of people gathered to worship in the name of Jesus, participates in many ways throughout the Mass. Some of the things we do are sing, listen and respond to the readings, pray for all people, and receive Holy Communion.

There are many people who help us during the celebration of the Mass. The different ways that people serve the Church in worship are called liturgical ministries.

The presider is the priest who celebrates the Eucharist for and with the people of God. He does and says the things Jesus did at the Last Supper. The deacon has a special role in proclaiming the gospel and in the preaching. He assists at the altar and leads the assembly in certain prayers.

Altar servers assist in many ways before, during, and after Mass. Readers proclaim the word of God and special ministers of the Eucharist help to distribute Holy Communion. Greeters or ushers often welcome us before Mass begins. Musicians help the whole assembly participate through song.

There are four parts to the Mass: the Introductory Rites, the Liturgy of the Word, the Liturgy of the Eucharist, and the Concluding Rite. (See chart on page 256.) The **Introductory Rites** is the part of the Mass that unites us as a community. It prepares us to hear God's word and to celebrate the Eucharist. During this time we ask God for mercy in the Penitential Rite. On Sundays we may sing or say the Gloria.

Illustrate one way you can help others to participate in your parish's Sunday celebration of the Mass.

## During the Liturgy of the Word, we listen and respond to the word of God.

After the Introductory Rites, we listen to the living word of God proclaimed from Scripture. The **Liturgy of the Word** is the part of the Mass in which we listen and respond to God's word. We hear about God's great love for his people. We hear about the life and teaching of Christ. We profess our faith and pray for all people in need.

To proclaim something is to announce it clearly and from the heart. To proclaim during the liturgy is to announce with faith. Our response to the readings proclaims our belief in God's word. After the first and second reading we respond "Thanks be to God." After the gospel we respond "Praise to you, Lord Jesus Christ." The homily is a proclamation, too. The words of the deacon or priest are a call to live the good news and to be witnesses to Christ.

Next, the assembly prays the general intercessions. Members of the assembly read the prayers, and we all respond "Lord, hear our prayer" or another suitable response.

As the Body of Christ united for worship, we pray for the needs of the whole Church, for the pope, and all Church leaders. We pray for our local community. We ask God to guide world leaders and those in public positions. We call on God to be with those who suffer from sickness and to help us care for those who are in need. We also pray that those who have died may experience God's love.

**Key Words**

**Introductory Rites** (p. 268)
**Liturgy of the Word** (p. 268)

### As Catholics...

The *lectionary* is a collection of Scripture readings that have been assigned to the various days of the Church year. We treat the lectionary with respect because it contains the word of God. We treat the *Book of the Gospels* with special reverence because it contains the good news of Jesus Christ.

How do the deacon and the priest show the importance of the Book of the Gospels?

With a partner name ways we can better listen to God's word. Share your ideas with the class.

## During the Liturgy of the Eucharist, we pray the great prayer of thanksgiving and receive the Body and Blood of Christ.

The **Liturgy of the Eucharist** is the part of the Mass in which the death and Resurrection of Christ are made present again. In this part of the Mass our gifts of bread and wine become the Body and Blood of Christ, which we receive in Holy Communion. The Liturgy of the Eucharist has three parts: the preparation of the gifts, the eucharistic prayer, and the communion rite.

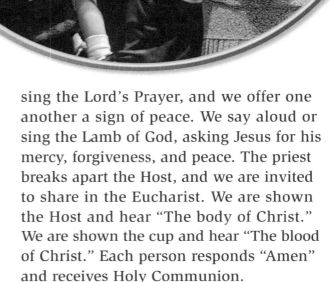

During the preparation of the gifts, the altar is prepared, and we offer gifts. These gifts include the bread and wine and the collection for the Church and for those in need.

The eucharistic prayer is truly the most important prayer of the Church. It is our greatest prayer of praise and thanksgiving.

In this prayer we offer God thanks and praise and sing "Holy, Holy, Holy." The priest calls on the Holy Spirit to bless the gifts of bread and wine, and he recalls Jesus' words and actions at the Last Supper. By the power of the Holy Spirit and through the words and actions of the priest, the bread and wine become the Body and Blood of Christ. This part of the prayer is called the **consecration**.

We then pray for the needs of the Church. We pray that all who receive the Body and Blood of Christ will be joined. We sing or say the great "Amen," and unite ourselves to this great prayer of thanksgiving which is prayed by the priest in our name and in the name of Christ.

The communion rite is the third part of the Liturgy of the Eucharist. We pray aloud or sing the Lord's Prayer, and we offer one another a sign of peace. We say aloud or sing the Lamb of God, asking Jesus for his mercy, forgiveness, and peace. The priest breaks apart the Host, and we are invited to share in the Eucharist. We are shown the Host and hear "The body of Christ." We are shown the cup and hear "The blood of Christ." Each person responds "Amen" and receives Holy Communion.

Every day we are called to give God thanks and praise. For what will you give thanks and praise today?

### The Concluding Rite sends us out to be the Body of Christ to others.

The Eucharist is nourishment. We can be weakened by sin or can find ourselves turning from God. The Eucharist renews our Baptism and restores our strength.

The Eucharist commits us to caring for the needs of others. Jesus gives himself freely to us in Holy Communion. He asks us to do the same. He sends us out from Mass to give ourselves freely to help others.

When we work to change the things that keep people from having what they need, we show the power of God's life in our lives and in the Church.

The last part of the Mass is called the **Concluding Rite**. In this rite we are blessed and sent forth to be Christ's servants in the world and to love others as he has loved us.

After the blessing, the deacon or priest says these or other words: "The Mass is ended, go in peace." We are sent out to make the world a better place to live. So we say, "Thanks be to God." We say these words to show that we are thankful and willing to do all that we can to live as the people of God.

**Key Words**

**Liturgy of the Eucharist** (p. 268)

**consecration** (p. 267)

**Concluding Rite** (p. 267)

## WE RESPOND

 In a group list some ways we can live as the people of God with our friends and in our neighborhoods.

_____

_____

_____

_____

_____

Act out one of these ways.

**Complete the following.**

1. The _____ is the part of Mass in which we are all blessed and sent forth to be Christ's servants in the world and to love one another as he has loved us.

2. The _____ is the part of the Mass that unites us as a community and prepares us to hear God's word and celebrate the Eucharist.

3. The _____ is the part of the Mass in which the death and Resurrection of Christ are made present again and our gifts of bread and wine become the Body and Blood of Christ.

4. The _____ is the part of Mass in which we listen and respond to God's word.

**Short Answers**

5. What is another name for the celebration of the Eucharist?

_____

6. What are three ways people can serve at Mass?

_____

7. What is our greatest prayer of praise and thanksgiving?

_____

8. What are two ways the Eucharist helps us to grow in holiness and act with justice?

_____

**Write a sentence to answer the question.**

9–10. What are the ways Jesus is present in the celebration of the Mass?

_____

_____

ASSESSMENT

Design a Web page for webelieveweb.com about the Mass. Show how the four parts of the Mass unite and strengthen the Body of Christ.

# We Respond in Faith

## Reflect & Pray

Lord Jesus, you are with us always. You come to us in a special way in the Eucharist. By receiving Holy Communion, help me to

_____. I want to share my faith in you

with the people I meet by _____.
Amen.

## Remember

- The Introductory Rites bring us together as a community.

- During the Liturgy of the Word, we listen and respond to the word of God.

- During the Liturgy of the Eucharist, we pray the great prayer of thanksgiving and receive the Body and Blood of Christ.

- The Concluding Rite sends us out to be the Body of Christ to others.

### Key Words

Introductory Rites
(p. 268)
Liturgy of the Word
(p. 268)
Liturgy of the
Eucharist (p. 268)
consecration (p. 267)
Concluding Rite (p. 267)

## OUR CATHOLIC LIFE

### Blessed Kateri Tekakwitha

Blessed Kateri Tekakwitha was a Native American who was born in New York State in 1656. She was a woman who took Jesus' call to holiness very seriously. She taught children. She cared for people who were ill or elderly, and she lived a life of prayer. She was devoted to Jesus and received Holy Communion frequently. She died at the age of twenty four. Her feast day in the United States is July 14.

BLESSED KATERI TEKAKWITHA of the IROQUOIS

# SHARING FAITH
## with My Family

## Sharing What I Learned

Discuss the following with your family:

- the Introductory Rites
- the Liturgy of the Word
- the Liturgy of the Eucharist
- the Concluding Rite.

## Sacrament Trading Cards

Design a trading card for the sacrament of the Eucharist using the pattern below. Use your knowledge about this sacrament to write "sacrament facts" on the back of the card. Collect all seven!

### A Family Prayer

Lord,
give to our hearts
the light of faith and the fire of love,
that we may worship in spirit and in truth
our God and Lord, present in this sacrament,
who lives and reigns for ever and ever.
Amen.

*from the Rite of the Eucharist*

## Eucharist

What is the importance of the sacrament?

_____

What do we see?

_____

What do we hear?

_____

Who leads us in the celebration?

_____

Visit Sadlier's

**www.WeBelieveweb.com**

**Connect to the Catechism**
For adult background and reflection, see paragraphs 1348, 1349, 1352, 1355, and 1396.

# Living As Prayerful People

## 12

## WE GATHER

**✟ Leader:** O God, come to my assistance.

**All:** Lord, make haste to help me.

**Side 1:** Glory to the Father, and to the Son, and to the Holy Spirit:

**Side 2:** as it was in the beginning, is now, and will be for ever. Amen.

**Leader:** "My help comes from the LORD,

**All:** the maker of heaven and earth."

(Psalm 121:2)

**Side 1:** "I raise my eyes toward the mountains. From where will my help come?

**Side 2:** My help comes from the LORD, the maker of heaven and earth.

**Side 1:** God will not allow your foot to slip; your guardian does not sleep.

**Side 2:** Truly, the guardian of Israel never slumbers nor sleeps.

**Side 1:** The LORD is your guardian; the LORD is your shade at your right hand.

**Side 2:** By day the sun cannot harm you, nor the moon by night."

(Psalm 121:1–6)

**Side 1:** Glory to the Father, and to the Son, and to the Holy Spirit:

**Side 2:** as it was in the beginning, is now, and will be for ever. Amen.

**All:** "My help comes from the LORD."

(Psalm 121:2)

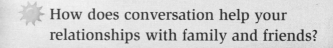 How does conversation help your relationships with family and friends?

## WE BELIEVE
### Jesus teaches us to pray.

Prayer is like a conversation. God calls to us in prayer, and we respond. Our prayer is a response to God's constant love for us.

In prayer we open our hearts and minds to God. We can pray alone or with others, in silence or aloud. Sometimes we do not use words to pray, but sit quietly trying to focus only on God.

Jesus taught us to pray with patience and complete trust in God. Jesus prayed in many ways. He thanked God the Father for his blessings and asked God to be with him. He prayed for the needs of others and forgave sinners in the name of his Father.

From the example of Jesus, most especially the Lord's Prayer, we learn to pray.

The Holy Spirit guides the Church to pray. Urged by the Holy Spirit, we pray these basic forms of prayer: blessing, petition, intercession, thanksgiving, and praise.

To bless is to dedicate someone or something to God or to make something holy in God's name. God blesses us with many gifts. Because God first blessed us, we can pray for his blessings on people and things.

Prayers of petition are prayers in which we ask something of God. Asking for forgiveness is the most important type of petition.

An intercession is a type of petition. When we pray a prayer of intercession, we are asking for something on behalf of another person or a group of people.

Prayers of thanksgiving show our gratitude to God for all he has given us. We show our gratitude most especially for the life, death, and Resurrection of Jesus.

Prayers of praise give glory to God for being God. They do not involve our needs or thanks. They are pure praise.

Think about what is happening in your life and in the world around you. Write your own prayer.

_____

_____

_____

_____

_____

Pray this prayer throughout the week.

## We are called to pray daily.

By praying throughout the day, we respond to God's desire to know us. Both personal prayer and communal prayer—prayer we pray as a community—help us to feel and remember God's presence.

The habit of daily prayer grows by making special times for prayer. We can pray in the morning and offer our entire day to God. Before and after meals we can give thanks to God for his many gifts. At night we can think about the ways we have or have not shown love for God and for others. We can see the ways God has been acting in our lives.

The habit of daily prayer also grows by joining in prayer with other members of the Church. The **Liturgy of the Hours** is a public prayer of the Church. It is made up of psalms, readings from Scripture and Church teaching, prayers, and hymns, and is celebrated at various times during the day. These prayers, especially morning prayer and evening prayer, help us to praise God throughout the entire day.

Of all days Sunday, the Lord's Day, is the most holy. We celebrate Christ's death and Resurrection in a special way on this day. All around the world Catholics gather with their parishes to celebrate the Eucharist. This Sunday celebration is at the very heart of our life in the Church.

We are obliged, or required, to participate in Sunday Mass, which may be celebrated any time from Saturday evening to Sunday evening.

In addition to Sunday, we are also obliged to participate in the Mass on holy days of obligation. A **holy day of obligation** is a day set apart to celebrate a special event in the life of Jesus, Mary, or the saints. The holy days of obligation celebrated in the United States can be found on page 262.

Imagine that you are in a peaceful place. Open your heart to God. Listen to what he is saying to you.

**Words**
**Liturgy of the Hours** (p. 268)
**holy day of obligation** (p. 268)

Many sacramentals remind us of the sacraments and of what God does for us through the sacraments. Sacramentals also make us more aware of God's presence in our lives and keep us focused on God. Blessing the food we eat, making the sign of the cross as we enter or leave a church, and seeing a crucifix in our home are all reminders of our faith and trust in God.

List some sacramentals that can help you to pray at home and in Church.

_____

_____

## Sacramentals are a part of the Church's prayer life.

Our prayer not only involves our thoughts and words. It involves gestures and objects, too. Blessings, actions, and objects that help us respond to God's grace received in the sacraments are sacramentals. Blessings are the most important **sacramentals**. Not only is the blessing itself a sacramental, but what is blessed can also become a sacramental.

Sacramentals are used in the liturgy and in personal prayer. Here are some examples of sacramentals:

- blessings of people, places, foods, and objects
- objects such as rosaries, medals, crucifixes, blessed ashes, and blessed palms
- actions such as making the sign of the cross and sprinkling blessed water.

## Catholics have a rich tradition of special practices and popular devotions.

Eucharistic adoration, which takes place outside the celebration of the Mass, is also part of the liturgy of the Church. Jesus' presence in the Eucharist is honored in various ways. After Holy Communion, the remaining consecrated Bread, or Hosts, are put aside in the tabernacle. This reserved Eucharist is called the Blessed Sacrament. The Blessed Sacrament can be brought to those who are sick and unable to participate in the Mass. It is also reserved for worship.

Many parishes have an Exposition of the Blessed Sacrament. In this ceremony the Blessed Sacrament, placed in a special holder called a monstrance, is presented for all to see. In a ceremony called Benediction, the community gathers to pray and to worship Jesus in the Blessed Sacrament.

Benediction of the Blessed Sacrament is sometimes a part of popular devotions.

Popular devotions are prayer practices that are not part of the Church's official public prayer, or liturgy. Popular devotions have grown from the practices of different groups of people. Catholics have rich and diverse prayer practices that have come from many cultures throughout the Church's history. Some of the popular devotions include novenas, stations of the cross, and pilgrimages.

Novenas include special prayers and are often followed by Benediction. The word *novena* comes from the Latin word meaning "nine." Novenas are special prayers or prayer services that occur nine times. Often they occur nine days in a row or on the same day of the week for nine weeks in a row.

Another popular devotion is the stations of the cross. Stations of the cross focus our attention on the passion and death of Jesus. By moving from one station to the next and praying the appropriate prayers, those gathered for this devotion join Jesus as he makes his way to his death on the cross. The stations of the cross can be found on page 266.

Pilgrimages, or prayer journeys, to holy places or shrines, and processions to honor Mary and the saints are also forms of devotion.

## WE RESPOND

In a group discuss some popular devotions in your community. Where can you find out more about them?

Key Word
**sacramentals** (p. 269)

The stations of the cross can be found on page 266.

## As Catholics...

Some devotions to Mary, the Blessed Mother, came about after her appearances to people in various countries. She appeared at Lourdes, France in 1858 and Fatima, Portugal in 1917.

Mary's appearances outside Mexico City in the year 1531 are very important to Catholics living in the Americas. In 1531 the Blessed Mother came to an Aztec man named Juan Diego. She spoke to him in his native language, and an image miraculously appeared on his cloak of her as a Native American. This image proved so powerful that the people, including Church leaders, believed that Mary had truly been there. She became known by this image as Our Lady of Guadalupe.

Every year we celebrate the feast of Saint Juan Diego on December 9 and of Our Lady of Guadalupe on December 12. How does your parish celebrate these special feasts?

**Procession for the Feast of the Assumption.**

**Parade in honor of Our Lady of Guadalupe.**

**Write True or False for the following sentences.
Then change the false sentences to make them true.**

1. _____ The Holy Spirit guides the Church to pray.

_____

_____

2. _____ A novena is a day we are obliged to participate in the Mass to celebrate a special event in the life of Jesus, Mary, or the saints.

_____

_____

3. _____ Catholics are obliged to participate in Sunday Mass.

_____

_____

4. _____ A sacramental is an effective sign given to us by Jesus through which we share in God's life, grace.

_____

_____

**Write the letter that best describes each type of prayer listed.**

5. _____ blessing

6. _____ intercession

7. _____ praise

8. _____ thanksgiving

a. prayer that shows our gratitude to God for all he has given us

b. prayer that dedicates someone or something to God or makes something holy in God's name

c. prayer that gives glory to God for being God

d. prayer in which we ask God for something on behalf of another person or a group of people

e. prayer in which we ask something of God

**Write a sentence to answer the question.**

**9–10.** How did Jesus teach us to live as prayerful people?

_____

_____

ASSESSMENT

Make a collection of your favorite Bible readings, prayers, hymns, and devotional practices. Use captions to explain these prayers and practices.

# We Respond in Faith

## Reflect & Pray

God calls us to pray. I can open my heart and my mind to God by

_____

Holy Spirit guide me to _____

_____

Amen.

### Key Words

**Liturgy of the Hours** (p. 268)

**holy day of obligation** (p. 268)

**sacramentals** (p. 269)

## Remember

- Jesus teaches us to pray.
- We are called to pray daily.
- Sacramentals are a part of the Church's prayer life.
- Catholics have a rich tradition of special practices and popular devotions.

## OUR CATHOLIC LIFE

### Las Posadas

Las Posadas is a Christmas novena. It means "The Inns." Catholics in Mexico and in many places in the United States participate in Las Posadas during the nine days before Christmas each year. Every evening, the people of a town or parish act out the story of Mary and Joseph on their way to Bethlehem. The actors that play Mary and Joseph go from house to house. They knock at the door and ask for shelter. But no one will let them in until the last day of Las Posadas. Then, the innkeeper welcomes them and all the people gather for a party. Las Posadas reminds us that we must always be ready to welcome Jesus into our lives and into our homes.

# SHARING FAITH
## with My Family

## Sharing What I Learned

Discuss the following with your family:

- forms of prayer
- daily prayer and the importance of Sunday
- sacramentals
- popular devotions.

## Family Faith Checklist

Ask your family to complete the Family Faith Checklist. Share your experiences.

### A Family Prayer

We give you thanks for all your gifts, almighty God,
living and reigning now and for ever. Amen.

*from Catholic Household Blessings and Prayers*

## Our Family

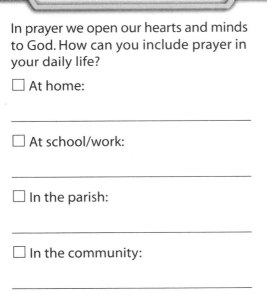

In prayer we open our hearts and minds to God. How can you include prayer in your daily life?

☐ At home:

_____

☐ At school/work:

_____

☐ In the parish:

_____

☐ In the community:

_____

Visit Sadlier's

**www.WeBelieveweb.com**

**Connect to the Catechism**
For adult background and reflection, see paragraphs 2765, 1174, 1670, and 1674.

# Advent

O Radiant Dawn, splendor of eternal light,
sun of justice.

# Advent is a season of joyful expectation and preparation for the coming of the Son of God.

## WE GATHER

✝ *O Radiant Dawn, Jesus, come and shine on us!*

Have you ever seen an exciting movie clip that ended with the words "Coming soon"? How did these words make you feel?

## WE BELIEVE

The word *Advent* means "coming." Jesus Christ, the Son of God who became one of us, is coming into our lives. During the four weeks of Advent, we prepare to celebrate Christ's coming.

- We hope for Christ's coming in the future, and we prepare by being his faithful followers today.

- We celebrate Christ's presence in the world today. He comes to us every day in the celebration of the Eucharist, in all the sacraments, and in the love we have for one another.

- We wait with joyful expectation to celebrate that Jesus first came to us over two thousand years ago in Bethlehem. We prepare to celebrate that coming of the Savior, the Son of God.

We use the color violet during Advent as a sign of waiting and joyful expectation. This color is also a sign of penance. So in Advent celebrating the sacrament of Reconciliation is an important way to prepare for the celebration of the coming of Christ.

During the weeks of Advent, we wait as the people did before Jesus' birth. They had waited many, many years for the Savior to come. During those years of waiting, God spoke to his people through the prophets.

Faithful followers of Jesus, working together and showing the love we have for one another

The prophets encouraged the people to live by the covenant. They told them that their God was loving and merciful, that he had not forgotten them. The prophets spoke of a Messiah who would be an anointed king, a just ruler, and a Savior. He would bring about a kingdom of peace and justice.

We believe that Jesus is the Messiah for whom they waited, but he is more. Jesus Christ is the Son of God who became one of us.

From December 17 through December 23, our hope and expectation grow. We are eager to celebrate the coming of the Messiah into the world. So during this time the Church prays the "O Antiphons." An antiphon is a short prayer. They are called the "O Antiphons" because they all begin with the one-letter word "O."

In each of the seven antiphons, we call on Jesus by different titles that come from the Old Testament prophets. In each of these short prayers we praise Christ for what he has done for us and call on him to come to all of God's people.

Modern day prophet, Cardinal Nguyen Van Thuan, president of the Pontifical Council for Justice and Peace

117

Today the O Antiphons are most familiar to us in the hymn "O Come, O Come Emmanuel." Each verse of the hymn parallels one of the antiphons.

From December 17 to December 23 the O Antiphons are recited or sung during Evening Prayer and sung at Mass before the gospel reading.

Look at the list of signs for each O Antiphon in this chart.

| Old Testament Title | | What it means to us | Sign of title |
|---|---|---|---|
| Dec. 17 | O Wisdom! | Jesus is our wise teacher. | oil lamp open book |
| Dec. 18 | O Lord of Israel! | Jesus is our leader. | burning bush stone tablet |
| Dec. 19 | O Flower of Jesse's Stem! | Jesse was the father of King David and the ancestor of Jesus. Jesus is the "flower" on the family tree. | vine or plant with flower |
| Dec. 20 | O Key of David! | Jesus opens the gates of God's Kingdom to us. | key broken chain |
| Dec. 21 | O Radiant Dawn! | Jesus is our light. | rising sun |
| Dec. 22 | O King of All Nations! | Jesus is the king who unites us all. | crown, scepter |
| Dec. 23 | O Emmanuel! | Emmanuel means "God with us." Jesus is with us always. | chalice and host |

For centuries these signs have been pictured in artwork. Check to see if your parish newsletter or Web site gives examples of these signs.

## WE RESPOND

The O Antiphons can help us get ready for the coming of Christ. Use one of the seven titles of Jesus to write a short prayer. You may want to thank Jesus or ask him to help you give witness to the good news in your daily life.

# ✝ We Respond in Prayer

**Leader:** Our help is in the name of the Lord.

**All:** Who made heaven and earth.

**Reader:** Once a woman said to Jesus, "I know that the Messiah is coming, the one called the Anointed; when he comes, he will tell us everything." Jesus told her in reply, "I am he" (John 4:25, 26).

**All:** Jesus, you are the Messiah.

**Leader:** O Wisdom! You guide creation with your strong yet tender care.

**All:** Come, show your people the way to salvation.

**Leader:** O Lord of Israel! You gave Moses the Law on Mount Sinai.

**All:** Come, stretch out your mighty hand to set us free.

**Leader:** O Flower of Jesse's Stem! You have been raised up as a sign for all people.

**All:** Come, let nothing keep you from coming to our aid.

**Leader:** O Key of David! You control the gates of heaven.

**All:** Come, lead your captive people to freedom.

**Leader:** O Radiant Dawn! You are the splendor of eternal light and the sun of justice.

**All:** Come, shine on those who dwell in darkness.

**Leader:** O King of All Nations! You are the only joy of every heart.

**All:** Come, save the creature you fashioned from the dust.

**Leader:** O Emmanuel! You are the desire of all nations and the Savior of all people!

**All:** Come, set us free, Lord our God.

# SHARING FAITH
## with My Family

## Sharing What I Learned

Discuss the following with your family:

- the season of Advent
- preparing for the coming of Christ
- the O Antiphons.

## Around the Table

Discuss with your family: How can our family show kindness and care to others during Advent? Here are some ideas. Add a few more of your own.

- Save money to give to a parish project that helps those in need.
- Buy a new toy to give to a toy drive.
- Bring a plate of cookies to someone who is homebound.
- Shovel snow for a neighbor.

- _____

## Family Prayer

On December 17, you may want to begin setting up your family nativity scene. From that day until December 23, put out a few figures at a time—first the stable or cave, then the animals, then Joseph and Mary. Save the figure of the Infant Jesus for Christmas Eve and the figures of the wise men for Epiphany Sunday in January. As you arrange the scene, pray the *We Respond in Prayer* found on the other side of this page.

Visit Sadlier's

www.WeBelieveweb.com

**Connect to the Catechism**
For adult background and reflection, see paragraph 524.

# Christmas

Advent · **Christmas** · Ordinary Time · Lent · Triduum · Easter · Ordinary Time

"A light will shine on us this day,
the Lord is born for us."

Mass at Dawn, Introductory Rites

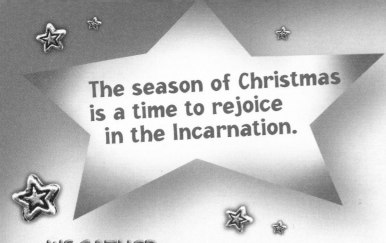

## The season of Christmas is a time to rejoice in the Incarnation.

### WE GATHER

 *Jesus, fill us with your light.*

Sometimes people may celebrate different events for different periods of time. For example, they may celebrate Valentine's Day for a day, birthdays for a whole weekend, and a family reunion for a whole week. How does your family celebrate different events?

### WE BELIEVE

What we celebrate on Christmas Day, and during the whole Christmas season, is the wonderful gift of God with us. During Advent and Christmas we hear Jesus called by the name Emmanuel. The name *Emmanuel* means "God with us." During Christmas we celebrate in a special way that God is with us today, now, and forever.

The season of Christmas is a time to rejoice in the Incarnation, the truth that the Son of God became man. We celebrate Christ's presence among us now as well as his first coming into the world over two thousand years ago. We recall that God so loved the world that he sent his only Son to be our Savior.

Many people do not know that we celebrate Christmas Day with three Masses: the Mass at Midnight, the Mass at Dawn, and the Mass during the Day. Each Mass helps us to celebrate the light of Christ in the world today.

**Mass at Midnight**   For the celebration of this Christmas Mass, all is dark and peaceful, and maybe even cold. The church is lit with candles. The priest opens with the words, "Father, you make this holy night radiant with the splendor of Jesus Christ our light." The gospel reading is the story of the birth of Jesus.

Christmas Mass, Mittersill, Austria

📖 Luke 2:1–14

Joseph and Mary had traveled to Bethlehem, the city of David, to be enrolled and counted in a census. "While they were there, the time came for her to have her child, and she gave birth to her firstborn son. She wrapped him in swaddling clothes and laid him in a manger, because there was no room for them in the inn." (Luke 2:6–7)

There were shepherds in the fields nearby. The angel of the Lord came to them and said:

"Do not be afraid; for behold, I proclaim to you good news of great joy that will be for all the people. For today in the city of David a savior has been born for you who is Messiah and Lord. And this will be a sign for you: you will find an infant wrapped in swaddling clothes and lying in a manger."

Suddenly there were many voices singing with the angel:

"Glory to God in the highest
      and on earth peace to those
         on whom his favor rests"
(Luke 2:10–12, 14).

Our great hymn the Gloria, or the Glory to God, is based on this song of the angels. We say or sing the Glory to God in Mass on Sundays all during the year, except during Advent and Lent. In the Masses of Christmas we sing this hymn with great joy. The light of Christ has come into the world and remained with us!

**Mass at Dawn**   For the celebration of this Christmas Mass, the sun is rising in the east. Just as the shepherds hurried to the stable, the faithful hurry to their parish churches. The priest opens with the words, "Father, we are filled with the new light by the coming of your Word among us."

You have heard many titles of Jesus. Messiah, Christ, Anointed One, Savior, and Lord are just a few. These titles are all ways to speak about the Son of God, the second Person of the Blessed Trinity who became one of us. "The Word among us" and "the Word made flesh" are also titles for Christ, but there are more. They are actually ways of explaining the Incarnation. In fact, the word *Incarnation* means "becoming flesh."

During the Christmas season we rejoice that the Word is among us, today and always.

CHRISTMAS

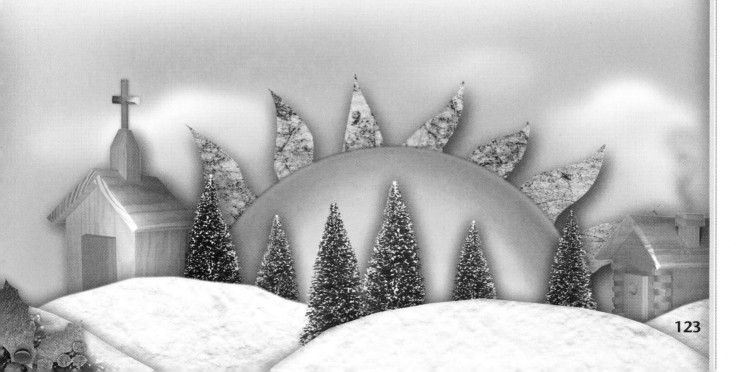

**Mass During the Day** For the celebration of this Christmas Mass, the bells probably continue to ring as people greet each other with joy. The priest begins, "God of love, Father of all, the darkness that covered the earth has given way to the bright dawn of your Word made flesh."

The gospel reading for this Mass is the beginning of the Gospel of John. Here is part of that reading.

"And the Word became flesh
and made his dwelling among us,
and we saw his glory,
the glory as of the Father's only Son,
full of grace and truth." (John 1:14)

Christmas does not end once these three Masses have been celebrated. The season of Christmas lasts until the Feast of the Baptism of the Lord, which is usually in the second week in January.

The days after Christmas are often called "The Twelve Days of Christmas" because the twelfth day after Christmas is the feast of Epiphany. Epiphany was originally celebrated on this twelfth day, January 6. Today in the United States Epiphany is celebrated on the second Sunday after Christmas.

People in all parts of the world celebrate Christmas and the feasts of the Christmas season. They celebrate using local customs and traditions. But however different the celebrations may be, they all help us to remember that Christ is our Light today, he is God-with-us today, the Word among us today and always.

## WE RESPOND

Work in groups to make a chart of the many ways people celebrate Christmas Day and the whole season of Christmas. Talk about whether or not these ways help us to remember the real meaning of Christmas.

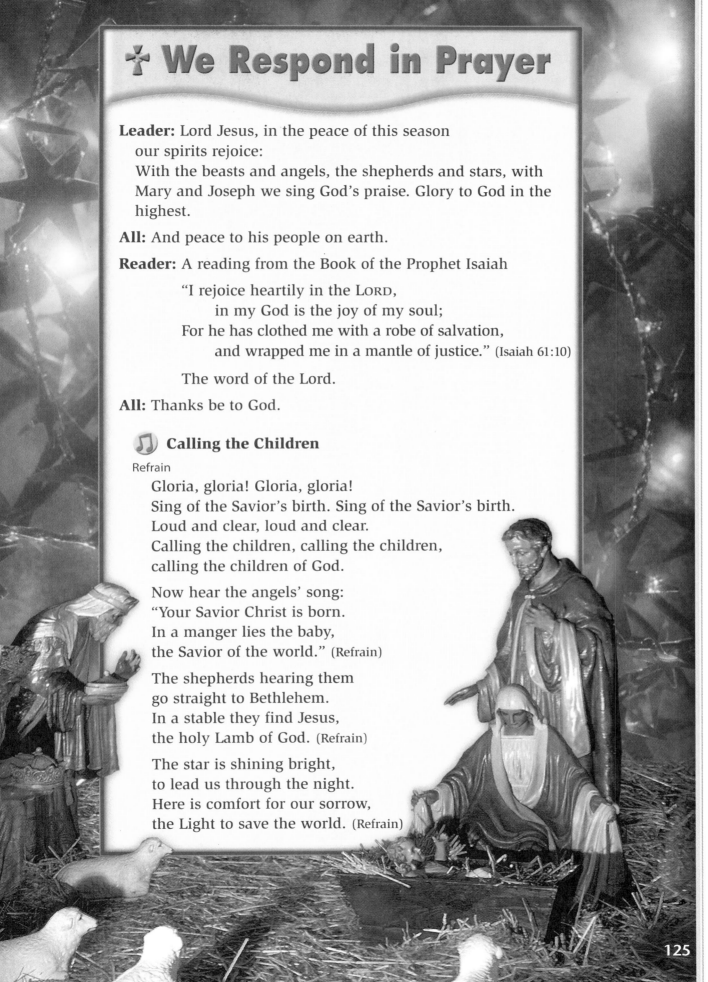

# ✝ We Respond in Prayer

**Leader:** Lord Jesus, in the peace of this season
our spirits rejoice:
With the beasts and angels, the shepherds and stars, with
Mary and Joseph we sing God's praise. Glory to God in the
highest.

**All:** And peace to his people on earth.

**Reader:** A reading from the Book of the Prophet Isaiah

"I rejoice heartily in the LORD,
in my God is the joy of my soul;
For he has clothed me with a robe of salvation,
and wrapped me in a mantle of justice." (Isaiah 61:10)

The word of the Lord.

**All:** Thanks be to God.

### 🎵 Calling the Children

Refrain

Gloria, gloria! Gloria, gloria!
Sing of the Savior's birth. Sing of the Savior's birth.
Loud and clear, loud and clear.
Calling the children, calling the children,
calling the children of God.

Now hear the angels' song:
"Your Savior Christ is born.
In a manger lies the baby,
the Savior of the world." (Refrain)

The shepherds hearing them
go straight to Bethlehem.
In a stable they find Jesus,
the holy Lamb of God. (Refrain)

The star is shining bright,
to lead us through the night.
Here is comfort for our sorrow,
the Light to save the world. (Refrain)

# SHARING FAITH
## with My Family

## Sharing What I Learned

Discuss the following with your family:

- the season of Christmas
- the Incarnation
- the three Masses of Christmas.

## Around the Table

Plan with your family ways to celebrate during the Christmas season. Write the following activities on slips of paper. Add some of your own ideas. During the Christmas season invite each family member to choose one of these activities.

☐ Take a walk or drive to see Christmas lights.

☐ Have a gathering for family and friends.

☐ Write thank-you notes for gifts.

☐ Call a grandparent or far-away relative.

☐ Read the Christmas story in Luke 2:1–20.

☐ Pray together, thanking God for gifts and blessings.

☐ Visit the nativity scene in your parish church.

☐ _____

## Family Prayer

During the Christmas season add the following prayer to your family's grace before or after meals.

**Leader:** The Word was made flesh, alleluia.
**All:** And dwells with us now, alleluia.
**Leader:** And we saw his glory, alleluia.
**All:** The glory of the Father's only Son, alleluia.
**Leader:** Full of grace and truth, alleluia.
**All:** He is Jesus, our God with us, alleluia, alleluia, alleluia!

Visit Sadlier's
**www.WE BELIEVE web.com**

**Connect to the Catechism**
For adult background and reflection, see paragraph 457.

**Write True or False for the following sentences.
Then change the false sentences to make them true.**

1. _____ In the sacrament of Confirmation we are sealed with the gift of the apostles.

_____

2. _____ Wisdom, understanding, right judgment, courage, knowledge, reverence, and wonder and awe are the fruits of the Holy Spirit.

_____

3. _____ The stations of the cross is a memorial, a meal, and a sacrifice.

_____

4. _____ There are four parts to the Mass: the Introductory Rites, the Liturgy of the Word, the Liturgy of the Eucharist, and the Concluding Rite.

_____

5. _____ Laying on of hands and anointing are signs of the Holy Spirit's presence.

_____

6. _____ In the Mass, the Church gathers as the Bread of Life.

_____

7. _____ After his Resurrection, the risen Jesus was made known to his disciples when he broke bread with them.

_____

8. _____ Consecration is a day we are obliged to participate in the Mass to celebrate a special event in the life of Jesus, Mary, or the saints.

_____

**Write the letter that best defines each term.**

9. _____ consecration

10. _____ sacramental

11. _____ Introductory Rites

12. _____ Confirmation

13. _____ real presence

14. _____ Liturgy of the Word

15. _____ sacrifice

16. _____ Liturgy of the Hours

**a.** a gift offered to God by the priest in the name of all the people

**b.** Jesus really and truly present in the Eucharist

**c.** the part of the Mass in which we listen and respond to God's word; we profess our faith and pray for all people in need

**d.** public prayer of the Church made up of psalms, readings from Scripture and Church teaching, prayers and hymns

**e.** the part of the eucharistic prayer when, by the power of the Holy Spirit and through the words and actions of the priest, the bread and wine become the Body and Blood of Christ

**f.** a blessing, action, or object that helps us respond to God's grace received in the sacraments

**g.** the sacrament in which we receive the Gift of the Holy Spirit in a special way

**h.** the part of the Mass that unites us as a community and prepares us to hear God's word and celebrate the Eucharist

**Answer the questions.**

**17–18.** Why is preparation an important part of Confirmation?

**19–20.** Name three sacramentals. How do these sacramentals help us grow in holiness?

# The Sacraments of Healing Restore Us

## The Power of Words

*"Sticks and stones may break my bones, but names can never hurt me."*

**A**nyone who has been teased or ridiculed knows the absurdity of this well-worn proverb. Words have tremendous power. In Jewish tradition they are likened to arrows which, once shot, cannot be retracted. Words can pierce the heart with painful hurt or penetrate it with soothing kindness. The choice lies in the one who speaks.

Families hold great potential to use words in hurtful or healing ways. Children learn by example. If children grow up in an atmosphere of criticism and cynicism, they will learn a language that includes put-downs, sarcasm, and gossip. On the other hand, words that come from a place of mutual love and respect teach care and concern. They offer empathy and a desire to understand.

One way to help gauge the use of our words is to consider their impact on others. Before saying something that is potentially hurtful, ask yourself: Is what I am about to say true? necessary? kind?

If the answer to even one of these is "No," then the words are not worth saying!

## What Your Child Will Learn in Unit 3

Unit 3 presents the sacraments of healing: the sacrament of Reconciliation and the sacrament of the Anointing of the Sick. The children learn the various parts of the sacrament of Reconciliation: contrition, confession, penance, and absolution. They find out about when and where the sacrament is celebrated, the roles of the priest and the penitent, the breakdown of the Rites for individual penitents and for several penitents. As the discussion of the sacrament of the Anointing of the Sick begins, the healing and saving work of Jesus is seen as a sign of his divinity. Through the Church, Jesus continues his healing work. The children learn where and when the sacrament is celebrated as well as its meaning and purpose. The parts of the Rite of Anointing are examined and the Eucharist as viaticum, the last sacrament of Christian life, is explained. The last chapter of Unit 3 presents Mary's role in God's plan of salvation. The children learn why the Church tells us that Mary is our greatest saint.

## Plan & Preview

▶ Have scissors, markers, pencils, or pens available for the various activities on the family pages.

▶ Your child will be asking you to help him or her assemble some scrapbook items that focus on the sacraments of Reconciliation and the Anointing of the Sick (*Chapters 15 & 17*).

## Bible Q & A

**Q:** Recently, a family member was seriously ill but thankfully has now fully recovered. Where can I find stories of Jesus healing and comforting to share with my children?

*—Athens, Texas*

**A:** There is not enough room to list them all. Try Luke chapters 8 and 9 in which you will find eight stories of Jesus healing others.

## From the Catechism

**"The family should live in such a way that its members learn to care and take responsibility for the young, the old, the sick, the handicapped, and the poor."**

*(Catechism of the Catholic Church, 2208)*

## Media Matters

Often, we look toward our pastor, political leaders, and parents for words to heal us during times of sorrow.

Over the next several days, participate in this exercise with your family. Assign each member of your family a different outlet of the media (TV, newspapers, magazines, radio, Internet). Ask each person to look, read, or listen for stories whose message either has the ability to hurt or the ability to heal its intended audience.

Gather as a family periodically throughout this exercise to discuss how these stories either hurt or healed and how they made you feel individually and as a family.

## WE GATHER

✝ **Leader:** God calls us to turn to him each day. Let us listen to this call in the word of God.

**Reader:** A reading from the Letter of Saint Paul to the Colossians

"Put on then, as God's chosen ones, holy and beloved, heartfelt compassion, kindness, humility, gentleness, and patience, bearing with one another and forgiving one another, . . . as the Lord has forgiven you, so must you also do." (Colossians 3:12–13)

The word of the Lord.

**All:** Thanks be to God.

🎵 **We Belong to God's Family**

(Refrain)
We belong to God's family.
Brothers and sisters are we,
singing together in unity about
one Lord and one faith, one family.

We all share a forgiveness that
flows from sea to sea,
gentle mercy that breaks all bonds
and sets the prisoner free. (Refrain)

☀ Why do you think forgiveness is important? What are some examples of ways we forgive and are forgiven?

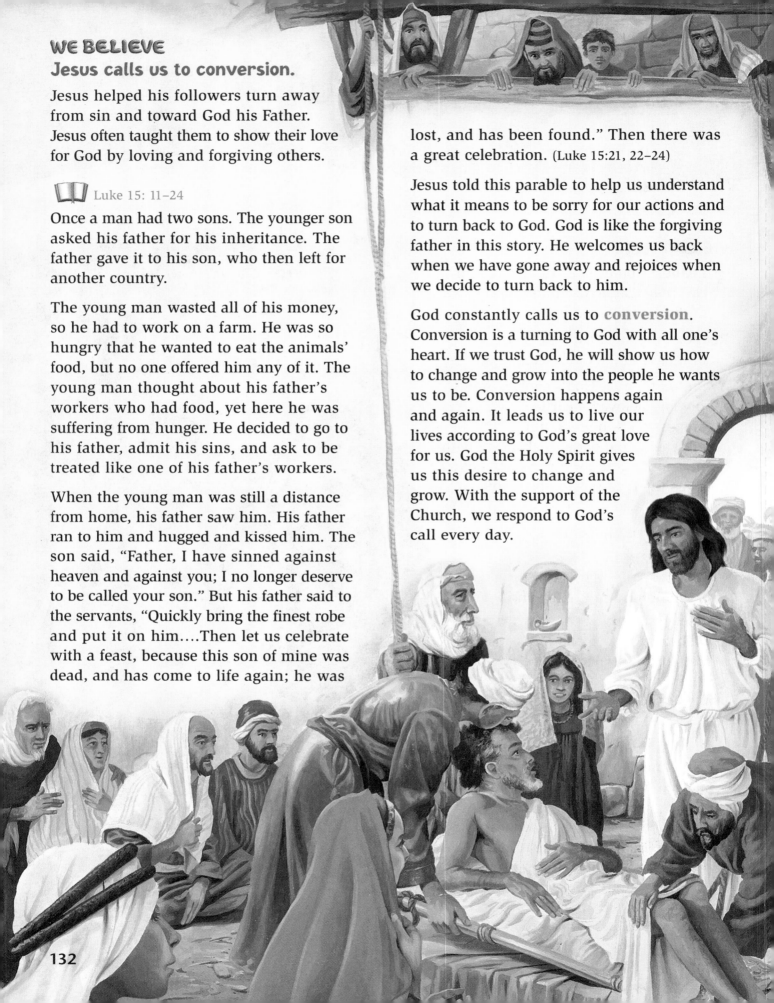

## WE BELIEVE
### Jesus calls us to conversion.

Jesus helped his followers turn away from sin and toward God his Father. Jesus often taught them to show their love for God by loving and forgiving others.

Luke 15: 11–24

Once a man had two sons. The younger son asked his father for his inheritance. The father gave it to his son, who then left for another country.

The young man wasted all of his money, so he had to work on a farm. He was so hungry that he wanted to eat the animals' food, but no one offered him any of it. The young man thought about his father's workers who had food, yet here he was suffering from hunger. He decided to go to his father, admit his sins, and ask to be treated like one of his father's workers.

When the young man was still a distance from home, his father saw him. His father ran to him and hugged and kissed him. The son said, "Father, I have sinned against heaven and against you; I no longer deserve to be called your son." But his father said to the servants, "Quickly bring the finest robe and put it on him….Then let us celebrate with a feast, because this son of mine was dead, and has come to life again; he was

lost, and has been found." Then there was a great celebration. (Luke 15:21, 22–24)

Jesus told this parable to help us understand what it means to be sorry for our actions and to turn back to God. God is like the forgiving father in this story. He welcomes us back when we have gone away and rejoices when we decide to turn back to him.

God constantly calls us to **conversion**. Conversion is a turning to God with all one's heart. If we trust God, he will show us how to change and grow into the people he wants us to be. Conversion happens again and again. It leads us to live our lives according to God's great love for us. God the Holy Spirit gives us this desire to change and grow. With the support of the Church, we respond to God's call every day.

Work in a group to write a modern-day story about being sorry and turning back to God and others.

*Story Script*

_____

Act out the story. Then discuss why this story might help people turn their hearts to God.

**Key Word**

conversion (p. 267)

## Jesus forgives as only God can do.

Some people did not understand Jesus' ministry of forgiveness and reconciliation. They were upset when Jesus spent time with sinners and forgave their sins.

 Mark 2:1–12

After traveling for some time, Jesus returned home. So many people gathered to hear him preach that there was no more room in the house. Four men carrying a paralyzed man came to see Jesus. Through an opening in the roof they let down the mat on which the paralyzed man was lying. When Jesus saw their faith, he said to the paralyzed man, "Child, your sins are forgiven."

Some of the people thought that Jesus should not be speaking this way because only God can forgive sins. Jesus knew what they were thinking. And so that they would know that he had authority to forgive sins Jesus said, "I say to you, rise, pick up your mat, and go home." The man rose, and walked away. They were all amazed because they had never seen anything like it. (Mark 2:2, 5, 11)

Jesus' words and actions brought many people to believe in him and have faith.

Jesus wanted all people to hear his call to conversion and receive his forgiveness. So Jesus shared his authority to forgive sins with his apostles. He said to them, "'Peace be with you. As the Father has sent me, so I send you.' And when he had said this, he breathed on them and said to them, 'Receive the holy Spirit. Whose sins you forgive are forgiven them, and whose sins you retain are retained'" (John 20:21–23). This forgiveness of sins took place when the apostles baptized those who believed.

What can you do each day to be more accepting and forgiving of others?

## Jesus continues to forgive us through the Church.

In Baptism we first receive God's forgiveness. We begin our new life in Christ. Yet we sometimes turn from God and are in need of his forgiveness. Sometimes the choices we make weaken God's life in us. When we think or do things that lead us away from God, we sin. **Sin** is a thought, word, deed or omission against God's law. Every sin weakens our friendship with God and others.

Sometimes people turn completely away from God's love. They commit very serious sin that breaks their friendship with God. This sin is called mortal sin. Those who commit mortal sin must freely choose to do something that they know is seriously wrong. However, God never stops loving people who sin seriously. The Holy Spirit calls them to conversion.

Less serious sin that weakens our friendship with God is called venial sin. Even though venial sins do not turn us completely away from God, they still hurt others, ourselves, and the Church. If we keep repeating them, they can lead us further away from God and the Church. However, God offers us forgiveness when we think or do things that harm our friendship with him or with others.

The Church celebrates God's forgiveness in one of the two sacraments of healing. In the sacrament of **Reconciliation**, our relationship with God and the Church is strengthened or restored and our sins are forgiven.

- We receive God's forgiveness. Our sins are forgiven by a priest in the name of Christ and the Church.

- We are reconciled with God. The life of grace in us is strengthened or made new. Our friendship with God becomes stronger.

- We are reconciled with the Church. Our relationship with the Body of Christ is made stronger.

- We are strengthened to live by the Ten Commandments and Jesus' teaching to love one another as he has loved us.

With a partner name some ways the Church can help us to be reconciling people.

_____

_____

Key Words

sin (p. 269)
Reconciliation (p. 269)

## We are reconciled with God and the Church.

As one body the whole Church benefits from our just and loving actions. The whole Church also suffers when one person turns from God. So the reconciliation of one member of the Church with God strengthens all of us. In the sacrament of Reconciliation, we are forgiven. We are also called to forgive others.

When we forgive others we grow as a loving and reconciling community. Reconciliation with God and the Church contributes to peace and reconciliation in the world. We are better able to stand up for what is right and to act with justice.

Justice is based on the belief that all people are equal. Acting with justice respects the rights of others and gives them what is rightfully theirs. All people are created in God's image and share the same human dignity. This makes us one human community, and sin affects that community.

Sin can lead to unjust situations and conditions in society. This is social sin. Some results of sin in society are prejudice, poverty, homelessness, crime, and violence. The Church speaks out against social sin, and we work to stop the things in society that allow unjust behaviors or conditions to exist. The Church encourages all people to turn to God and live lives of love and respect.

## As Catholics...

Part of being reconciled with the Church is admitting that we have not lived as God calls us to live. During Mass the whole assembly confesses that we have sinned. A prayer we often pray begins:

"I confess to almighty God, and to you, my brothers and sisters."

In this prayer, which can be found on page 252, we ask all the members of the Church to pray for us and our forgiveness. During the next week pray that all people will experience God's love and mercy.

## WE RESPOND

Write a poem or a song about the meaning of being reconciled and the importance of celebrating the sacrament of Reconciliation.

_____

_____

_____

_____

_____

_____

_____

_____

**Write True or False for the following sentences.**
**Then change the false sentences to make them true.**

1. _____ The sacrament by which our relationship with God is strengthened or restored and our sins are forgiven is called Confirmation.

_____

_____

2. _____ Jesus shared his authority to forgive sins with his apostles.

_____

_____

3. _____ Reconciliation with God and the Church contributes to peace in the world.

_____

_____

4. _____ Reconciliation is a sacrament of initiation.

_____

_____

**Circle the letter of the correct answer.**

5. _____ is a turning to God with all one's heart.

   **a.** Repentance  **b.** Sin  **c.** Conversion

6. _____ is a thought, word, deed, or omission against God's law.

   **a.** Conversion  **b.** Sin  **c.** Reconciliation

7. Jesus continues to forgive us through _____.

   **a.** parables  **b.** the Church  **c.** sin

8. The unjust actions of one person affect _____ of the Church.

   **a.** all    **b.** some    **c.** none

**Write a sentence to answer the question.**

**9–10.** What is the importance of Reconciliation?

_____

_____

ASSESSMENT

Jesus told parables to help people understand God's power, love, and mercy. Write a parable to help others understand the need to be reconciled with God and the Church.

# We Respond in Faith

## Reflect & Pray

Lord, help me to focus my life on you. Help me _____

_____

_____

Be always with me, guiding and leading me back to you.

**Key Words**

conversion (p. 267)
sin (p. 269)
Reconciliation (p. 269)

## Remember

- Jesus calls us to conversion.
- Jesus forgives as only God can do.
- Jesus continues to forgive us through the Church.
- We are reconciled with God and the Church.

## OUR CATHOLIC LIFE

### Saint Dominic

Born in Spain in 1170, Dominic began school at the age of seven. He spent many years studying and was eventually ordained a priest. At first he led a quiet life of prayer, but then he became involved in preaching a message of faith and conversion. He called many people to turn to God and live by Christ's example. Dominic helped many Christians return to the teachings of Christ and the Church. He began a new religious community devoted to preaching. It is called the Order of Preachers, and is also known as the Dominicans. Dominic urged his fellow priests to study the Bible and spend time in prayer. Many wanted to follow Dominic's way of life, and his order spread throughout Europe. Today there are Dominicans in all parts of the world, preaching the good news and calling people to conversion. Saint Dominic's feast day is August 8.

SAINT DOMINIC

# SHARING FAITH
## with My Family

## Sharing What I Learned

Discuss the following with your family:

- conversion
- Jesus' forgiveness
- sin
- Reconciliation.

## A Sacraments Scrapbook

Work with your family to collect prayers, poems, songs, Scripture, pictures, photographs, and so on, that reflect the sacrament of Reconciliation. Place your findings on sheets of paper to include in your Sacraments Scrapbook.

## A Family Prayer

Hear us, Lord,
for you are merciful and kind.
In your great compassion,
look on us with love.

*from Rite of Penance*

Visit Sadlier's
**www.WEBELIEVEweb.com**

**Connect to the Catechism**
For adult background and reflection, see paragraphs 1427, 1441, 1442, and 1445.

# The Celebration of Reconciliation

## 16

## WE GATHER

✝ **Leader:** Let us be still a moment and think about the need for God's forgiveness in our lives.

**Reader:** A reading from the holy Gospel according to Luke

**Reader 1:** Once tax collectors and sinners were listening to Jesus teach. "But the Pharisees and scribes began to complain, saying, 'This man welcomes sinners and eats with them.' So to them he addressed this parable."

**Reader 2:** "What man among you having a hundred sheep and losing one of them would not leave the ninety-nine in the desert and go after the lost one until he finds it? And when he does find it, he sets it on his shoulders with great joy and, upon his arrival home, he calls together his friends and neighbors and says to them, 'Rejoice with me because I have found my lost sheep.'"

**Reader 3:** "I tell you, in just the same way there will be more joy in heaven over one sinner who repents than over ninety-nine righteous people who have no need of repentance." (Luke 15:2–7)

The Gospel of the Lord.

**All:** Praise to you, Lord Jesus Christ.

🎵 **With Open Hands/ Abierto Está Me Corazón**

Refrain:
With open hands and open hearts
we come before you, O God above.
Your loving kindness fills all the earth;
eternal is your love.

Abierto está me corazón
para encontrarte mi Dios de amor.
Yen todas partes tu cariño está;
eterno es tu amor.

Have mercy on me, O God of goodness,
according to your abundant love.
Wash me clean from all my sins;
restore to me your joy! (Refrain)

☀ What are ways that we can show that we are sorry?

## WE BELIEVE
### The sacrament of Reconciliation strengthens our relationship with God and others.

The Church calls the sacrament of Reconciliation by different names. For instance, it has been called the sacrament of conversion, of Penance, of confession, and of forgiveness. Each of these names tells us something about the meaning of the sacrament. No matter how we name it, this sacrament includes four major parts: contrition, confession, penance, and absolution.

**Contrition** is heartfelt sorrow for our sins. It includes the desire to sin no more. Being truly sorry for our sins leads us to conversion, to turn back to God the Father.

**Confession** is naming and telling our sins to the priest. An examination of conscience helps us to know what we need to confess. Our **conscience** is our ability to know the difference between good and evil, right and wrong. This gift from God helps us to make decisions and to judge our decisions and actions.

When we examine our conscience, we determine whether the choices we have made showed love for God, ourselves, and others. We ask the Holy Spirit to help us judge the goodness of our thoughts, words, and actions.

Serious sins must be confessed and forgiven in order to share in God's friendship and grace again. The forgiveness of less serious sins strengthens our weakened friendship with God.

A **penance** is an action that shows we are sorry for our sins. It is sometimes a prayer or act of service. A penance is a way of making right the harm we may have caused. Accepting this penance is a sign we are turning back to God and are willing to change our lives.

In **absolution** our sins are absolved, or forgiven. In the name of Christ and the Church and through the power of the Holy Spirit, a priest grants the forgiveness of sins. This forgiveness brings reconciliation with God and the Church.

Use the questions on page 253 to reflect on your relationship with God and others.

Write one question you could use each day to reflect on the ways you have shown love for others.

_____

_____

_____

_____

_____

Key Word

conscience (p. 267)

## In the sacrament of Reconciliation, the Church celebrates God's forgiveness.

The Church requires us to celebrate the sacrament of Reconciliation at least once a year if we have committed serious sin. However, we are called to participate in the sacrament often. The Church has two usual ways to celebrate the sacrament of Reconciliation. One way, or rite, is used when an individual meets with a priest for the celebration. The other rite is used when a group gathers to celebrate the sacrament with one or more priests. (See pages 254–255.)

Gathering with a group to celebrate the sacrament clearly shows that the sacrament is a celebration of the whole Church. Yet whether we celebrate Reconciliation individually or in a group, we are joined to the whole Church.

Most parishes have a regular schedule for celebrations of the sacrament of Reconciliation. Normally there is a special place in church where a penitent, someone seeking God's forgiveness, can meet with the priest for individual confession and absolution. The penitent can either sit with the priest and speak to him directly, or kneel and speak with him from behind a screen.

The priest can never, for any reason, tell anyone what we have confessed. He is bound to the secrecy of the sacrament. This secrecy is called the seal of confession.

> Name some times your parish celebrates the sacrament of Reconciliation.

141

## In the sacrament of Reconciliation we trust in God's mercy.

During the celebration of Reconciliation, the words of the penitent and of the priest show our trust in God and our thankfulness. An **act of contrition** is a prayer that allows us to express our sorrow. In this prayer we promise to try not to sin again. We can say we are sorry in many ways. The Church gives us several prayers to use as acts of contrition. Here is one prayer you may know.

### Act of Contrition

My God,
I am sorry for my sins with all my heart.
In choosing to do wrong
and failing to do good,
I have sinned against you
whom I should love above all things.
I firmly intend, with your help,
to do penance,
to sin no more,
and to avoid whatever leads me to sin.
Our Savior Jesus Christ
suffered and died for us.
In his name, my God, have mercy.

Only a priest can hear our confession and forgive our sins. He has received the sacrament of Holy Orders and acts in the name of Christ and the Church and through the power of the Holy Spirit. During the absolution, the priest, acting with the authority of Christ and in the name of the Church, extends his hand and prays,

"God, the Father of mercies,
through the death and resurrection of
   his Son
has reconciled the world to himself
and sent the Holy Spirit among us
for the forgiveness of sins;
through the ministry of the Church
may God give you pardon and peace,
and I absolve you from your sins
in the name of the Father, and of the Son,
and of the Holy Spirit."

The penitent answers: "Amen."

The words of absolution remind us that our reconciliation comes about by the mercy of the Father, the saving action of Jesus Christ, and the presence of the Holy Spirit.

Design a symbol to describe each of the four parts of the sacrament of Reconciliation. Your symbols can include pictures, actions, or words. Share your symbols with the class.

grow as his children. Together we can turn our minds and hearts to God by

- following Jesus' example and sharing his good news
- trusting in God when we may be struggling in school or at home
- caring for the needs of others
- praying daily.

We are the Church. When we act with mercy, others may seek God's mercy. If we help people in the community to understand one another and to work to settle differences peacefully, they may experience reconciliation with one another. Each of us can lead others to turn to God, to rely on him, and to live as he calls us to live.

## WE RESPOND

God continually calls us to be a community of faith focused on him and his love. Discuss ways to respond this week.

**Key Word**

act of contrition (p. 267)

## Together we turn our hearts and minds to God.

God constantly calls us to him. By God's gift of grace, we can turn to God and open our hearts to him. To do this we need to think about the ways we are living as members of the Church. We need to think about what we can change or strengthen in our lives.

The community of faith helps us to turn our lives to God. We are not alone as we try to

## As Catholics...

At every Mass, we have the opportunity to ask forgiveness of our sins as a community. When we pray, "Lord, have mercy. Christ, have mercy. Lord, have mercy" we are seeking forgiveness. This asking of forgiveness together prepares us to celebrate the Eucharist as the one Body of Christ.

**Review**

**Write the letter that best describes each part of the sacrament of Reconciliation.**

1. _____ contrition
2. _____ confession
3. _____ penance
4. _____ absolution

   a. true sorrow for the sins we have committed and the intention to sin no more

   b. our sins are forgiven in the name of Christ and the Church and through the power of the Holy Spirit

   c. an action that helps us to show sorrow for our sins

   d. telling our sins to the priest

**Short Answers**

5. The Church calls the sacrament of Reconciliation by different names. List three of the names. _____

6. What ability does our conscience give us?

   _____

7. How can the sacrament of Reconciliation be celebrated?

   _____

8. What is one way we can turn our minds and hearts to God?

   _____

**Write a sentence to answer this question.**

9–10. Why is it important to celebrate the sacrament of Reconciliation?

   _____

   _____

ASSESSMENT

Put together a presentation about the sacrament of Reconciliation for children who will be celebrating this sacrament for the first time. Your purpose is to help the children understand the meaning of the sacrament and the ways it is celebrated. You may want to include illustrations, charts, songs, and stories.

# We Respond in Faith

## Reflect & Pray

Lord, You are my shepherd, you

_____

_____

Give me the strength to follow you always.

**Key Words**
conscience (p. 267)
act of contrition (p. 267)

## Remember

- The sacrament of Reconciliation strengthens our relationship with God and others.

- In the sacrament of Reconciliation, the Church celebrates God's forgiveness.

- In the sacrament of Reconciliation we trust in God's mercy.

- Together we turn our hearts and minds to God.

## OUR CATHOLIC LIFE

### Retreat Days

The word *retreat* comes from military language. When an army retreats, it does not run away. It leaves the battle in order to plan better ways of fighting. This is what we do when we join friends and parish members on a retreat. We leave our ordinary way of life for a short time so that we can pray and think about our lives as Christians. We learn and plan ways to follow Christ. Some retreats last for one day. Sometimes retreats last a week or even a month.

The sacrament of Reconciliation is an important part of a retreat. We have the time we need to ask Jesus for help and guidance. We receive God's forgiveness and are strengthened to follow Christ in our daily lives.

# SHARING FAITH
## with My Family

## Sharing What I Learned

Discuss the following with your family:

- the four parts of Reconciliation
- examination of conscience
- the celebration of the sacrament of Reconciliation
- turning our hearts and minds to God.

## Sacrament Trading Cards

Design a trading card for the sacrament of Reconciliation using the pattern below. Use your knowledge about this sacrament to write "sacrament facts" on the back of the card. Collect all seven!

### A Family Prayer

Lord,
turn to us in mercy
and forgive us all our sins
that we may serve you in true freedom.

We ask this through Christ our Lord.
Amen.

*from the Rite on Penance*

## Reconciliation

What is the importance of the sacrament?

_____

What do we see?

_____

What do we hear?

_____

Who leads us in the celebration?

_____

Visit Sadlier's
**www.WeBelieveweb.com**

**Connect to the Catechism**
For adult background and reflection, see paragraphs 1468–1469, 1484, 1470, and 1474.

# Jesus, the Healer

## 17

## WE GATHER

✝ **Leader:** Let us bless the Lord,
who went about doing good
and healing the sick.
Blessed be God now and for ever.

**All:** Blessed be God for ever.

🎵 **Psalm 23: The Lord Is My Shepherd**

Refrain:
The Lord is my shepherd;
there is nothing I shall want.

**Reader:** Listen to the words of the holy
Gospel according to Matthew.

"Jesus went around to all the towns and
villages, teaching in their synagogues,
proclaiming the gospel of the kingdom,
and curing every disease and illness. At
the sight of the crowds, his heart was
moved with pity for them because they
were troubled and abandoned, like sheep
without a shepherd." (Matthew 9:35–36)

The Gospel of the Lord.

**All:** Praise to you, Lord Jesus Christ.

Refrain:
The Lord is my shepherd;
there is nothing I shall want.

**Leader:** May the almighty and merciful
God bless and protect us,
The Father, and the Son, and the
Holy Spirit.

**All:** Amen.

☀ When family members or friends are
ill, what can we do to help them?

147

## WE BELIEVE
### Jesus heals those who are sick.

Healing was an important part of Jesus' ministry from the very beginning. Jesus' amazing love and power healed people. Those who were sick would come to Jesus to be cured. Sometimes their families or friends would ask Jesus to heal them.

Act out this story.

John 4:46–53

**Narrator:** "Now there was a royal official whose son was ill in Capernaum. When he heard that Jesus had arrived in Galilee from Judea, he went to him and asked him to come down and heal his son, who was near death. Jesus said to him,

**Jesus:** 'Unless you people see signs and wonders, you will not believe.'

**Narrator:** The royal official said to him,

**Royal Official:** 'Sir, come down before my child dies.'

**Narrator:** Jesus said to him,

**Jesus:** 'You may go; your son will live.'

**Narrator:** The man believed what Jesus said to him and left. While he was on his way back, his slaves met him and told him that his boy would live. He asked them when he began to recover. They told him,

**Servants:** 'The fever left him yesterday, about one in the afternoon.'

**Narrator:** The father realized that just at that time Jesus had said to him, 'Your son will live,' and he and his whole household came to believe."

Many people grew to believe in Jesus because of his healing. Jesus felt great love for those who were suffering, and he healed many of them. Jesus desired to heal people from sin, too. Often when he cured the sick, he also forgave their sins. Jesus forgave the sins of people because he knew that sin kept them from loving God.

The healing and forgiving actions of Jesus were signs of his power to save us and bring us God's life. They showed that he was the Son of God and that God has power over sickness and sin. By his death, Resurrection, and Ascension, Jesus has victory over death. Because of Jesus, suffering and death no longer have power over us. He is our Savior.

## Jesus' apostles preach and heal in his name.

Jesus' healing was a sign of God's presence and action in the lives of the people. Jesus wanted all people to feel God's power and presence, so he shared his ministry with the apostles. Jesus sent them to different towns and villages to share the message of the Kingdom of God. He sent them out to preach repentance and to cure the sick.

The apostles traveled, teaching and healing in Jesus' name. "They anointed with oil many who were sick and cured them." (Mark 6:13)

This healing ministry of the apostles took on even greater meaning after Jesus' death and Resurrection. After his Resurrection Jesus told them to preach the gospel to the whole world. He told them that they would "lay hands on the sick, and they will recover" (Mark 16:18).

After the Holy Spirit came upon them at Pentecost, the apostles went out preaching and baptizing. Strengthened by the gift of the Holy Spirit, the apostles healed many people and brought them to believe in the risen Christ.

The apostles continued to preach the gospel and heal in Christ's name. Many more were baptized and the Church continued to grow.

Design a magazine cover for an issue entitled "Jesus the Healer." Use symbols, pictures, and words. What articles would be featured in the issue? What current happenings or stories might be included?

## As Catholics...

Jesus calmed the stormy seas, made the blind to see, walked on water, changed water into wine, and even raised the dead to life. These amazing signs were beyond human power. They are called miracles.

Jesus' miracles were a sign to all people that he was the Son of God and that the Father had sent him to save his people. The miracles were special signs that strengthened people's trust and belief in God. These miracles showed people that God's Kingdom had begun in Jesus himself.

This week read through the gospels with your family to find two stories of Jesus' miracles.

JESUS
the Healer

VOLUME 2

U.S.A. $5.99
CANADA/FOREIGN $6.99

## The Church continues Jesus' healing ministry.

From the time of the apostles, the faithful have turned to the Church for healing and comfort. We see in this account from the letter of Saint James, the beginning of the sacrament of the Anointing of the Sick.

📖 James 5:13–15

James wrote to one of the early Christian communities about the need for healing. He said that anyone who is suffering should pray. Anyone who is in good spirits should sing praise. Anyone who was sick should call on the priests of the Church, "and they should pray over him and anoint [him] with oil in the name of the Lord, and the prayer of faith will save the sick person, and the Lord will raise him up" (James 5:14–15).

All the sacraments bring us closer to God and one another. However, as a sacrament of healing, the Anointing of the Sick celebrates in a special way Jesus' healing work.

Jesus' healing comes to us through the Church. In the sacrament of the **Anointing of the Sick**, God's grace and comfort are given to those who are seriously ill or suffering because of their old age. Members of the Church who should definitely receive this sacrament are those who are near death.

Those who celebrate this sacrament receive strength, peace, and courage to face the difficulties that come from serious illness. The grace of this sacrament

- renews their trust and faith in God
- unites them to Christ and to his suffering
- prepares them, when necessary, for death and the hope of life forever with God.

The grace of this sacrament may also restore them to health.

🧍 How does your parish offer comfort and support to those who are ill?

**Key Word**
**Anointing of the Sick** (p. 267)

## We are all called to care for those who are sick.

All who are baptized are joined together in the Body of Christ. What happens to one member affects us all. When a member of the Church is suffering or in pain, he or she is not alone. The whole Church suffers with the person. This is why being kind and considerate to those who are ill is so important. Out of love for Christ and the members of the Church, we help others to feel better. We try to provide them with the things they need. We join them in the celebration of the sacraments. These actions are a way to share in Jesus' healing work.

Family and friends are called to support their loved ones by comforting them with words of faith and by praying for them. The sick should be encouraged to receive the Anointing of the Sick when it is necessary.

The Church cares for all those who are sick, not only those who are seriously ill. We support those who are sick in our families and parishes. We can visit those who are sick and pray with them. Our families, classes, or youth groups can spend time getting to know people in our community who need hope and encouragement. Priests, deacons, and other representatives of the parish visit the sick. They read with them from the Bible, pray with them, bless them, and offer them Holy Communion.

The whole Church remembers in prayer those who are sick, especially when we gather at Sunday Mass. We pray for the strength and healing of those who are sick in the general intercessions of the Mass. This is also a good time to remember their family members and those who care for them.

The priest brings these items to celebrate the sacrament of the Anointing of the Sick in a home, hospital, or emergency situation.

The stole is a vestment the priest wears.

A small container holds the oil of the sick that the priest uses for anointing.

The priest may have a small aspergillum, or container, for sprinkling holy water.

A book has the prayers and Scripture readings for the sacrament.

## WE RESPOND

Work with a partner to make a list of ways people can reach out to those who are sick or elderly.

_____

_____

_____

_____

As a group plan your own social outreach to those who are sick or elderly.

**Write True or False for the following sentences.
Then change the false sentences to make them true.**

1. _____ Jesus' healing was a sign of the apostles' presence in the lives of the people.

   _____

   _____

2. _____ Anointing of the Sick is a sacrament of initiation.

   _____

   _____

3. _____ In Reconciliation God's grace is given to those who are seriously ill or suffering because of their old age.

   _____

   _____

4. _____ Jesus healed people by his love and power.

   _____

   _____

**Short Answers**

5. Jesus' healing of the sick and forgiving of sins were signs of what?

   _____

6. How did Jesus' healing ministry continue after his death and Resurrection?

   _____

7. What do those who celebrate the sacrament of the Anointing of the Sick receive?

   _____

8. What are two ways that the Church can care for those who are sick?

   _____

**Write a sentence to answer the question.**

9–10. What is the importance of the Anointing of the Sick?

   _____

ASSESSMENT

Research what your parish does to offer comfort and support to the seriously ill and to the elderly. Write a summary of your findings.

# We Respond in Faith

## Reflect & Pray

Jesus, be with our loved ones in their times of illness, especially

_____

Help us to _____

_____

Amen.

**Anointing of the Sick**
(p. 267)

## Remember

- Jesus heals those who are sick.
- Jesus' apostles preach and heal in his name.
- The Church continues Jesus' healing ministry.
- We are all called to care for those who are sick.

## OUR CATHOLIC LIFE

### The Hospice Movement

Hospice care provides support for those who are dying. It gives loving care to those who are terminally ill. The word *hospice* comes from a word that means "hospitality." For centuries Catholic religious communities have given hospitality to travelers, the poor, widows, and orphans. A hospice is a shelter for those in need.

An early example of a hospice as a shelter for the dying is St. James Hospice in London. The Sisters of Charity established it in 1905. In North America, New Haven, Connecticut was the site of the first hospice in 1974. Since then, over two thousand hospices have been opened. Some of these offer home care for patients and their families. Other hospices provide residential care for the terminally ill and support for their loved ones.

# SHARING FAITH
## with My Family

## Sharing What I Learned

Discuss the following with your family:

- Jesus' healing ministry
- the healing ministry of the apostles
- Anointing of the Sick
- the sick and suffering are special to God.

## A Sacraments Scrapbook

Work with your family to collect prayers, poems, songs, Scripture, pictures, photographs, and so on, that reflect the sacrament of the Anointing of the Sick. Place your findings on sheets of paper to include in your Sacraments Scrapbook.

## A Family Prayer

May the Lord bless us, protect us from all evil, and bring us to everlasting life. Amen.

*from the Rite of Pastoral Care of the Sick*

May the Lord bless us, protect us from all evil, and bring us to everlasting life. Amen.

(from the Rite of Pastoral Care of the Sick)

Visit Sadlier's

**www.WeBelieveweb.com**

**Connect to the Catechism**
For adult background and reflection, see paragraphs 1503, 1506, 1509, and 2288.

# The Celebration of the Anointing of the Sick

## 18

## WE GATHER

**Leader:** Blessed be the God of mercy and love.

**All:** Blessed be God for ever.

**Reader:** A reading from the holy Gospel according to Mark

"And people were bringing children to him that he might touch them, but the disciples rebuked them. When Jesus saw this he became indignant and said to them, 'Let the children come to me; do not prevent them, for the kingdom of God belongs to such as these' . . . Then he embraced them and blessed them, placing his hands on them." (Mark 10:13–14, 16)

The Gospel of the Lord.

**All:** Praise to you, Lord Jesus Christ.

**Leader:** Jesus, come to me.

**All:** Jesus, come to me.

**Leader:** Jesus, bless me.

**All:** Jesus, bless me.

**Leader:** Let us pray for all children who are sick.

God of love,
ever caring,
ever strong,
stand by us in our time of need.

Watch over your children who are sick,
look after them in every danger,
and grant them your healing and peace.

We ask this in the name of Jesus the Lord.

**All:** Amen.

When are some times you need support and comfort? How do you ask for it? Who offers it to you?

Italian School (17th Century)
*Christ Healing the Blind Man of Jericho*

## WE BELIEVE
### Jesus is with us when we are suffering.

At one time or another in our lives, we will probably get sick. During these times of sickness, we may become lonely or worried. We may even wonder if God remembers us. Yet God always remembers those who are sick and suffering. They are very special to God. As Christians, we believe that when we are suffering Jesus is with us sharing in our pain. He understands our pain and suffering because he suffered and died on the cross.

Our care for those who are suffering around the world helps us to grow closer to Jesus. Jesus taught us that when we care for those who are ill, we care for him. He said, "whatever you did for one of these least brothers of mine, you did for me" (Matthew 25:40).

Trust in God, prayer, and hope can help all of us through the difficult times. We learn to rely on God and our faith community. Our family, our friends, and our parish community can help us to realize that Jesus' friendship always strengthens us. We can learn from Jesus that we can care for one another.

In groups discuss ways we can encourage others to trust in God.

### The Anointing of the Sick continues Jesus' saving work of healing.

When people are very sick, they may become anxious and discouraged. They need the special help of God's grace to stay strong and keep their faith alive. In the sacrament of the Anointing of the Sick, Christ comforts them and suffers with them.

All of us in the Church have a responsibility to those who are seriously weakened by sickness or old age. We need to pray for and with them. We need to encourage those in need to celebrate the sacrament of the Anointing of the Sick. In this sacrament the Church community does two very important things. We support those who fight against sickness, and we continue Jesus' saving work of healing.

The sacrament is meant for all the faithful who need it. Children, adults, and the elderly are all invited to be strengthened by God's grace in times of serious sickness. The sacrament is meant to help people in their daily living of the faith. So the Church encourages its members to welcome the grace of this sacrament.

The sacrament can be celebrated more than once. For instance, if someone who has been anointed grows more ill, the sacrament can be celebrated again. Or, if a person recovers after being anointed but becomes seriously ill at another time, he or she can receive the sacrament again. When someone is preparing to have serious surgery, he or she can celebrate the sacrament with family, friends, and parish. Those of the faithful who are elderly and growing weaker may also want to be anointed.

Priests have a responsibility to make sure that the sacraments of Reconciliation and the Eucharist are available to those who are sick. Deacons and special ministers of the Eucharist can visit the sick to pray with them and bring them Holy Communion. These visits are a sign of the support and concern of the whole community.

## As Catholics...

The oil used for the sacrament of the Anointing of the Sick is called the oil of the sick. It is generally olive oil that has been blessed by the bishop at the Chrism Mass. This is a very special Mass during which the bishop prepares with special blessings the chrism used for the anointings in Baptism and Confirmation. He also blesses the oil of the sick and the oil of catechumens, which is used during the time before the person's Baptism.

Do you know when the Chrism Mass is celebrated? Ask someone in your parish who might know.

In groups discuss what a motto is and why people use mottoes. Name some different mottoes you know. Then develop a motto that will encourage sick people to receive the Anointing of the Sick.

## The Church celebrates the Anointing of the Sick.

Like all sacraments, the Anointing of the Sick is a celebration of the whole community of the faithful. However, most times the sacrament is celebrated outside of the Mass in hospitals, in homes, at the site of an accident, or wherever someone is in need of it.

The main parts of the Anointing of the Sick are the prayer of faith, the laying on of hands, and the anointing with oil.

The *prayer of faith* has been an important part of the Church's celebration of the sacrament from the beginning of the Church. The whole Church is represented by the priest, family, friends, and parish members gathered to pray. Trusting in God's mercy, they offer several intentions and ask for help for those who are sick.

*Laying on of hands* In silence, the priest lays his hands on the person who is sick. Many times Jesus healed the sick by the laying on of his hands or by simply touching them. The priest's laying on of hands is a sign of blessing and a calling of the Holy Spirit upon the person.

Because the oil has been blessed, the *anointing with oil* is a sign of the power and presence of the Holy Spirit. It is also a sign of healing and strengthening.

The anointing takes place while the priest prays the following prayer.

The priest anoints the forehead first saying "Through this holy anointing may the Lord in his love and mercy help you with the grace of the Holy Spirit."
All respond "Amen."

Then he anoints the hands saying "May the Lord who frees you from sin save you and raise you up."
All respond "Amen."

The Anointing of the Sick usually begins with a Liturgy of the Word and is followed by Holy Communion. In this way those being anointed are further strengthened and nourished by the word of God and by the Body and Blood of Christ. Holy Communion also joins them to their parish community with whom they are unable to celebrate the Eucharist.

Write a prayer for those who are ill. Pray that they may find God's peace and hope.

_____

_____

_____

_____

_____

_____

_____

Now pray your prayer quietly.

## Jesus is with those who hope for eternal life.

People receive the sacrament of the Anointing of the Sick during a serious illness. It is often called the sacrament of the sick. Jesus came to give us life, and we receive his life in the sacraments. He helps us to understand that suffering and death are part of the journey to eternal life. We know that when we die with Christ, we will also rise with him. To help us in this journey through death to eternal life, Jesus Christ gives us himself in the Eucharist.

As a person's life on earth is about to end, he or she receives the Eucharist as viaticum. Viaticum is called the sacrament of the dying. In Latin *viaticum* means "food for the journey." It strengthens the person as he or she prepares for death and the hope of eternal life. The person receives the Body of Christ trusting that Jesus will welcome him or her home.

Jesus told his followers: "Whoever eats my flesh and drinks my blood has eternal life, and I will raise him on the last day" (John 6:54). Jesus acts through his Church to make this promise come true. The sacraments of Reconciliation, Anointing of the Sick, and the Eucharist as viaticum are sometimes celebrated together and are called the "last sacraments."

### WE RESPOND

 **I Am the Bread of Life**

I am the Bread of life.
You who come to me shall not hunger;
and who believe in me shall not thirst.
No one can come to me unless the
Father beckons.

Refrain:
And I will raise you up,
and I will raise you up,
and I will raise you up on the last day.

**Choose a word(s) from the box to complete each sentence.**

| laying on of hands    viaticum    faith    anointing with oil |

**1.** The _____ is a sign of healing, strengthening, and the power and presence of the Holy Spirit.

**2.** Jesus healed the sick by the

_____ or by simply touching them.

**3.** The prayer of _____ is a way for the Church to show its hope and trust in God.

**4.** The Eucharist as _____ strengthens those who are dying.

**Underline the correct answer.**

**5.** As Christians, we believe that Jesus is **(with/against)** us when we are suffering.

**6.** The Anointing of the Sick can be celebrated **(once/more than once)**.

**7.** Reconciliation, Anointing of the Sick, and the Eucharist as viaticum are sometimes celebrated together and are called the **(first/last)** sacraments.

**8.** There are **(three/four)** main parts to celebrating the Anointing of the Sick.

**Write a sentence to answer the question.**

**9–10.** Why does the Church celebrate the sacrament of the Anointing of the Sick?

_____

_____

ASSESSMENT

Jesus taught us that when we care for those who are ill, we care for him. Make a mural that illustrates ways that the Church cares for those who are ill. Share your mural with your class.

# We Respond in Faith

## Reflect & Pray

Saint Paul tells us that "the weakness of God is stronger than human strength" (1 Corinthians 1:25).

Jesus, when I feel weak help me by _____

_____

And when I want to give up hope, give me _____

_____

## Remember

- Jesus is with us when we are suffering.
- The Anointing of the Sick continues Jesus' saving work of healing.
- The Church celebrates the Anointing of the Sick.
- Jesus is with those who hope for eternal life.

## OUR CATHOLIC LIFE

### The Alexian Brothers

This religious community of brothers began to care for the sick of Europe in the twelfth century. At that time, the sick and the dying were not cared for in hospitals. Their families sometimes were unable to take care of them because of fear of contagious diseases. In the fourteenth century a serious disease spread through Europe, and the brothers risked their lives to care for the many people who became sick.

The brothers continued to devote themselves to those who were poor or sick. They chose Saint Alexius, who had worked among the poor, as their patron. From then on, they were known as the Alexian Brothers. They are still devoted to those who are sick. They serve in hospitals and clinics all over the world.

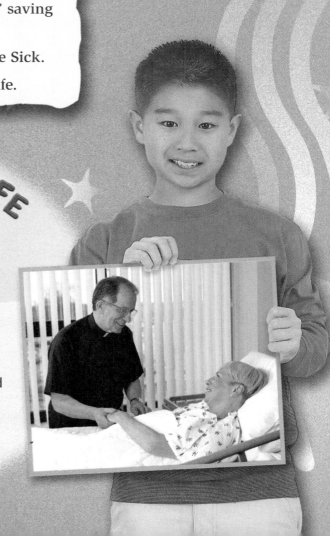

# SHARING FAITH
## with My Family

## Sharing What I Learned

Discuss the following with your family:

- our role in caring for the sick
- the purpose of the sacrament of the Anointing of the Sick
- the celebration of the sacrament
- viaticum.

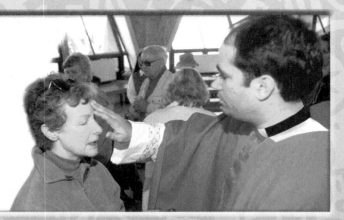

## Sacrament Trading Cards

Design a trading card for the sacrament of the Anointing of the Sick using the pattern below. Use your knowledge about this sacrament to write "sacrament facts" on the back of the card. Collect all seven!

### A Family Prayer

God of love,
ever caring, ever strong,
stand by us in our time of need.
Amen.

*from Catholic Household Blessings and Prayers*

**Anointing of the Sick**

What is the importance of the sacrament?

_____

What do we see?

_____

What do we hear?

_____

Who leads us in the celebration?

_____

Visit Sadlier's

**www.WeBelieveweb.com**

**Connect to the Catechism**
For adult background and reflection, see paragraphs 1521, 1520, 1522, and 1517.

# Mary, Model of Discipleship

## 19

## WE GATHER

✝ **Leader:** We know Mary as the mother of Jesus and our mother, too. Mary cares about us. She will bring all our needs to Jesus, her son. Think quietly about anything you might be worried about. Is there anything important that you might need? Let us bring our needs to our mother, Mary. Let us ask her to bring them to her son.

**Leader:** The response to the following prayers is: "Mary, bring them to Jesus."

**Reader 1:** For those who are in need in the world . . .

**Reader 2:** For those who are in need in our country . . .

**Reader 3:** For those who are in need in our parish . . .

**Reader 4:** For those who are in need in our families . . .

**Leader:** Anyone who wishes may name a need. (Response as above.)

**Leader:** Pray for us, Mother Mary, in the name of your Son, Jesus.

**All:** Amen.

☀ Who are some people in your community whom you admire? What is it about these people that makes you want to follow their example?

163

## WE BELIEVE
### Mary is Jesus' first disciple.

Mary, the mother of Jesus, is also his first and most faithful disciple. Mary believed in Jesus from the moment that God asked her to be the mother of his Son.

We first learn about Mary at the Annunciation. The **Annunciation** is the name given to the angel's visit to Mary at which the announcement was made that she would be the mother of the Son of God.

Luke 1:26–38

God sent the angel Gabriel to the town of Nazareth in Galilee to a young Jewish woman. Her name was Mary, and she was promised in marriage to a man named Joseph.

The angel said to Mary, "Hail, favored one! The Lord is with you" (Luke 1:28). Mary did not understand what the angel meant, so the angel said, "Do not be afraid, Mary, for you have found favor with God. Behold, you will conceive in your womb and bear a son, and you shall name him Jesus" (Luke 1:30–31).

Mary questioned how this could be possible. The angel told Mary that she would conceive her child by the power of the Holy Spirit. "Therefore the child to be born will be called holy, the Son of God." (Luke 1:35)

And Mary said, "Behold, I am the handmaid of the Lord. May it be done to me according to your word" (Luke 1:38).

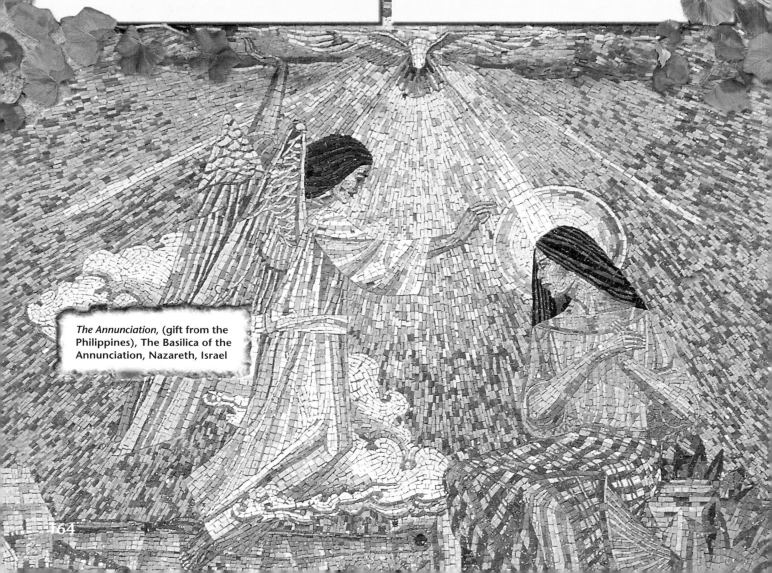

*The Annunciation,* (gift from the Philippines), The Basilica of the Annunciation, Nazareth, Israel

Mary was chosen by God from among all the women of history to be the mother of his Son. She did not know what to expect or how people would react. Yet Mary's faith and love for God brought her to accept his invitation.

Mary loved and cared for Jesus as he grew and learned. She supported Jesus throughout his ministry. She even stood by the cross as he died. Along with Jesus' followers she waited in prayer and with hope for the coming of the Holy Spirit. In all of these ways Mary is the perfect example of discipleship, and she is a model for all of us.

Like Mary we need to be open to the ways God may be calling us. Mary teaches us to trust in God's will for us. When we trust God, we show that we believe in his love for us.

 With a partner discuss situations in which we show trust in God. Write one way you can encourage others to trust in God.

_____

_____

_____

### Mary is most blessed among women.

When the angel Gabriel visited Mary, he told her something amazing about her cousin Elizabeth. Elizabeth, who had not been able to have children, was pregnant with a son, even in her old age.

 Luke 1:39–45

Mary went to visit her cousin Elizabeth and Elizabeth's husband Zechariah. "When Elizabeth heard Mary's greeting, the infant leaped in her womb, and Elizabeth, filled with the holy Spirit, cried out in a loud voice and said, 'Most blessed are you among women, and blessed is the fruit of your womb.'" (Luke 1:41–42).

Elizabeth then told Mary, "Blessed are you who believed that what was spoken to you by the Lord would be fulfilled" (Luke 1:45). Mary's response to Elizabeth is known as the Magnificat. This prayer can be found on page 248. A version of the prayer is also found as a song called the Canticle of Mary.

### 🎵 The Canticle of Mary

My soul proclaims the greatness of
    the Lord.
My spirit sings to God, my saving God,
Who on this day above all others
    favored me
And raised me up, a light for all to see.

As Catholics, what we believe about Mary is based on what we believe about her son, Jesus Christ. Mary was blessed by God and chosen to be the mother of his Son. For this reason, she was free from original sin from the moment she was conceived. This belief is called the **Immaculate Conception**.

Throughout her life Mary loved and obeyed God. Because Mary did not sin, she had a pure heart. God blessed Mary in another way. We believe that when Mary's work on earth was done, God brought her body and soul to live forever with the risen Christ. This belief is called the **Assumption**.

 Words
**Annunciation** (p. 267)
**Immaculate Conception** (p. 268)
**Assumption** (p. 267)

# Mary is the greatest of all the saints.

Because of Mary's closeness to Jesus, the Church honors her as the greatest of all the saints. Saints are followers of Christ who lived lives of holiness on earth and now share in eternal life with God in heaven.

The Church has many titles for Mary. These titles help us to understand Mary's role in our lives and in the life of the Church.

**Blessed Virgin** We learn from the Annunciation account that Mary was not yet married when the angel visited her. She was a virgin. Her son was conceived by the power of the Holy Spirit. Mary was truly blessed by God with the gift of his Son. We also believe that Mary remained a virgin throughout her married life. We call Mary the Blessed Virgin, the Blessed Virgin Mary, and the Blessed Mother.

**Mother of God** As the mother of Jesus, Mary went through the joys of having a baby. She cared for her son and loved him. She prayed with him, and was an example to him of love and obedience to God. However, Jesus was truly human and truly divine. He is the Son of God, the second Person of the Blessed Trinity who became man. So Mary is the Mother of God.

**Mother of the Church** Mary is Jesus' mother. She is the mother of the Church, too. As Jesus was dying on the cross he saw his mother and his disciple John at his feet. Jesus said to Mary, "Woman, behold, your son." He said to John, "Behold, your mother" (John 19:26, 27). Mary is the mother of all those who believe in and follow Jesus Christ. Mary is the Mother of the Church and our mother, too.

There are many more titles for Mary. We hear some of these titles when we pray a litany of Mary. The word *litany* comes from the Greek word for prayer. Often litanies of Mary are made up of a list of Mary's titles followed by a short request for her help. For example, we pray "Queen of Peace, pray for us."

What are some ways you call on Mary? What are some other titles for Mary that you know?

## As Catholics...

We honor Saint Joseph for his love and care of Mary and Jesus. We do not know many things about him. However, we know that he was a just man who listened to the angel sent by God.

We call Jesus, Mary, and Joseph the Holy Family. As Jesus' foster father, Joseph took care of him. Joseph and Mary prayed with Jesus and taught him the Jewish faith.

Saint Joseph's feast days are March 19 and May 1. Find out some ways the Church honors him.

## The Church remembers and honors Mary.

Catholics all over the world honor Mary through prayer. However, we do not worship or adore Mary. Our worship and adoration belong only to God, the Father, Son, and Holy Spirit. We are devoted to Mary and the saints because of the ways they have responded to God's great love. We ask Mary to pray for us and to speak to her son on our behalf.

In its prayer and liturgy the Church remembers the ways God blessed Mary. We celebrate the special times in her life as the mother of the Son of God. The Church has many feast days in Mary's honor, some of which are listed on page 250.

There are also popular devotions to Mary. Like litanies and novenas, praying the rosary is one of these devotions. We can pray the rosary alone or with others.

The rosary is usually prayed using a set of beads with a crucifix attached. We pray the rosary by praying the Our Father, Hail Mary, and Glory to the Father over and over again.

This creates a peaceful rhythm of prayer during which we can reflect on special times in the lives of Jesus and Mary.

The mysteries of the rosary recall these special times. We remember a different mystery at the beginning of each set of prayers, or decade, of the rosary. You can find the mysteries of the rosary on page 250.

## WE RESPOND

Mary said yes to God throughout her life. Illustrate one way you can follow Mary's example and say yes to God today.

**5.** Pray a Glory to the Father after each set of ten small beads.

**6.** Pray the Hail, Holy Queen to end the rosary.

**4.** Pray a Hail Mary at every small bead.

**3.** Pray an Our Father at every large bead.

**2.** Then pray the Apostles' Creed.

**1.** Start with the Sign of the Cross.

**Short Answers**

1. Mary has many titles. List three. _____

2. How does the Church remember the ways God blessed Mary? _____

_____

3. What is the Canticle of Mary? _____

4. What is the rosary? _____

**Write the letter that best defines each term.**

5. _____ Annunciation

6. _____ saints

7. _____ Assumption

8. _____ Immaculate Conception

a. followers of Christ who lived lives of holiness on earth and now share in eternal life with God in heaven

b. the belief that Mary was free from original sin from the moment she was conceived

c. the name given to the angel's visit to Mary and the announcement that she would be the mother of the Son of God

d. the belief that when Mary's work on earth was done, God brought her body and soul to live forever with the risen Christ

e. recalling special times in the lives of Jesus and Mary

**Write a sentence to answer the question.**

9–10. How is Mary a model of holiness?

_____

_____

ASSESSMENT

Write a news story with the headline, "Mary Said Yes to God." The story should describe how Mary is a model of discipleship. Share your news story about Mary with your class.

# We Respond in Faith

## Reflect & Pray

Son of God, thank you for being born of a woman. Through Mary, your mother, we have _____

_____

Into Mary's loving hands, we _____

_____

Amen.

**Annunciation** (p. 267)
**Immaculate Conception** (p. 268)
**Assumption** (p. 267)

## Remember

- Mary is Jesus' first disciple.
- Mary is most blessed among women.
- Mary is the greatest of all the saints.
- The Church remembers and honors Mary.

## OUR CATHOLIC LIFE

### The National Shrine of the Immaculate Conception

In 1847, Pope Pius IX proclaimed Mary as "patroness of the United States" under the title of her Immaculate Conception. Later, the bishops of the United States made plans to build a national shrine in Washington, D.C. to honor Mary. It is known as the Basilica of the National Shrine of the Immaculate Conception.

This national shrine is a large church where people from all over come to pray. Within the Basilica there are sixty beautifully decorated chapel areas. Many are dedicated to Our Lady as she is known in countries around the world. Some of these are: Our Lady of Czestochowa (Poland), Our Mother of Africa (Africa), Our Lady of Vailankanni (India), Our Lady of Guadalupe (Mexico and the Americas), and Our Lady of Bistrica (Croatia).

# SHARING FAITH
## with My Family

### Sharing What I Learned

Discuss the following with your family:

- the Annunication
- the Immaculate Conception
- the Assumption
- titles of Mary.

### Family Faith Checklist

Ask your family to complete the Family Faith Checklist. Share your experiences.

### A Family Prayer

We turn to you for protection,
holy Mother of God.
Listen to our prayers
and help us in our needs.
Save us from every danger,
glorious and blessed Virgin.

*from Catholic Household Blessings and Prayers*

## Our Family

Mary said "yes" to God and became our model of holiness. How will you say "yes" to God?

☐ At home:

_____

☐ At school/work:

_____

☐ In the parish:

_____

☐ In the community:

_____

Visit Sadlier's

**www.WeBelieveweb.com**

**Connect to the Catechism**
For adult background and reflection, see paragraphs 494, 492, 963, and 971.

# Lent

## 20

Advent · Christmas · Ordinary Time · Lent · Triduum · Easter · Ordinary Time

"Yet even now, says the LORD,
return to me with your whole heart."

Joel 2:12

171

## Lent is a season of preparation for the great celebration of Easter.

### WE GATHER

✝ *Holy Spirit, help us to follow Christ.*

What are some ways to become a better student, team player, or class member? Why is it important to try to improve?

### WE BELIEVE

During Lent the whole Church prepares for the great celebration of Christ's Paschal Mystery in the Easter Triduum. This season is the final time of preparation for those who will celebrate the sacraments of initiation at Easter. It is also a time for all who are already baptized in the Church to prepare to renew their Baptism at Easter. The whole Church thinks and prays about the new life Christ shares with us in Baptism.

The season of Lent begins on Ash Wednesday and lasts forty days. On Ash Wednesday we are marked on our foreheads with blessed ashes. These ashes are a sign of sorrow for our sins and of hope of having life forever with God. During Lent we use deep shades of purple and violet in our churches and during our worship. This is a sign of our need for reconciliation with God. The color also helps us to remember that joy and happiness will come from Christ's death and Resurrection.

Lent is a season of simple living. We make a special effort to pray, to do penance, and to do good works. We are called to do these things all year long. During Lent, however, they take on added meaning as we prepare to renew our Baptism.

**Prayer**   During Lent we try to give more time to God, and prayer helps us to do this. In Lent we may devote extra time to daily prayers and worship. We can spend more time reading and reflecting on Scripture. We can pray especially for those who are preparing to receive the sacraments of Christian initiation. We can gather with our parishes for the stations of the cross (found on page 266) and for the celebration of the sacrament of Reconciliation.

**Penance**   Lent is a time of conversion, of turning to God with all our hearts. God constantly calls us to be with him and to respond to his love. Lent is a special time to think about the ways we follow God's law. It is a time to change our lives so that we can be better disciples of Christ.

Penance is an important part of this conversion. Doing penance helps us to turn back to God and to focus on the things that are important in our lives as Christians. Doing penance is a way to show that we are sorry for our sins. Our penance restores our friendship with God and the Body of Christ, the Church.

We may do penance by giving up things we enjoy, like a favorite food or activity. We can also do without, or fast, from these things. Catholics of certain ages do penance by fasting from food on Ash Wednesday and not eating meat on the Fridays during Lent.

**Good works**   During Lent we also show special concern for those in need. A way to do penance is to practice a work of mercy or to give of our time in a special way. We follow Jesus' example of providing for the hungry and caring for the sick. We try to help other people get the things they need and to make sure that people have what is rightfully theirs. Many parishes have food and clothing drives during this time of year. Families may volunteer at soup kitchens, visit those who are sick, and practice other works of mercy. We remember that good works should happen all year long.

In what ways can you grow closer to Christ and others this Lent?

I will pray by _____

_____

I will turn to God by _____

_____

I will care for the needs of others by

_____

**Passion (Palm) Sunday** After five weeks of preparing through prayer, penance, and doing good works, Lent is nearly over. The Sunday before the Easter Triduum is known as Passion Sunday. This Sunday is also called Palm Sunday. We recall Jesus' passion: the judgment to put him to death, his carrying of the cross, and his suffering and dying on the cross. We also celebrate his joyous entrance into Jerusalem just days before he was to die.

 Matthew 21:1–11

Jesus and his disciples were traveling to Jerusalem for the great feast of Passover. As they neared the city, Jesus sent two disciples ahead to find a mule on which he could ride. They did as Jesus ordered. When they returned they placed their cloaks upon the animal, and Jesus sat upon it.

"The very large crowd spread their cloaks on the road, while others cut branches from the trees and strewed them on the road. The crowds preceding him and those following kept crying out and saying:

'Hosanna to the Son of David;
    blessed is he who comes in the
        name of the Lord;
    hosanna in the highest.'

And when he entered Jerusalem the whole city was shaken and asked, 'Who is this?' And the crowds replied, 'This is Jesus the prophet, from Nazareth of Galilee.'" (Matthew 21:8–11)

The original Hebrew meaning of the word *hosanna* is "O Lord, grant salvation." But it had come to be an acclamation of joy and welcome. The crowds were overjoyed to see Jesus.

On Passion Sunday, a joyful procession takes place to celebrate Jesus' entrance into Jerusalem. We may gather away from the church building, and palm branches are blessed with holy water. We listen to the story of Jesus' entrance into Jerusalem, and a short homily may be given. The procession then begins to the church. We all sing hosanna and wave our branches to praise and welcome Jesus as the crowds of Jerusalem once did.

When we arrive at the church, Mass begins. During the Liturgy of the Word the gospel reading is the Passion of our Lord Jesus Christ. This is one of the longest gospel readings we hear all year long. It helps to prepare us for the celebration of the Easter Triduum that will begin four days later on Holy Thursday evening.

The palm branches that are blessed on Passion Sunday remind us that Lent is a time of renewal and hope. After Mass many people place these branches near the cross or crucifix in their home. The palm branches often remain there until the celebration of Passion Sunday the following year. These branches are also burned before Lent of the next year to make ashes for the Ash Wednesday celebration.

## WE RESPOND

In your family or parish are there any other traditions or practices regarding the palm branches?

What are some other signs of new life and hope that help people to follow Christ?

Passion Sunday

# ✝ We Respond in Prayer

**Leader:** The Lord calls us to days of penance
and mercy. Blessed be the name of the Lord.

**All:** Now and for ever.

**Reader:** A reading from the Book of Joel
"Yet even now, says the LORD,
return to me with your whole heart,
with fasting, and weeping, and mourning;
Rend your hearts, not your garments,
and return to the LORD, your God.
For gracious and merciful is he,
slow to anger, rich in kindness." (Joel 2:12–13)
The word of the Lord.

**All:** Thanks be to God.

 **Sign Us with Ashes**

Refrain

Sign us with ashes, the sign of your cross.
Give us the grace to know your mercy, Lord.
Renew our spirits and open our hearts.
Help us remember the love you gave us.

Help us pray so we might be closer
to you and to God's family. (Refrain)

Help us fast so we might know the want
of those within God's family. (Refrain)

Help us give so we might share of what
we have to serve God's family. (Refrain)

LENT

175

# SHARING FAITH
## with My Family

## Sharing What I Learned

Discuss the following with your family:

- the season of Lent
- the importance of prayer, penance, and good works
- Passion Sunday, sometimes called Palm Sunday.

## Around the Table

Your family can remember each Sunday of Lent with these symbols.

**First Sunday:** Place a white candle on a table. Ask Jesus, the Light, to guide your family.

**Second Sunday:** Tape a 2-inch band of purple paper around the candle. Remember that God's love surrounds you this week.

**Third Sunday:** Paste a gold paper cross to the paper. Look to the cross for hope this week.

**Fourth Sunday:** Write names of family members on a small card. Prop it up near the candle and pray for one another this week.

**Fifth Sunday:** Turn the card over and write the name "Jesus" on it. Prop it up as before. Pray the name of Jesus often this week.

**Passion Sunday:** Cut pieces of blessed palm and arrange them on the table around the candle. Thank God for the blessings of this Lenten season.

## Family Prayer

Encourage your family to say this prayer at meals, especially on Fridays in Lent. Also share ways that your family will put fasting and sharing into practice.

Blessed are you, Lord, God of all creation: you make us hunger and thirst for holiness. Blessed are you, Lord, God of all creation: you call us to true fasting: to set free the oppressed, to share our bread with the hungry, to shelter the homeless and to clothe the naked.

Visit Sadlier's

**www.WeBelieveweb.com**

**Connect to the Catechism**
For adult background and reflection, see paragraph 559.

# Triduum

"Jesus knew that his hour had come
to pass from this world to the Father.
He loved his own in the world and
he loved them to the end."

John 13:1

# The Easter Triduum is our greatest celebration of the Paschal Mystery.

## WE GATHER

✝ *Jesus, remember us when you come into your Kingdom.*

Think of someone in your family who you care about and love very much. How do you let him or her know your love?

## WE BELIEVE

All during his life Jesus showed his love for his disciples. Jesus' greatest act of love for us was his dying for our sins. However, Jesus' death was not the end of his love for us. Three days after his death Jesus rose to new life. His death and Resurrection restores our relationship with God. They make it possible for us to have life forever with God. We celebrate Christ's Paschal Mystery of dying and rising to new life during the Easter Triduum. These three days are the holiest days of the year.

It is a Jewish tradition to mark the day as beginning at sundown and ending at sundown of the next day. Since Jesus followed this tradition, the Church also counts Sundays and solemnities from one evening to the next. So the Triduum begins on Holy Thursday evening and ends on the evening of Easter Sunday.

**Holy Thursday** The Evening Mass of the Lord's Supper on Holy Thursday begins the Easter Triduum. This celebration is not simply a remembering of the events of the Last Supper. It is a celebration of the life that Jesus gives us in the Eucharist. We are thankful for the unity that we have because of the Eucharist. We celebrate the love and service Christ calls us to everyday.

At the Last Supper Jesus washed his disciples' feet as a sign of his love for them. Jesus calls each of us to love and serve others, too. During the Mass on Holy Thursday, we have a special ceremony of the washing of the feet. This commits us to follow the example of Jesus' love and service. During this Mass we also take a special collection for those who are in need.

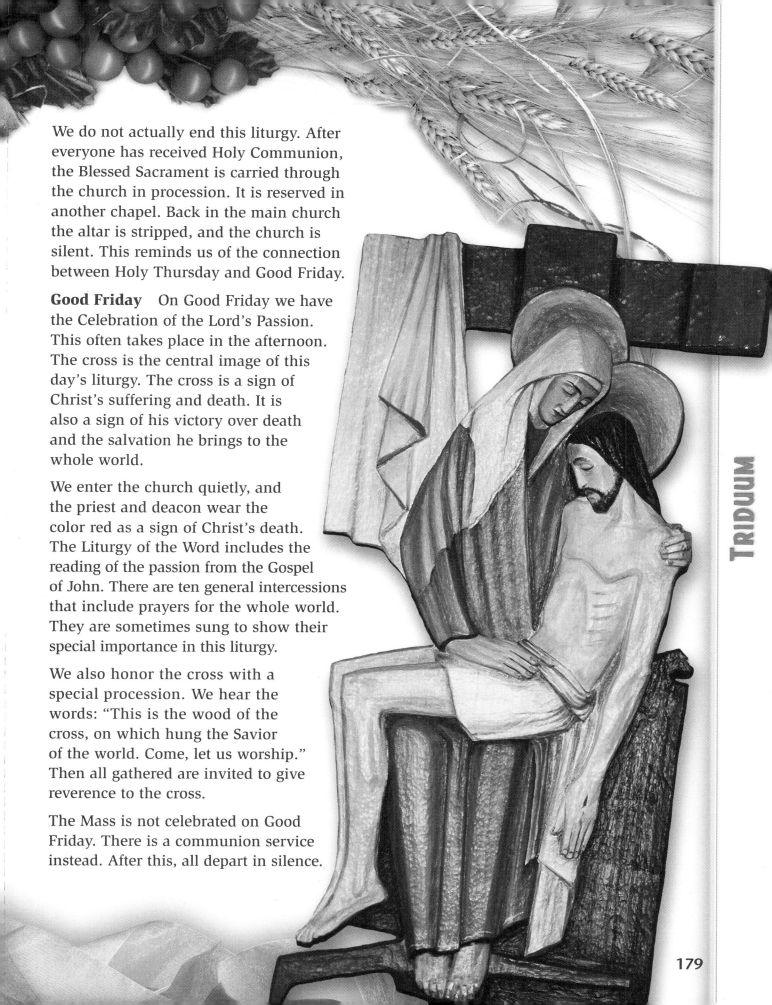

We do not actually end this liturgy. After everyone has received Holy Communion, the Blessed Sacrament is carried through the church in procession. It is reserved in another chapel. Back in the main church the altar is stripped, and the church is silent. This reminds us of the connection between Holy Thursday and Good Friday.

**Good Friday**   On Good Friday we have the Celebration of the Lord's Passion. This often takes place in the afternoon. The cross is the central image of this day's liturgy. The cross is a sign of Christ's suffering and death. It is also a sign of his victory over death and the salvation he brings to the whole world.

We enter the church quietly, and the priest and deacon wear the color red as a sign of Christ's death. The Liturgy of the Word includes the reading of the passion from the Gospel of John. There are ten general intercessions that include prayers for the whole world. They are sometimes sung to show their special importance in this liturgy.

We also honor the cross with a special procession. We hear the words: "This is the wood of the cross, on which hung the Savior of the world. Come, let us worship." Then all gathered are invited to give reverence to the cross.

The Mass is not celebrated on Good Friday. There is a communion service instead. After this, all depart in silence.

TRIDUUM

**Holy Saturday** During the day we spend time thinking and praying. We remember that Jesus died to save all people, and we thank God for this gift. In the evening we gather with our parish for the celebration of the Easter Vigil.

We begin in darkness, waiting for the light of Christ. When we see the light of the large paschal candle, we sing with joy. At this vigil there are many readings in the Liturgy of the Word. We hear again all the wonderful things God has done for his people. We have not sung the Alleluia since Lent began, but we sing it now with great joy. Jesus has indeed risen from the dead! One high point of this vigil is the celebration of the sacraments of initiation. We welcome new members into the Church and praise God for the new life we have all received in Christ. We renew our own baptismal promises and rejoice in the newness of our own lives. We continue to share in Christ's life in the celebration of the Eucharist that follows.

The third day of the Triduum begins Saturday evening and continues until the evening of Sunday. Parishes gather on Easter Sunday for the celebration of the Mass. We sing with joy that the Lord is risen!

## WE RESPOND

Illustrate the Easter Triduum. Show that it is one celebration that spans three days from evening to evening.

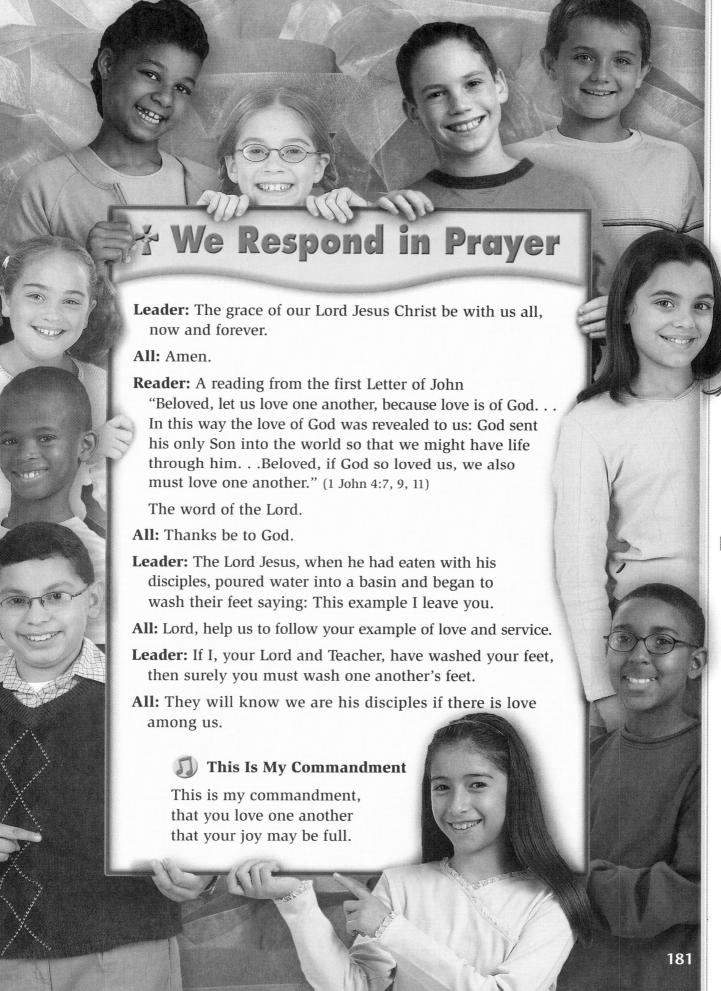

## ✦ We Respond in Prayer

**Leader:** The grace of our Lord Jesus Christ be with us all, now and forever.

**All:** Amen.

**Reader:** A reading from the first Letter of John
"Beloved, let us love one another, because love is of God. . . In this way the love of God was revealed to us: God sent his only Son into the world so that we might have life through him. . .Beloved, if God so loved us, we also must love one another." (1 John 4:7, 9, 11)

The word of the Lord.

**All:** Thanks be to God.

**Leader:** The Lord Jesus, when he had eaten with his disciples, poured water into a basin and began to wash their feet saying: This example I leave you.

**All:** Lord, help us to follow your example of love and service.

**Leader:** If I, your Lord and Teacher, have washed your feet, then surely you must wash one another's feet.

**All:** They will know we are his disciples if there is love among us.

🎵 **This Is My Commandment**

This is my commandment,
that you love one another
that your joy may be full.

# SHARING FAITH
## with My Family

CHAPTER 21 GRADE 5

## Sharing What I Learned

Discuss the following with your family:

• the Evening Mass of the Lord's Supper

• the celebration of the Lord's Passion

• the Easter Vigil.

## Around the Table

Ask your family to think about ways to observe the days of the Triduum at home. Here are some suggestions.

• Keep Good Friday simple and focused on Jesus by eating soup (no meat) and bread.

• Try to keep your home as quiet as possible, with no TV, radio, or stereos—not even in the car!

• Look for traditional recipes to use for your Easter celebrations.

• Join together to clean your home before the Easter celebrations.

• Add your own ideas.

_____

_____

## Family Prayer

Invite your family to pray this prayer during the Triduum, the great Three Days.

We should glory in the cross of our
   Lord Jesus Christ,
for he is our salvation, our life, and
   our resurrection;
through him we are saved and made free.

*(Holy Thursday Introductory Rites)*

Visit Sadlier's
**www.WeBelieveweb.com**

**Connect to the Catechism**
For adult background and reflection, see paragraph 654.

**Choose a word or phrase from the box to complete each sentence.**

| | | | |
|---|---|---|---|
| Assumption | Immaculate Conception | conscience | contrition |
| Anointing of the Sick | Reconciliation | rosary | conversion | sin |

1. When we examine our _____, we determine whether the choices we have made showed love for God, ourselves, and others.

2. God constantly calls us to turn back to him. A turning to God with all one's heart is called _____.

3. _____ is the sacrament by which God's grace and comfort are given to those who are seriously ill or suffering because of their old age.

4. The mysteries of the _____ recall special times in the lives of Jesus and Mary.

5. An act of _____ is a prayer that allows us to express our sorrow and promise to try not to sin again.

6. A thought, word, deed, or omission against God's law is a _____.

7. In the sacrament of _____ our relationship with God and the Church is strengthened or restored and our sins are forgiven.

8. The belief that Mary was free from original sin from the moment she was conceived is called the _____.

**Fill in the circle beside the correct answer.**

9. A prayer, a work of mercy, or an act of service that shows we are sorry for our sins is called _____.

   ○ a confession    ○ absolution    ○ a penance

10. Reconciliation, the Anointing of the Sick, and the Eucharist as _____ are often celebrated together by those who are sick.

    ○ litany    ○ viaticum    ○ initiation

11. Unjust situations and conditions in society such as prejudice, poverty, and violence are examples of _____.

    ○ mortal sin    ○ venial sin    ○ social sin

12. Because of _____, the priest cannot tell anyone what we have confessed in the sacrament of Reconciliation.

    ○ absolution    ○ the seal of confession    ○ the act of contrition

13. The _____ is also known as the Canticle of Mary.

    ○ Magnificat    ○ Annunciation    ○ Assumption

14. In the Anointing of the Sick we proclaim our faith in God's _____.

    ○ justice    ○ mercy    ○ litany

15. The main parts of the Anointing of the Sick are the prayer of faith, the _____, and the anointing with oil.

    ○ laying on of hands    ○ absolution    ○ examination of conscience

16. We hear many of the titles for Mary when we pray _____.

    ○ the Our Father    ○ a litany    ○ an act of contrition

**Answer the questions.**

17–18. How does celebrating the sacrament of Reconciliation help us to grow as the Body of Christ?

19–20. What are some ways that the sacrament of the Anointing of the Sick offers God's grace and comfort to those who are ill, and to those who love and care for them?

# We Love and Serve As Jesus Did

# UNIT 4 SHARING FAITH as a Family

## Virtues for Our Time

**P**rudence, temperance, fortitude, and justice. These words might sound outdated to some, but these four cardinal virtues are still very important in modern life and in the building of healthy families.

**Prudence** calls for a way of living based on wisdom and discernment. Being prudent means choosing carefully and avoiding paths that are harmful or destructive.

**Temperance** can be defined as holding back and refraining from overindulgence. At a time when families find themselves overwhelmed by too much to do and too much to take care of, this virtue is both practical and desirable.

**Fortitude** denotes strength, something parents and caregivers need in great measure as they raise their children. Fortitude is also a virtue to foster in young people in order to help them stay grounded in positive values and beliefs.

**Justice** is so rooted in the four gospels that it is mentioned, on average, in every tenth line. Christian discipleship means standing in solidarity with those who are poor, those who suffer, and those who are powerless.

## What Your Child Will Learn in Unit 4

The last unit of Grade 5 *We Believe* calls the children to live their lives as disciples of Jesus Christ. They examine the theological virtues of faith, hope, and love and learn the Beatitudes. In this unit the sacrament of Matrimony is introduced. Children learn about the celebration of the sacrament and the importance of the family. The presentation of the sacrament of Holy Orders begins with Jesus sharing his ministry in a special way with his apostles. The children learn more about the different ways bishops, priests, and deacons serve the Church. The last chapter of the unit is aptly titled, "One, Holy, Catholic, and Apostolic." These four characteristics are the marks of the Church. What better way to sum up this years emphasis on the sacraments than by examining the very nature of the Church that celebrates these special signs of God's love and forgiveness.

## Plan & Preview

▶ Pieces of cardboard or stiff paper can be used for the Sacrament Trading Cards. The front and back of the cards are glued to the board, forming a sturdy trading card.

## A Story in Faith
### Catherine A. Nardella

It was impossible to be around Catherine A. Nardella and not feel that any day was a little brighter, or that there was a lot more to enjoy in life. Yet it was on a bright, sunny day in September that Catherine lost her life. She was an insurance consultant for a firm in New York

### From the Catechism

**"The Christian home is the place where children receive the first proclamation of the faith."**
*(Catechism of the Catholic Church, 1666)*

City and worked high up in the World Trade Center. There was no chance of escape when the terrorists flew into the buildings on September 11, 2001 with two hijacked planes.

"Steward" perhaps best describes Cathy. She was a driving force of the group of people in her parish who wanted to give more of their time and talents in service to others. In doing so, Cathy and those involved in the stewardship program embodied the hospitality of Jesus. "Hospitality" is another good word to describe Cathy. No one was more warm and gracious to friend and stranger alike.

At a memorial service, her friends, family, co-workers, and parishioners remembered her and the life that she lived. So many of them remembered her sense of dedication and her sense of fun. Father Peter Funesti, a priest in her parish, said it best. "Jesus gave people respect by the way he treated them. He responded to people out of their need. So did Cathy. We will miss her always."

Catherine A. Nardella

# Faith, Hope, and Love

## WE GATHER

✝ **Leader:** Loving God, fill our hearts with peace and share your love with us. Blessed be the name of the Lord.

**All:** Now and for ever.

**Reader:** A reading from the first Letter of Saint Paul to the Corinthians

". . . If I have all faith so as to move mountains, but do not have love, I am nothing. If I give away everything I own . . . but do not have love, I gain nothing.

Love is patient, love is kind . . . faith, hope, love remain, these three; but the greatest of these is love."

(1 Corinthians 13:2–4, 13)

The word of the Lord.

**All:** Thanks be to God.

🎵 **God's Greatest Gift**

Love, love, Jesus is love.
God's greatest gift is the
    gift of love.
All creation sings together,
    praising God for love.

☀ What are some choices you have had to make recently? Were your decisions easy or difficult to make? How did your decisions affect you and others?

## WE BELIEVE

### We believe in God and all that the Church teaches.

Every day Christ calls us to follow him and to live by his teachings. Every day we have the opportunity to act as Jesus' disciples. The choices that we make show whether or not we follow Jesus' example. Sometimes we do not even realize that we are making a choice. We show love and respect because we are in the habit of doing it. A **virtue** is a good habit that helps us to act according to God's love for us.

The *theological virtues* of faith, hope, and love bring us closer to God and increase our desire to be with God forever. They are called theological because "theo" means God and these virtues are gifts from God. They make it possible for us to have a relationship with God—the Father, the Son, and the Holy Spirit.

The virtue of **faith** enables us to believe in God and all that the Church teaches us. Faith helps us to believe all that God has told us about himself and all that he has done. The gift of faith helps us to believe that God is with us and is acting in our lives.

God makes faith possible, but faith is still a choice we make. Jesus once said, "Blessed are those who have not seen and have believed" (John 20:29). We choose to respond to God's gift of faith. We choose to believe. Faith leads us to want to understand more about God and his plan for us, so that our belief in him can grow stronger.

Our faith is the faith of the Church. It is through the community of the Church that we come to believe. Through this community of faith we learn what it means to believe. Our faith is guided and strengthened by the Church.

Jesus' followers once asked him to "increase our faith" (Luke 17:5). They understood that faith could grow by the power of God. To grow in faith, we need to read the Bible, pray to God to make our faith stronger, and give witness to our faith by the way we live. We give witness to Christ when we speak and act based upon the good news. As Christ's disciples we are called to show others our belief in God and to help them believe.

With a partner use each of the letters below to describe faith.

F _____

A _____

I _____

T _____

H _____

How can you grow in faith this week?

Pray together this Act of Faith.

> O God, we believe in all that Jesus
>    has taught us about you.
> We place all our trust in you
>    because of your great love for us.

### As Catholics...

The theological virtues are the foundation of the human virtues. The human virtues are habits that come about by our own efforts. They lead us to live a good life. They result from our making the decision, over and over again, to live by God's law. These human virtues guide the way we think, feel, and behave. Four of these are called "cardinal" virtues: prudence, justice, fortitude, and temperance.

Find out more about each of these virtues.

188

## We trust in God and are confident in his love and care for us.

The virtue of **hope** enables us to trust in God's promise to share his life with us forever. Hope makes us confident in God's love and care for us. Hope keeps us from becoming discouraged or giving up when times are difficult. Hope helps us to trust in Christ and to rely on the strength of the Holy Spirit.

Hope is a gift that helps us to respond to the happiness that God offers us now and in the future. Hope helps us work to spread the Kingdom of God here on earth, and to look forward to the kingdom in heaven.

From the beginning of his ministry, Jesus gave people a reason to hope in God's mercy. God had not forgotten his people. He had sent his only Son to be with them and to share his life and love with them. Jesus brought them God's forgiveness and healing. He gave them the hope of peace and life with God.

The Beatitudes, which can be found on page 258, are a very important teaching of Jesus. Each beatitude begins with the word *blessed* which means "happy." In the Beatitudes Jesus describes the happiness that comes to those who follow his example of living and trusting in God's care. The Beatitudes describe the ways Christ's disciples should think and act. They are a promise of God's blessings. They give us reason to hope in the Kingdom of God, also called the kingdom of heaven.

Share one thing that gives you hope.

Pray together this Act of Hope.

O God, we never give up on your love. We have hope and will work for your kingdom to come and for a life that lasts forever with you in heaven.

**Key Words**

virtue (p. 269)

faith (p. 268)

hope (p. 268)

## We are able to love God and one another.

During his ministry Jesus taught the people about the meaning of the Ten Commandments. He gave them the Beatitudes as a model for living and working toward future happiness. Jesus showed the people that God's law is a law of love.

Once Jesus was asked what commandment of God's law was the greatest. Jesus responded by saying "You shall love the Lord, your God, with all your heart, with all your soul, and with all your mind. This is the greatest and the first commandment. The second is like it: You shall love your neighbor as yourself" (Matthew 22:37–39).

Love is possible because God loves us first. All love comes from God. God's love for us never ends. He is always there for us, especially through the Church community. The virtue of love enables us to love God and to love our neighbor. Love is the greatest of all virtues. All the other virtues come from it and lead back to it. Love is the goal of our lives as Christians.

Before he died Jesus told his disciples, "I give you a new commandment: love one another. As I have loved you, so you also should love one another. This is how all will know that you are my disciples, if you have love for one another" (John 13:34–35).

Jesus showed us how to love. He kept his promises, lived by the virtues, took care of his family and friends, and treated all people with respect. He listened to people and cared for their needs, even when he was tired. He stood up for the rights of others and helped them to find peace and comfort.

How can people be recognized as Jesus' disciples? Work in groups and act out some ways.

Pray together this Act of Love.

O God, we love you above all things. Help us to love ourselves and one another as Jesus taught us to do.

Key Word
love (p. 268)

## The saints are models for living the life of virtue.

From the very beginning of the Church, Christ's disciples have given witness to their faith in him. They spread the good news of Jesus Christ, followed the teaching of the apostles, and lived as a community of believers.

Many of these early disciples were martyrs, people who died rather than give up their belief in Christ. The word martyr comes from the Greek word for "witness." We remember and honor these martyrs, and the many others throughout history who have given their lives for their faith.

In the sixteenth century, Christian missionaries first brought the faith to Vietnam. During the next three centuries, Christians in Vietnam suffered for their beliefs. Many were martyred, especially during the years of 1820 to 1840. In 1988, Pope John Paul II proclaimed a group of one hundred seventeen of these martyrs as saints.

Saint Josephine Bakhita

The majority of those honored were lay-people. There were also many priests, some bishops, and religious sisters and brothers. Many of them were missionaries. Andrew Dung-Lac was a Vietnamese priest who was martyred, along with Father Peter Thi.

Andrew Trong Van Tram was a soldier and later an officer in the army. He had to keep his faith a secret. In 1834 the authorities discovered that Andrew, who was Catholic, was helping the missionaries. His position as an officer was taken away from him, and he was

Saint Andrew Trong Van Tram

put in prison. He was given the chance to be freed if he would stop practicing his faith. He refused to do so, and in 1835 he was killed for his belief.

Anthony Dich Nguyen was a wealthy farmer who contributed to the Church.

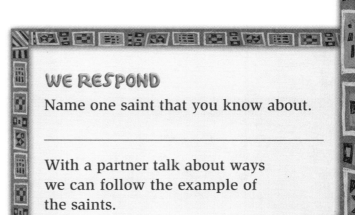

Saint Anthony Dich Nguyen

He helped the missionaries of the Paris Foreign Mission Society who served in Vietnam. He hid priests who were trying to escape government persecution. Anthony was arrested and beaten because of his faith and because he sheltered these Catholic priests.

These holy people made it possible for future generations of Vietnamese to know Christ and learn the faith. The feast day of the martyrs of Vietnam is November 24. We also remember and honor some of these martyrs with their own feast days: Andrew Dung-Lac and Peter Thi on December 21 and Andrew Trong Van Tram on November 28.

We look to the saints as examples for living the virtues of faith, hope, and love. Saint Josephine Bakhita also lived a life of holiness. Find out more about her and the lives of other saints.

## WE RESPOND
Name one saint that you know about.

_____

With a partner talk about ways we can follow the example of the saints.

**Write the letter of the definition that matches each term.**

1. _____ faith
2. _____ love
3. _____ hope
4. _____ martyrs

a. enables us to trust in God's promise to share his life with us

b. disciples who died rather than give up their belief in Christ

c. enables us to believe in God and all that the Church teaches us

d. the greatest of all virtues that enables us to love God and our neighbor

e. a habit that comes about by our own efforts

**Write True or False for the following sentences.**
**Then change the false sentences to make them true.**

5. _____ The new commandment teaches us to love only ourselves.

_____

_____

6. _____ The theological virtues are gifts from God that make it possible for us to have a relationship with God.

_____

_____

7. _____ A virtue is a good habit that helps us to act according to our wants.

_____

_____

8. _____ Love is the greatest of all virtues.

_____

_____

**Write a sentence to answer the question.**

**9–10.** What does Jesus teach us in the Beatitudes?

_____

_____

ASSESSMENT

Write your own Acts of Faith, Hope, and Love. Share these prayers with your class or family.

# We Respond in Faith

## Reflect & Pray

Jesus, thank you for the saints. Help me to live like the saints by

_____

_____

Saint _____, pray for me that I may grow in faith, hope, and love.

**Key Words**

**virtue** (p. 269)
**faith** (p. 268)
**hope** (p. 268)
**love** (p. 268)

## Remember

- We believe in God and all that the Church teaches.
- We trust in God and are confident in his love and care for us.
- We are able to love God and one another.
- The saints are models for living the life of virtue.

## OUR CATHOLIC LIFE

### Canonization Process

The Church has a special process to honor people who have lived very holy lives and have witnessed to Jesus Christ. This process is called canonization. During this process Church leaders examine the life of each person whose name has been submitted for sainthood. The Church leaders gather proof that this person has lived a life of faith and holiness. When someone is canonized a saint, the Church officially names him or her a saint. His or her name is entered into the worldwide list of saints recognized by the Catholic Church. We remember and celebrate each canonized saint on a special day during the Church year.

Padre Pio was canonized a saint in 2002.

# SHARING FAITH
## with My Family

## Sharing What I Learned

Discuss the following with your family:

- the virtues of faith, hope, and love
- the Beatitudes
- Jesus' greatest commandment
- saints who lived lives of virtue.

## Family Faith Checklist

Ask your family to complete the Family Faith Checklist. Share your experiences.

### A Family Prayer

Lord,
grant your people your protection and grace.
Give them health of mind and body,
perfect love for one another,
and make them always faithful to you.
Grant this through Christ our Lord.
Amen.

*from the Book of Blessings*

## Our Family

Who is your favorite saint? How did that saint witness to his or her faith in Christ? How can you give witness to Jesus Christ?

☐ At home:

_____

☐ At school/work:

_____

☐ In the parish:

_____

☐ In the community:

_____

Visit Sadlier's

**www.WeBelieveweb.com**

**Connect to the Catechism**
For adult background and reflection, see paragraphs 1814, 1817, 1822, and 828.

# Called to Live As Jesus' Disciples

## WE GATHER

✝ **Leader:** Lord, may we follow your call to do good in whatever work we do.

**Reader:** A reading from the holy Gospel according to John

"Whoever believes in me will do the works that I do, and will do greater ones than these, because I am going to the Father. And whatever you ask in my name, I will do, so that the Father may be glorified in the Son." (John 14:12–13)

The Gospel of the Lord.

**All:** Praise to you, Lord Jesus Christ.

**Leader:** Lord you ask us to continue your work. Be with us as we share your love and peace with others.

**All:** Lord, make me an instrument of your peace:
where there is hatred, let me sow love;
where there is injury, pardon;
where there is doubt, faith;
where there is despair, hope;
where there is darkness, light;
where there is sadness, joy.

O divine Master, grant that I may not
  so much seek
to be consoled as to console,
to be understood as to understand,
to be loved as to love.
For it is in giving that we receive,
it is in pardoning that we are pardoned,
it is in dying that we are born
  to eternal life.

Amen. (Saint Francis of Assisi)

☀ Think of a time when a group that you were part of was given a job to do. What was the job? How did the group get it done?

## WE BELIEVE
### Jesus calls the baptized to serve him in the priesthood of the faithful.

When Jesus was baptized at the Jordan, the Spirit of the Lord came upon him. This anointing by the Holy Spirit marked Jesus as priest, prophet, and king. Our anointing at Baptism makes us sharers in Christ's role as priest, prophet, and king.

So all those who are baptized share in Christ's priestly mission. This is known as the **priesthood of the faithful**. In the priesthood of the faithful, each and every one of us is called to

- worship God

- spread the good news of Jesus Christ

- serve one another and the Church.

In the sacrament of Holy Orders, priests and bishops become members of the ordained priesthood. They participate in Christ's priestly mission in a unique way. They receive the grace to act in the name of and in the person of Christ.

Being part of the priesthood of the faithful is not the same thing as being an ordained priest. However, members of the priesthood of the faithful work with ordained priests to lead and care for God's people. These women and men help us to participate in Christ's priestly mission. They help us to learn the faith, to worship, and to care for the needs of others.

As members of the priesthood of the faithful, we continue to learn about Jesus and the teachings of the Church. We try to live by these teachings each day. We are called to protect people's rights and care for those in need. With God's grace and the help of our community, we can focus on loving God and others.

Illustrate one way people can show they are part of the priesthood of the faithful.

**Key Words**
priesthood of the faithful (p. 269)
laypeople (p. 268)

## The laity share in the mission to bring the good news of Christ to the world.

Because all Christians share in the priesthood of the faithful, we all share a common vocation, too. Our common vocation is to grow in holiness and spread the message of Jesus' life and saving work. God calls each of us to live out our common vocation in a particular way. We do this as laypeople, religious, or ordained ministers.

**Laypeople** are all the baptized members of the Church who share in the mission to bring the good news of Christ to the world. Laypeople are also known as the Christian faithful or the laity. Most Catholics are members of the laity and follow God's call either in the single life or in marriage.

Single people and married people serve God and the Church in many ways. They share God's love in their families and parishes. A husband and wife share God's love with each other and form a new Christian family. Much of their time is focused on loving and caring for their families.

Single people can share their gifts and talents with others through their work. Sometimes they care for their brothers or sisters or take on extra responsibility in caring for their parents. They may also dedicate their time to their parishes and communities.

You are a member of the Christian faithful. You are called to share the good news at home, in school, and in your neighborhood.

You can take part in your parish celebrations. You can live as Jesus taught. You can be an example of Christian living for others. With your family and your parish, you can care for the needs of others. You can stand up for what is right. You can help others to see Christ's love and his presence in the world.

Laypeople have a responsibility to bring the good news of Christ to their work and communities. They do this when they treat others fairly and justly. They also have a responsibility to act and make decisions based on the teachings of Jesus and on their faith.

The Christian faithful are called to be active in their parishes. We

- participate in the celebration of the sacraments and parish programs

- serve on the pastoral council, in the parish school or religious education program, or in youth ministry

- perform different liturgical ministries during the Mass.

The laity serve in their dioceses, too. They may work in offices for education, worship, youth, and social ministries.

Imagine yourself ten years from now. In what ways do you see yourself taking part in the work of the Church? Act these out for the group.

## Women and men in religious life serve Christ, their communities, and the whole Church.

God calls some women and men to the religious life. **Religious** refers to the women and men who belong to communities of service to God and the Church. They are known as religious sisters, brothers, and priests. They devote themselves to Christ's work through the work of their communities.

Religious make vows, or promises, to God. By taking these vows religious try to follow Jesus' example of living each day for God. The vows that religious sisters, brothers, and priests often make are:

*Chastity* They choose to live a life of loving service to the Church and their community. They do not marry. Instead they promise to devote themselves to the work of God and to the Church as members of their communities.

*Poverty* They promise to live simply as Jesus did. They agree to share their belongings and to own no personal property.

*Obedience* They promise to listen carefully to God's direction in their lives by obeying the leaders of the Church and of their communities. They serve wherever their community and the Church need them. Religious try to live the way Christ did and follow God's will.

Many religious live as a family in one community. They pray together, work together, and share their meals. Other religious may live away from their community and work where they are needed.

Some communities are set apart from the rest of society. These religious usually live in places called monasteries. They devote their lives to praying for the world. Whether they farm, prepare food to sell, or work on computers, their work is a way of prayer.

Other communities combine prayer with a life of service outside their communities. These religious sisters, brothers, and priests may serve in many different parish ministries. They may also be teachers, missionaries, doctors, nurses, or social workers. In these ways they can directly help those who are poor, elderly, suffering, or in any type of need.

Together the laity, religious, and ordained ministers make up the Church. No one group is more important or special than another. The Church needs all its members to be able to continue Jesus' work.

Talk about the ways religious sisters, brothers, and priests may serve in your community.

## Friendships prepare us for future vocations.

For most of us discovering our vocation is a process that takes many years. We are encouraged to pray and think about our talents and abilities. The Holy Spirit will guide and help us as we pray about our future. Our families, friends, and parish also support us as we try to find out what God is calling us to do.

You might not realize it, but you are actually preparing for your future vocation. The ways that you are responding to God and other people in your life right now are preparing you to respond to God in the future.

Right now you are discovering the importance of responsibility, faithfulness, and self-respect. These values are essential in all of your relationships. You are also learning about love and service in your families and with your friends.

Friendships are an important part of finding out what it means to be faithful to Christ and one another. Good friends are true to each other. They are honest. They keep their promises. They stand up for each other. However, friends sometimes make mistakes. They may forget something important or hurt each other's feelings. But they learn to forgive each other. They encourage each other to be fair and loving in the future.

Good friends help us to live as disciples of Christ at home, in school, and in our neighborhood. They also prepare us to serve God in whatever vocation we accept and follow.

## As Catholics...

All of us are called to share in the mission of the Church. We can do this by our prayers, words, and actions. We are called to share the good news of Christ and to live lives of holiness. Lay people, religious, and ordained ministers can also do this as missionaries.

Missionaries serve here in our own country and in places all over the world. They may spend weeks, months, or even years doing mission work. They live with the people they serve and share their love with them. Some missionaries learn the customs and traditions of the people they serve. They may even learn a new language so that they can teach about Jesus and the Catholic faith.

Find out what missionary opportunities your parish and diocese offer.

Key Word
**religious** (p. 269)

## WE RESPOND

God calls us to our vocation. Here are ways we can listen to God's call.

☐ prayer

☐ advice from good people

☐ recognizing our God-given abilities and talents

Listen in each of these ways. Check the box when you have listened to God in this way.

Pray together the Prayer for Vocation found on page 259.

**Circle the letter of the correct answer.**

1. _____ are baptized members of the Church who share in the mission to bring the good news of Christ to the world.

   **a.** Laypeople    **b.** Vows    **c.** Vocations

2. _____ are men and women who belong to communities in which they dedicate their lives to the service of God and the Church.

   **a.** Christian faithful     **b.** Laity

         **c.** Religious

3. _____ are an important part of finding out what it means to be faithful to Christ and one another.

   **a.** Vocations    **b.** Laity    **c.** Friendships

4. The _____ is Christ's priestly mission in which all those who are baptized share.

   **a.** Laypeople    **b.** ordained priesthood

         **c.** priesthood of the faithful

**Short Answers**

5. Name three things that help us to live out the priesthood of the faithful.

   _____

6. As Christians, what is our common vocation?

   _____

7. Name three ways that laypeople can be active and serve in their parish community.

   _____

8. What are the three vows, or promises, that religious sisters, brothers, and priests might make to God?

   _____

**Write a sentence to answer the question.**

9–10. How do friendships prepare us for future vocations?

   _____

ASSESSMENT

How do the Christian faithful, religious, and ordained ministers serve God and the Church? Design a brochure that illustrates ways the Christian faithful, religious, and ordained ministers serve God and the Church.

# We Respond in Faith

## Reflect & Pray

Jesus, you said that your kingdom is already here and that it is growing. To help spread your kingdom, we ask that you

_____

_____

**Key Words**

priesthood of the
faithful (p. 269)
laypeople (p. 268)
religious (p. 269)

## Remember

- Jesus calls the baptized to serve him in the priesthood of the faithful.

- The laity share in the mission to bring the good news of Christ to the world.

- Women and men in religious life serve Christ, their communities, and the whole Church.

- Friendships prepare us for future vocations.

## OUR CATHOLIC LIFE

### Pastoral Administrators

Some religious sisters and brothers as well as laypeople serve as pastoral administrators. When a parish does not have a priest to serve the people, the bishop of the diocese appoints a pastoral administrator to serve the parish. This person is responsible for parish life and business. She or he makes sure the parish community is being offered religious education, worship, and social outreach programs. The administrator often leads the faith community in prayer services and community outreach. The bishop assigns a priest to celebrate the Mass and other sacraments with the parish, or the community joins with another parish for the celebration of the sacraments.

# SHARING FAITH
## with My Family

## Sharing What I Learned

Discuss the following with your family:

- the priesthood of the faithful
- the laity
- religious life
- good friendships.

## Family Faith Checklist

Ask your family to complete the Family Faith Checklist. Share your experiences.

### Our Family

What are the ways you will answer Jesus' call to share in the priesthood of the faithful?

☐ At home:

_____

☐ At school/work:

_____

☐ In the parish:

_____

☐ In the community:

_____

## A Family Prayer

Dear God,
You have a great and loving plan
    for our world and for me.
I wish to share in that plan fully,
    faithfully, and joyfully.

*from the Prayer for Vocation*

**Connect to the Catechism**
For adult background and reflection, see paragraphs 1546, 900, 917, and 959.

# Matrimony: A Promise of Faithfulness and Love

## WE GATHER

✝ **Leader:** : Let us bless the Lord,
by whose goodness we live
and by whose grace we love one another.
Blessed be God for ever.

**All:** Blessed be God for ever.

**Reader:** A reading from the Book of Deuteronomy

"Hear, O Israel! The LORD is our God, the LORD alone! Therefore, you shall love the LORD, your God, with all your heart, and with all your soul, and with all your strength. Take to heart these words which I enjoin on you today. Drill them into your children. Speak of them at home and abroad, whether you are busy or at rest."
(Deuteronomy 6:4–7)

The word of the Lord.

**All:** Thanks be to God.

**Leader:** May the God of hope fill us with every joy in believing.
May the peace of Christ abound in our hearts.
May the Holy Spirit enrich us with his gifts, now and for ever.

**All:** Amen.

What words would you use to explain what faithfulness means? How would you describe faithful friends?

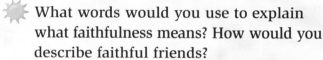

## WE BELIEVE
### Marriage was part of God's plan from the very beginning.

When God created the first humans, he made them male and female. God created them to be different but equal, and he found this very good. The differences between girls and boys, women and men are good. These differences are part of God's plan. Even though we are different, we are equal. We share the same human dignity that comes from being made in God's image.

God told the first man and woman to "Be fertile and multiply" (Genesis 1:28). In this way God blessed the first man and woman to bring new life into the world. He wanted them to have children and to share in his plan for creating the human family.

We learn from the Old Testament that marriage was part of God's plan from the very beginning. "That is why a man leaves his father and mother and clings to his wife, and the two of them become one body." (Genesis 2:24)

We learn from the New Testament that Jesus showed the importance of marriage by attending a wedding in Cana and helping the couple who had been married. Since that time marriage has been an effective sign of Jesus' love and presence. Jesus' love is made present through the love of a husband and wife. This is what the Church celebrates in the sacrament of Matrimony.

In the sacrament of **Matrimony**, a man and woman become husband and wife. They promise to be faithful to each other for the rest of their lives. They

- promise to love and be true to each other always

- lovingly accept their children as a gift from God

- are strengthened by God's grace to live out their promises to Christ and each other.

With members of the Church community present, their love is blessed and strengthened by the grace of this sacrament.

Discuss why it is important to keep our promises. Then quietly pray and ask God to help all people live out their promises to him and to one another.

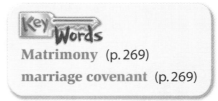

**Matrimony** (p. 269)

**marriage covenant** (p. 269)

## The marriage covenant is built on Christ's love for the Church.

Christians believe there is a new covenant between Jesus Christ and the Church. It is based on the Son of God's complete love for his Church. Jesus promises to love us always and be with us. In return, we, the Church, promise to love Jesus and one another. We promise to follow and be faithful to his teachings and the teachings of the Church.

The Church sees marriage as a covenant, too. The **marriage covenant** is the life-long commitment between a man and woman to live as faithful and loving partners. The marriage covenant reminds us of Christ's covenant with the Church.

The love between a husband and a wife is a sign of Christ's love for his Church. The love between a husband and wife is meant to be generous, faithful, and complete. A married couple promises to share and express this love only with each other.

Christ will always love us. He will forever keep his promise to share God's life and love with us. So Christ's love for the Church is permanent. In the same way, the marriage covenant is meant to be permanent, too.

Once Jesus was teaching about marriage, and he said "what God has joined together, no human being must separate" (Matthew 19:6). Christ and the Church teach us that the marriage covenant is not to be broken.

Married couples can turn to their family and parish community for prayer and support. They can turn to the sacraments of Eucharist and Reconciliation to strengthen and heal their relationship.

Often during difficult times children do not understand what is happening to their parents. They may be confused and sad. So it is important for them to understand that they are not to blame for these difficulties. And they are not responsible if their parents get separated or divorced. Though separation and divorce are very painful, God continues to offer his healing to all who need it.

Write two ways you can be a loyal and trustworthy family member, friend, or neighbor.

_____

_____

**In the sacrament of Matrimony, a man and woman promise to always love and be true to each other.**

In all the other sacraments, Jesus acts through his ordained ministers to offer the grace of the sacrament. But in the sacrament of Matrimony, the bride and groom are the celebrants. Jesus acts through the couple and through their promise to always love and be true to each other. The priest or deacon is the official witness of the sacrament, and he blesses the union that God has joined together.

The celebration of the sacrament of Matrimony often takes place within the Mass. When it does, the Liturgy of the Word includes readings selected by the couple themselves. The Rite of Marriage takes place after the gospel is proclaimed.

The deacon or priest asks the couple three important questions. Are they free to give themselves in marriage? Will they love and honor each other as husband and wife for the rest of their lives? Will they lovingly accept children from God and raise them in the faith?

After answering these questions, the bride and groom then pledge their love for each other by exchanging their vows. They may say words such as these: "I take you to be my husband (or wife). I promise to be true to you in good times and in bad, in sickness and in health. I will love you and honor you all the days of my life."

The deacon or priest receives the couple's promises and asks God to strengthen their love and faithfulness and to fill them with many blessings. The rings are then blessed, and the couple exchanges them as a sign of their love and fidelity. **Fidelity** is faithfulness to a person and to duties, obligations, or promises. In marriage, fidelity is loyalty and the willingness to be true to each other always.

The whole assembly prays the general intercessions, and the Mass continues with the Liturgy of the Eucharist. After the Lord's Prayer, the priest faces the couple and prays a special prayer asking for God's favor on this new marriage. The bride and groom, if they are Catholic, receive Holy Communion. Their communion is a sign of their union with Jesus who is the source of their love.

 In the Rite of Marriage the priest prays "Let them be living examples of Christian life." Name some ways that married couples can show others what it means to be an example of Christian life.

_____

_____

## Families are very important communities.

The sacrament of Matrimony is a sacrament of service. Those who celebrate this sacrament are strengthened to serve God and the Church. They are called to live out their fidelity to God and each other in their home, in their jobs, and in their neighborhoods. By creating a loving family, married couples express their love. When they share the goodness of their love with others, their own love for each other and for Christ grows.

Being part of a family means having duties and responsibilities. Parents and guardians try to provide a safe, loving home for the children. They protect and care for their children. Parents and guardians are the first teachers of their children. They are called to live by their faith and to share their belief with their children. Children learn what it means to be a disciple of Christ and member of the Church by the example of their parents, guardians, and family members.

Children have many duties and responsibilities, too. They are called to honor their parents and guardians by loving and obeying them. They are to do the just and good things that are asked of them, and to cooperate with their parents and guardians. They try to help out around the house by doing chores and showing their appreciation for their family members and all of their relatives.

As children grow older, the ways they show their love and appreciation often change. But the love between children and their parents and guardians is meant to stay strong and to continue to grow.

**Key Word**
fidelity (p. 268)

## As Catholics...

Christian families are called to be communities of faith, hope, and love. Every family is called to be a domestic church, or a "church in the home." It is in the family that we can first feel love and acceptance. We can experience Jesus' love when our family members love and care for us. We can learn to forgive and be forgiven, to grow in faith as we pray and worship together. In our families we can learn to be disciples of Jesus and to help and comfort those in need.

Talk with your family about the ways that you can be a domestic church.

## WE RESPOND

Design a billboard to show others what wonderful things can happen in families where there is love for God and one another.

**Short Answers**

1. How do children learn what it means to be a disciple of Christ and a member

   of the Church? _____

2. What is the role of the priest or deacon in the sacrament of Matrimony?

   _____

3. What are the three questions the couple is asked by a priest or deacon at
   the beginning of the Rite of Marriage?

   _____

4. How does the marriage covenant remind us of Christ's love for the Church?

   _____

**Write True or False for the following sentences.
Then change the false sentences to make them true.**

5. _____ Marriage is an effective sign of
   Jesus' love and presence.

   _____

6. _____ Fidelity is the sacrament in which
   a man and woman become husband and
   wife, and promise to be faithful to each
   other for the rest of their lives.

   _____

7. _____ The sacrament of Matrimony is
   a sacrament of Christian initiation.

   _____

8. _____ Being part of a family means
   having duties and responsibilities.

   _____

**Write a sentence to answer the question.**

**9–10.** In the Rite of Marriage, what do the bride and groom promise each other?

_____

ASSESSMENT

What entries might be included in the Table of Contents for a guide on
the sacrament of Matrimony and the meaning of Christian marriage?

# We Respond in Faith

## Reflect & Pray

Jesus, you gave us the sacrament of Matrimony to help us live our vocations as Christians. We pray that we can support married

couples by _____

Send us your Spirit to guide us as we _____

_____

### Key Words

**Matrimony** (p. 269)
**marriage covenant** (p. 269)
**fidelity** (p. 268)

## Remember

- Marriage was part of God's plan from the very beginning.

- The marriage covenant is built on Christ's love for the Church.

- In the sacrament of Matrimony, a man and woman promise to always love and be true to each other.

- Families are very important communities.

## OUR CATHOLIC LIFE

### Saint Margaret

Margaret was an English princess born in 1045. When she was older, she and her mother moved to Scotland where Margaret eventually married King Malcolm. As Queen of Scotland, Margaret worked to make Scotland a better place. She gave her husband wise advice and helped him to live a life of virtue. Margaret and Malcolm had eight children. She was devoted to her family, her faith, and the people. She took great effort to get good teachers and have churches built so that the people could learn and practice their faith. Margaret was a great example to other wives and mothers of her time as well as to us today. We honor Saint Margaret on her feast day, November 16.

# SHARING FAITH
## with My Family

## Sharing What I Learned

Discuss the following with your family:

- the sacrament of Matrimony
- the marriage covenant
- fidelity
- family duties and responsibilities.

## Sacrament Trading Cards

Design a trading card for the sacrament of Matrimony using the pattern below. Use your knowledge about this sacrament to write "sacrament facts" on the back of the card. Collect all seven!

### A Family Prayer

May the Holy Spirit of God always fill your hearts with his love. Amen.

*from the Rite of Marriage*

### Matrimony

What is the importance of the sacrament?

_____

What do we see?

_____

What do we hear?

_____

Who leads us in the celebration?

_____

Visit Sadlier's

www.WEBELIEVEweb.com

**Connect to the Catechism**
For adult background and reflection, see paragraphs 1605, 1616, 1644, and 1657.

# Holy Orders: A Promise of Service for the People of God

## WE GATHER

**✝ Leader:** Christ, you call us to follow you every day of our lives. Give us the courage to trust in you as your first disciples did.

**Reader 1:** A reading from the holy Gospel according to Matthew

"As he was walking by the Sea of Galilee, he saw two brothers, Simon who is called Peter, and his brother Andrew, casting a net into the sea; they were fishermen. He said to them, 'Come after me, and I will make you fishers of men.' At once they left their nets and followed him."

(Matthew 4:18–20)

**Reader 2:** "As Jesus passed on from there, he saw a man named Matthew sitting at the customs post. He said to him, 'Follow me.' And he got up and followed him." (Matthew 9:9)

The Gospel of the Lord.

**All:** Praise to you, Lord Jesus Christ.

## ♪ Come, Follow Me

Refrain:
Come, follow me, come, follow me.
I am the way, the truth, and the life.
Come, follow me, come, follow me.
I am the light of the world, follow me.

You call us to serve with a generous
    heart;
in building your kingdom each one
    has a part.
Each person is special in your
    kingdom of love.
Yes, we will follow you, Jesus!
(Refrain)

☀ Who are some people who help you to grow in faith? How do they help you to believe in and follow Christ?

## WE BELIEVE
## Jesus shares his ministry in a special way with the apostles.

From the beginning of his ministry, Jesus Christ invited all types people to be his disciples. After a night of prayer, Jesus "called his disciples to himself, and from them he chose Twelve, whom he also named apostles." (Luke 6:13) Jesus chose the apostles to share in his ministry in a special way.

Jesus sent the apostles out to share his message. He sent them to preach and to cure people in his name. He told them, "whoever receives the one I send receives me" (John 13:20).

Once the apostles argued among themselves about who was the greatest. Jesus told them that whoever wanted to be great must be a servant to the others. He told them, "I am among you as the one who serves" (Luke 22:27). Jesus wanted his apostles to follow his example and to lead others by serving them.

*Christ Appearing to His Disciples at the Mount of Galilee*
Duccio di Buoninsegna (1278–1319)

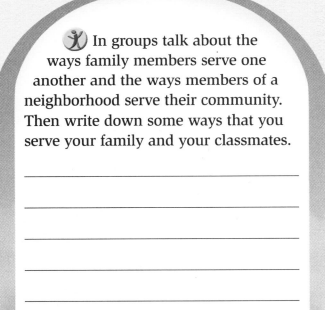

In groups talk about the ways family members serve one another and the ways members of a neighborhood serve their community. Then write down some ways that you serve your family and your classmates.

_____

_____

_____

_____

_____

Before he returned to his Father, Jesus promised his apostles that they would receive the gift of the Holy Spirit. The Holy Spirit would help them to remember all that Jesus had said and done.

After his death and Resurrection, the risen Jesus gave the apostles the authority to continue his work. He commissioned them, or sent them out, saying, "'Peace be with you. As the Father has sent me, so I send you.' And when he said this, he breathed on them and said to them, 'Receive the holy Spirit'" (John 20:21–22).

With these words Jesus trusted the apostles with his own work, and they received their mission. Jesus sent them out to all parts of the world to lead his community and to bring people to share in his kingdom. They were to teach and to baptize people. The Holy Spirit strengthened the apostles to carry out their mission.

## Holy Orders is the sacrament through which the Church continues the apostles' mission.

Everywhere they went the apostles gathered believers into local Church communities. With the help of each local Church, they chose leaders and ministers for the community. The apostles laid hands on those chosen and commissioned them.

Some of these leaders acted on behalf of the apostles by preaching the good news of Jesus Christ and sharing the teachings of the apostles. They continued the apostles' ministry and were the successors of the apostles. They eventually became known as bishops.

The local leaders who worked with the bishops became known as priests. And those who assisted in the worship and service of the community were called deacons.

As the Church continued to grow, the bishops, the successors of the apostles, commissioned others to continue the ministry of the apostles. In this way, the leadership of the Church throughout history can be traced back to the apostles.

**Holy Orders** is the sacrament in which men are ordained to serve the Church as deacons, priests, and bishops. It is a sacrament of service to others. While there are many ministries in the Church, deacons, priests, and bishops are the only ordained ministers. Those who receive Holy Orders take on a special mission in leading and serving the people of God.

**Holy Orders** (p. 268)

In the sacrament of Holy Orders:

- Men are ordained by the bishop's laying on of hands and prayer of consecration.

- Those ordained receive the grace necessary to carry out their ministry to the faithful.

- The Church, through its ordained ministers, continues the mission that Jesus Christ first gave to his apostles.

Some men, single or married, are ordained permanent deacons. They share in Christ's mission and remain deacons for life. They may work to support themselves and their families. Other men are ordained deacons as a step in their preparation for the priesthood. These men remain unmarried and continue their study to become ordained priests.

With a partner discuss ways that the members of your parish work with the priests and deacons who serve you.

## As Catholics...

The pope is the bishop of Rome because he is the successor of the apostle Peter, who was the first leader of the Church of Rome. As the bishop of Rome, the pope has a special responsibility to care for and lead the Church. The bishops are called to work with the pope to lead and guide the whole Church. The bishops, with the pope as their head, are called to watch over all those under their care, especially those who are in need in any way.

## Bishops, priests, and deacons serve the Church in different ways.

The **bishops** are the successors of the apostles. They are called to continue the apostles' mission of leadership and service in the Church. The bishops are the chief teachers, leaders, and priests of the Church.

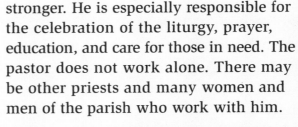
Bishop

A bishop usually leads and cares for a diocese. A diocese is a local community of Christian faithful. A diocese is made up of parish communities, schools and colleges, and even hospitals.

While bishops are fully and completely responsible for the care of the whole Church, they do not do this alone. The bishop of a diocese appoints priests to represent him and carry out his ministry in the parishes. The bishop also appoints deacons, religious and lay women and men to work with the priests in caring for the people of his diocese.

**Priests** are ordained by their bishops and are called to serve the Christian faithful by leading, teaching, and most especially celebrating the Eucharist and other sacraments. Priests are coworkers with their bishops.

Bishops usually appoint one priest to serve as the pastor of a parish. The pastor is responsible to see that the life of the parish grows

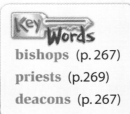
Missionary Priest

stronger. He is especially responsible for the celebration of the liturgy, prayer, education, and care for those in need. The pastor does not work alone. There may be other priests and many women and men of the parish who work with him.

**Deacons** are men who are not priests but are ordained by their bishops to the work of service for the Church. They have an important role in worship, leadership, and social ministries.

Deacons are called to serve the community in worship. They may preach the word of God and baptize new members of the Church. They may witness marriages and preside at Christian burials. At Mass they proclaim the gospel, preach, prepare the altar, distribute Holy Communion, and send the gathered community out to serve others.

Deacons help the parish to reach out to people in the community. They have a special responsibility to care for those who are suffering or who are in need.

Deacon

There are many people who minister to and lead the members of your parish community. As a class name some of them and explain their ministries.

**Key Words**

bishops (p. 267)

priests (p.269)

deacons (p. 267)

## The laying on of hands and prayer of consecration are the main parts of the sacrament of Holy Orders.

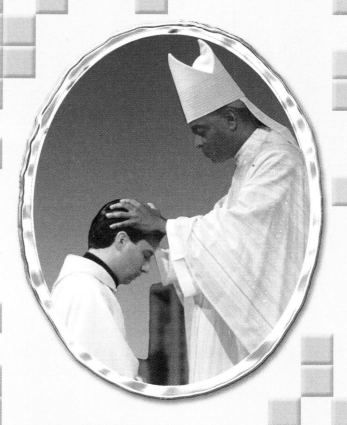

The sacrament of Holy Orders is a wonderful celebration for the Church. The whole community in the diocese gathers for the celebration. A bishop is always the celebrant of this sacrament. Only a bishop can ordain another bishop, a priest, or a deacon.

The celebration of Holy Orders always takes place during the celebration of the Mass. The ordination of deacons, priests, and bishops is similar. The Liturgy of the Word includes readings about ministry and service. After the gospel reading, those to be ordained are presented to the bishop celebrant.

The celebrant speaks about the roles these men will have in the Church. He reflects on the ways they are called to lead and serve in Jesus' name. He talks about their responsibilities to teach, to lead, and to worship.

The laying on of hands and the prayer of consecration are the main parts of the sacrament of Holy Orders. It is through these two actions that the candidates or the bishop-elect are ordained. During the laying on of hands, the bishop celebrant prays in silence. The bishop celebrant then prays the prayer of consecration. Through this prayer these men are consecrated or dedicated for a particular service in the Church. The bishop celebrant extends his hands, and by the power of the Holy Spirit consecrates the candidates or the bishop-elect to continue Jesus' ministry. The newly ordained are forever marked by Holy Orders.

## WE RESPOND

Design a sign of service to show others that you are a follower of Christ and member of the Church. It might be an object, logo, or image.

**Choose a word(s) from the box to complete each sentence.**

| Deacons | Bishops | Holy Orders | Priests | Eucharist |

1. _____ is the sacrament in which men are ordained to serve as deacons, priests, and bishops.

2. _____ are ordained ministers who serve the Christian faithful by leading, teaching, and most especially celebrating the Eucharist and other sacraments.

3. _____ are men who are not priests but are ordained to the work of service for the Church.

4. _____ are the successors of the apostles who are ordained to continue the apostles' mission of leadership and service in the Church.

**Short answers**

5. How did the Holy Spirit help the apostles carry out Jesus' mission?

_____

6. Who is the celebrant of Holy Orders?

_____

7. What was the apostles' mission?

_____

8. What are the two main parts of the sacrament of Holy Orders?

_____

**Write a sentence to answer the question.**

9–10. What is the importance of the sacrament of Holy Orders?

_____

ASSESSMENT

You have been asked to write a guide of frequently asked questions about the sacrament of Holy Orders. What questions would you include? List possible responses for each question.

# We Respond in Faith

## Reflect & Pray

Jesus told his disciples, "The harvest is abundant but the laborers are few" (Luke 10:2). Jesus, help us to work for your kingdom by

_____

Help our bishops, priests, and deacons to _____

_____

**Holy Orders** (p. 268)
**bishops** (p. 267)
**priests** (p. 269)
**deacons** (p. 267)

## Remember

- Jesus shares his ministry in a special way with the apostles.

- Holy Orders is the sacrament through which the Church continues the apostles' mission.

- Bishops, priests, and deacons serve the Church in different ways.

- The laying on of hands and the prayer of consecration are the main parts of the sacrament of Holy Orders.

# OUR CATHOLIC LIFE

## Saint
## Andrew Kim Taegon

Andrew Kim Taegon was baptized a Catholic in Korea when he was fifteen years old. He later traveled over a thousand miles to China to study for the priesthood. He became Korea's first native priest. He was famous for the faith and the witness he gave to Christ.

At that time, the Church in Korea was under persecution. Father Andrew helped many Christians escape to China. He also tried to bring some French missionaries to Korea. He prepared a map and other information for them. Because he tried to continue the work of Christ and the Church he was captured and put to death. Saint Andrew Kim Taegon was the first of 103 Korean Catholics to be martyred for their faith. He was only twenty-five years old when he was killed. His feast day is September 20.

# SHARING FAITH
## with My Family

## Sharing What I Learned

Discuss the following with your family:

- the mission of Jesus' apostles
- the sacrament of Holy Orders
- the role of bishops, priests, and deacons
- the celebration of Holy Orders.

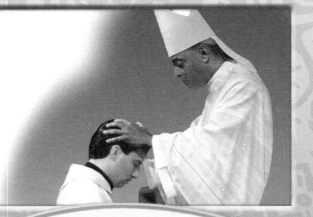

## A Family Prayer

Fill the hearts of your missionaries with
  the Holy Spirit,
so that, becoming all things to all people,
they may lead many to you, the Father of all,
to sing your praises in your holy Church.
Amen.

*from the Book of Blessings*

## Sacrament Trading Cards

Design a trading card for the sacrament of Holy Orders using the pattern below. Use your knowledge about this sacrament to write "sacrament facts" on the back of the card. Collect all seven!

Holy Orders

## Holy Orders

What is the importance
of the sacrament?

_____

What do we see?

_____

What do we hear?

_____

Who leads us in the celebration?

_____

Visit Sadlier's

**www.WeBelieveweb.com**

**Connect to the Catechism**
For adult background and reflection, see
paragraphs 551, 1562, 1554, and 1573.

# One, Holy, Catholic, and Apostolic

## WE GATHER

**Leader:** Blessed be the name of the Lord.

**All:** Now and for ever.

**Reader:** A reading from the Letter of Saint Paul to the Ephesians

". . . you are fellow citizens with the holy ones and members of the household of God, built upon the foundation of the apostles and prophets with Christ Jesus himself as the capstone." (Ephesians 2:19, 20).

The word of the Lord

**All:** Thanks be to God.

**Leader:** The Church is one

**All:** Make us one, Lord.

**Leader:** The Church is holy.

**All:** Share your holiness with us, Lord.

**Leader:** The Church is catholic.

**All:** Lord, help us to share your good news with people everywhere.

**Leader:** The Church is apostolic.

**All:** Lord, thank you for the faith of the apostles passed on to us through all generations.

Bless us always. Amen.

What are some qualities or characteristics that describe you? How can these qualities and characteristics help you to grow closer to your family and community?

## WE BELIEVE
### The Church is one and holy.

In the sacraments we profess our faith. In the celebration of the Eucharist, we do this when we pray the Nicene Creed. In the Nicene Creed we state that "we believe in one holy catholic and apostolic Church." These four characteristics are the **marks of the Church**. The Church is one, holy, catholic, and apostolic.

The first mark is that the Church is one. The Church is one because all its members believe in the one Lord, Jesus Christ. The Church is one because we all share the same Baptism, and together are the one Body of Christ.

The Church is one because we are guided and united by the one Holy Spirit. The Church is one because of the leadership of the pope and bishops, the sacraments we celebrate, and the laws of the Church that help us to live as members of the Church.

The second mark of the Church is that it is holy. God alone is good and holy. Christ shares God's holiness with us today through the Church, where we are first made holy in Baptism. Throughout our lives God and the Church call us to holiness. Our holiness comes from the gift of grace that we receive in the sacraments. It comes from the gifts of the Holy Spirit and from the practice of the virtues. Our holiness grows as we respond to God's love in our lives, and from living as Christ asks us to live.

We are not perfect. We do not always live according to Christ's example or God's law for us. Yet we always have the chance to begin again. The sacraments help us to turn to God and his love. When we follow Jesus' example to pray, respect all people, live fairly, and work for justice and peace, we grow in holiness.

✍ Write one thing you can do this week that will lead you to holiness.

_____

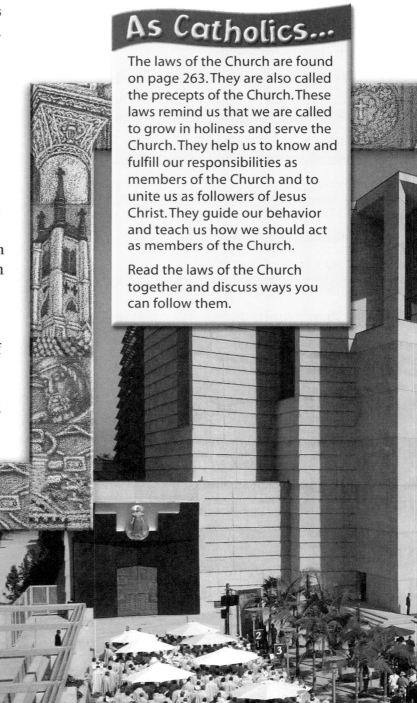

### As Catholics...

The laws of the Church are found on page 263. They are also called the precepts of the Church. These laws remind us that we are called to grow in holiness and serve the Church. They help us to know and fulfill our responsibilities as members of the Church and to unite us as followers of Jesus Christ. They guide our behavior and teach us how we should act as members of the Church.

Read the laws of the Church together and discuss ways you can follow them.

**Key Word**
marks of the Church
(p. 269)

## The Church is catholic and apostolic.

The third mark of the Church is that it is catholic. The word *catholic* means "universal." The Church is world wide, and it is open to all people everywhere. The Church has been universal since its very beginning.

Some of the apostles traveled to different parts of the world they knew. They preached the gospel message. The Church continued to grow, and today there are Catholics all across the world.

The Church is truly catholic, or universal. It is made up of people from all over the world. Often Catholics have different ways of living, dressing, and celebrating. These different customs are part of the Church's life. They add beauty and wonder to the Church. Yet with all of our differences, we are still one. We are united by our faith in Jesus and by our membership in the Church. We are the Body of Christ and the people of God.

We experience the Church as world-wide in our parishes, too. In this family of faith we are joined with Catholics who may be very different from us. Together we grow and celebrate our faith.

Because the Church is catholic, it is missionary, too. The Church welcomes all people as Jesus Christ did. We are to tell everyone about the saving love of Christ and the Church.

The fourth mark of the Church is that it is apostolic. The word apostolic comes from the word *apostle*. The Church is *apostolic* because it is built on the faith of the apostles. The faith we profess and practice is based on the Apostles' Creed, which we still pray today.

The Church is apostolic because the life and leadership of the Church is based on that of the apostles. Jesus chose the apostles to care for and lead the community of believers. Today the pope and bishops carry out the apostles' mission, and all baptized Catholics share in this work.

In groups discuss ways that as a Church we can welcome others and share our faith with them.

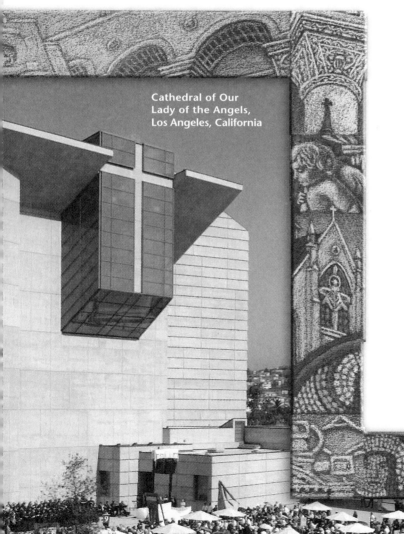

Cathedral of Our Lady of the Angels, Los Angeles, California

## The Church respects all people.

Christians are people of faith who believe in and follow Jesus Christ. Among Christians there are Catholics, Orthodox Christians, and Episcopalians. There are Lutherans, Methodists, Presbyterians, Baptists, and many others.

Yet despite the many differences among Christians, there are some very important things that we have in common. Christians are baptized and believe that Jesus is both divine and human. They believe that Jesus died and rose to save us from sin. Christians also share the belief that the Bible was inspired by the Holy Spirit.

The Catholic Church is the Church founded by Christ himself. However, we respect all Christians and see the goodness in other Christian communities. We are working with other Christian communities to bring about the unity of the Church. This work to promote the unity of all Christians is called **ecumenism**.

The differences among Christians are serious, but the Church is committed to the work of ecumenism. Each year in January the Church celebrates a week of prayer for Christian Unity. We pray that all Christians may be one. Prayer services and discussion groups are held. Together Christians try to grow in love and understanding.

Not everyone in the world believes in Jesus as Christians do, but that does not mean that they are not people of faith. We respect the right of others to practice and live their faith in different ways.

The Christian faith has a special connection to the Jewish faith. Jesus himself grew up as a Jew. So the Jewish

Ecumenical Prayer Service Toronto, Canada

people are our ancestors in faith. Many Christian beliefs and practices come from the Jewish faith. Today Jewish people everywhere continue to live their faith in the one true God.

Imagine that you are asking Jesus to give a talk on "Faith in Our World." What questions would you ask him?

_____

_____

_____

_____

_____

In groups discuss ways that Church we can welcome others and share our faith with them.

## The Church works for justice and peace.

Justice means respect for the rights of others. When we are just we give people the things that are rightfully theirs. Justice is based on the simple fact that all people have human dignity. All people have the value and worth that come from being created in God's image.

Jesus respected the dignity of others and protected their rights. He began his ministry by saying,

"The Spirit of the Lord is upon me,
  because he has anointed me
    to bring glad tidings to the poor.
He has sent me to proclaim liberty to captives
  and recovery of sight to the blind,
    to let the oppressed go free,
and to proclaim a year acceptable to the Lord"
  (Luke 4:18–19).

Jesus then did all these things. He worked to be sure that people had what they needed. He healed the sick and fed the hungry. He listened to people when they told him about their needs. Jesus stood up for those who were neglected or ignored by society.

The whole Church continues Jesus' work for justice. The pope and our bishops remind us to respect the rights of all people. We can work to change the things in society that allow unjust behaviors and conditions to exist. Together we can visit those who are sick or elderly. We can volunteer in soup kitchens or homeless shelters. We can help those from other countries to find homes and jobs and to learn the language. We can write to the leaders of our state and country asking them for laws that protect children and those in need.

Justice is sharing the resources that come from God's creation with those who do not have them. God asks us to protect and take care of creation—people, animals, and the resources of the world. He asks us to be stewards of creation. **Stewards of creation** are those who take care of everything that God has given them. God intended all people to use the goods of his creation.

Justice is using the resources we have in a responsible way. We cannot use so much food, water, and energy that there is not enough for others. The world is not only God's gift to us. It is also his gift for the generations of people to come. We must work together to protect our environment and the good of all God's creation.

## WE RESPOND

Discuss what you and your families can do during the summer months to show your respect for the rights of others at home, in your neighborhood, and around the world.

**Key Words**

ecumenism (p. 267)
stewards of creation (p. 269)

**Write the mark of the Church that best completes each sentence.**

1. The Church is _____ because God shares his holiness with us in the sacraments, and through the gifts of the Holy Spirit and the virtues.

2. The Church is _____ because all of its members believe in the one Lord, Jesus Christ, are led by the pope and bishops, and participate in the sacraments.

3. The Church is _____ because it is built on the faith of the apostles. The Church's life and leadership is based on that of the apostles.

4. The Church is _____ because it is universal and missionary. All people are welcomed to believe in Jesus Christ.

**Short Answers**

5. How are all Christians alike?

_____

6. What is a steward of creation?

_____

7. What is one way the Church works for justice?

_____

8. How does the Catholic Church practice ecumenism?

_____

**Write a sentence to answer the question.**

9–10. What are some things that unite Catholics?

_____

_____

ASSESSMENT

Make a commercial that advertises the four marks, or characteristics of the Church. Share your commercial with your class or family.

# We Respond in Faith

## Reflect & Pray

What do you think a year acceptable to the Lord is like? How can you continue Jesus' work of justice in the world?

Lord, I know that the Holy Spirit is upon me. I can work with others to help those who are poor, lead those who are lost, and bring peace to all people.

Help us to _____

_____

**marks of the Church** (p. 269)

**ecumenism** (p. 267)

**stewards of creation** (p. 269)

## Remember

- The Church is one and holy.
- The Church is catholic and apostolic.
- The Church respects all people.
- The Church works for justice and peace.

## OUR CATHOLIC LIFE

Tell your story here.

Place your photo here.

# SHARING FAITH
## with My Family

## Sharing What I Learned

Discuss the following with your family:

- the four marks of the Church
- ecumenism
- the call to work for justice and peace
- stewards of creation.

## Family Faith Checklist

Ask your family to complete the Family Faith Checklist. Share your experiences.

### Our Family

God gave human beings the responsibility to protect and care for God's gift of creation. How can you protect and take care of all that God has given to us?

☐ At home:

_____

☐ At school/work:

_____

☐ In the parish:

_____

☐ In the community:

_____

## A Family Prayer

Lord,
we pray for your people who
 believe in you.
May they enjoy the gift of your love,
share it with others,
and spread it everywhere.
We ask this in the name of Jesus
 the Lord.
Amen.

*from the Book of Blessings*

**Connect to the Catechism**
For adult background and reflection, see paragraphs 813, 823, 830, 831, 857, 855, and 2442.

## WE GATHER

✝ *Lord, we praise you with our hearts and voices.*

What are some exciting or joyful school or neighborhood events that you have been a part of? What make these times so happy and full of fun?

## WE BELIEVE

On Easter Sunday the celebration of the Mass is very festive. It is a joyous time with bells ringing and flowers filling the church. There are other signs of new life, too. During this Mass we listen to the gospel reading about Jesus' Resurrection.

📖 Mark 16:1–10

**Narrator**: "When the sabbath was over, Mary Magdalene, Mary, the mother of James, and Salome bought spices so that they might go and anoint him. Very early when the sun had risen, on the first day of the week, they came to the tomb. They were saying to one another,

**Women**: 'Who will roll back the stone for us from the entrance of the tomb?'"

**Narrator**: "When they looked up, they saw that the stone had been rolled back; it was very large. On entering the tomb they saw a young man sitting on the right side, clothed in a white robe, and they were utterly amazed." He said to them,

**Young man**: "Do not be amazed! You seek Jesus of Nazareth, the crucified. He has been raised; he is not here. Behold, the place where they laid him. But go and tell his disciples and Peter, 'He is going before you to Galilee; there you will see him, as he told you.'"(Mark 16:1–7)

**Narrator**: The women ran from the tomb not knowing what to think. Later that morning the risen Christ appeared to Mary Magdalene, and she went and told his other disciples. But they did not believe. Christ appeared to two other disciples, and still the others did not believe. But when the risen Christ appeared to the apostles, the apostles and disciples finally believed.

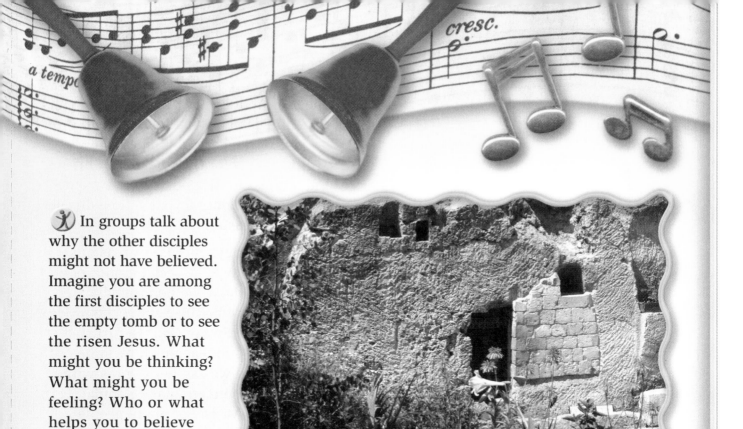

In groups talk about why the other disciples might not have believed. Imagine you are among the first disciples to see the empty tomb or to see the risen Jesus. What might you be thinking? What might you be feeling? Who or what helps you to believe in the risen Christ?

We celebrate Christ's Resurrection every Sunday. The risen Christ is among us, and there are signs of new life all around us. However, the Easter season is a special time to remember and rejoice over the new life we have in Christ.

The deep purple used during Lent is changed to a brilliant white and joyous gold. White and gold are the colors of light, life, and Resurrection. Gold is the most precious metal there is, and we often use it as a sign of God and heaven.

We sing, "Alleluia!" The word *alleluia* means "Praise God!" All during Lent, we did not sing or say alleluia in the liturgy.

Now during the Easter season, we say it and sing it over and over again! Jesus is risen, alleluia! He has conquered death forever, alleluia!

In the Easter season the first reading during the Mass is from the Acts of the Apostles, not the Old Testament. The Acts of the Apostles records the life of the apostles after Jesus' Ascension into heaven. It tells of the beginning of the Church. During this reading we hear of the wonderful way the first Christians spread the good news of Christ and formed a community of faith.

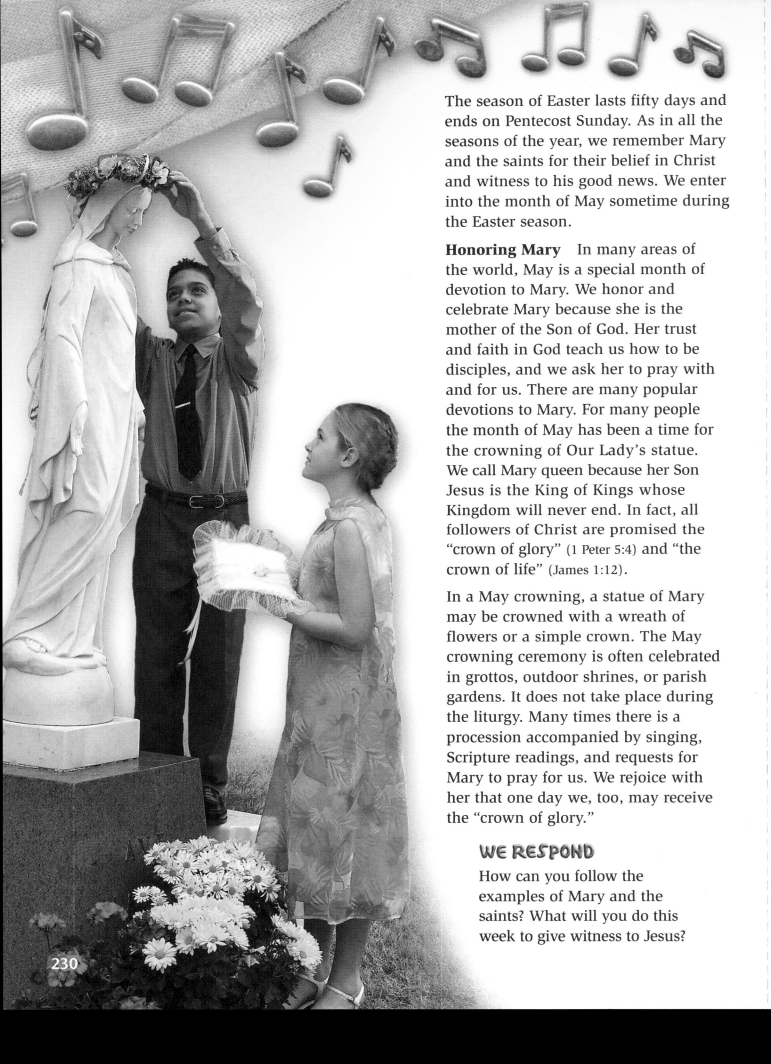

The season of Easter lasts fifty days and ends on Pentecost Sunday. As in all the seasons of the year, we remember Mary and the saints for their belief in Christ and witness to his good news. We enter into the month of May sometime during the Easter season.

**Honoring Mary** In many areas of the world, May is a special month of devotion to Mary. We honor and celebrate Mary because she is the mother of the Son of God. Her trust and faith in God teach us how to be disciples, and we ask her to pray with and for us. There are many popular devotions to Mary. For many people the month of May has been a time for the crowning of Our Lady's statue. We call Mary queen because her Son Jesus is the King of Kings whose Kingdom will never end. In fact, all followers of Christ are promised the "crown of glory" (1 Peter 5:4) and "the crown of life" (James 1:12).

In a May crowning, a statue of Mary may be crowned with a wreath of flowers or a simple crown. The May crowning ceremony is often celebrated in grottos, outdoor shrines, or parish gardens. It does not take place during the liturgy. Many times there is a procession accompanied by singing, Scripture readings, and requests for Mary to pray for us. We rejoice with her that one day we, too, may receive the "crown of glory."

## WE RESPOND

How can you follow the examples of Mary and the saints? What will you do this week to give witness to Jesus?

# ✝ We Respond in Prayer

**Leader:** We praise you, Lord, in this daughter of Israel,

**All:** Mary, your faithful one and our mother.

**Reader:** A reading from the holy Gospel according to Luke

"When Elizabeth heard Mary's greeting, the infant leaped in her womb, and Elizabeth, filled with the holy Spirit, cried out in a loud voice and said, 'Most blessed are you among women, and blessed is the fruit of your womb. And how does this happen to me, that the mother of my Lord should come to me?'" (Luke 1:41–43)

The Gospel of the Lord.

**All:** Praise to you Lord, Jesus Christ.

**Leader:** Pray for us, holy Mother of God.

**All:** That we may become worthy of the promises of Christ.

🎵 **Holy Mary**

Refrain

Holy Mary, we come to honor you.
We crown you this day,
the queen of our hearts.
Mary, you are filled with the Lord's own grace.
Salve Regina, Holy Mary.

We crown you this day
the mother of our Savior.
You show us the way
to Jesus Christ our Lord. (Refrain)

We crown you this day
the virgin blest and chosen.
The gift of your life
has shown us how to love. (Refrain)

# SHARING FAITH
## with My Family

## Sharing What I Learned

Discuss the following with your family:

- the meaning of the Easter season
- the signs of Easter in our church and liturgy
- May as a month to honor Mary.

## Around the Table

Ask your family to try one of the following Easter season activities. Draw a cross in front of the one chosen. Then write the date you plan to do this activity as a family.

_____ Give old toys and clothing away or have a yard sale for the benefit of a worthy cause.

_____

_____ Visit one person at a senior care center and bring this person flowers.

_____

_____ Discuss ways your family can care for the world around you.

_____

_____ Take a walk and find some signs of new life.

_____

## Family Prayer

The octave of Easter is the first eight days of Easter, including Easter Sunday. It is also called Easter Week. Each one of these octave days of Easter is celebrated as a solemnity, or as another day of Easter. In a very real way, it is a week of Sundays!

During Easter Week bless your home with the following prayer.

**Leader**: God, fill our hearts and home with peace.

Blessed be the name of the Lord.

**All**: Now and for ever.

**Leader**: Christ, risen from the dead, is our hope, joy, and comfort. May all who enter this home find Christ's light and love.

**All**: Amen.

Visit Sadlier's

**www.WeBelieveweb.com**

**Connect to the Catechism**
For adult background and reflection, see paragraph 655.

# SHARING FAITH
## in Class and at Home

## Small Steps

"This is terrible," Joanne said to herself. She had been staring at the image on the computer screen for a long time. It was a picture of a small child with a bloated stomach and large, sad eyes. The picture was part of an online news article about children suffering from hunger. Joanne printed the news article.

That night Joanne showed the article to her family. They talked about those who were poor and suffering. Joanne asked, "Can we do something to help?" "Maybe we can," Mother said.

Joanne's mother went to the kitchen drawer and pulled out an envelope. "This came in the mail from the parish," she explained. In the envelope was information about a Catholic relief agency. The relief agency provided help for people around the world who were poor and suffering. Joanne asked if the family could donate money. The members of Joanne's family discussed ways they could spend less money each month. They would donate whatever they saved to the relief agency. When Joanne went to bed that night, she felt better. Joanne and her family had not solved all of the problems of the world, but they had taken a small step.

"For in one Spirit we were all baptized into one body. . . . If [one] part suffers, all the parts suffer with it; if one part is honored, all the parts share its joy."

1 Corinthians 12:13; 26

## Think It Over

• What other small steps can Joanne and her family take to help those who are suffering?

• What small steps can you take?

## Because *We Believe*

The work, or *mission,* of the Church is to share the good news of Jesus Christ and to spread the Kingdom of God. As members of the Church, we all help the Kingdom to grow when we work for justice and peace in our homes, neighborhoods, and the world.

Jesus is our greatest example of service to others. During his life he cared for the poor and those who felt neglected. He listened to people and welcomed those who were considered outcasts. He prayed for those in need, visited the sick, and provided food for the hungry. Jesus spent his life serving others.

What we do for other people, we do for Jesus. The Corporal and Spiritual Works of Mercy are acts of love in which we care for the physical needs of people as well as the needs of their hearts, minds, and souls. When we perform the Works of Mercy, we give witness to Jesus.

How do we show we believe this?

When we serve others we show our love and care for them.

## With Your Class

Jesus often reached out to people who others rejected or ignored. Even his disciples did not want him to have anything to do with certain people.

Talk about groups of people who today are rejected in some way. How can we see them as Jesus does?

Complete this chart:

*"Education in the faith . . .* happens when family members help one another to grow in faith by the witness of a Christian life."
(*Catechism of the Catholic Church, 2226*)

| Group of people | | | |
|---|---|---|---|
| How they are rejected | | | |
| How Jesus would help them | | | |

## With Your Family

Read page 233 together. Talk about the mission of the Church and what it means to give witness to Jesus.

Look through a newspaper, magazine or news sites on the Internet together, and answer these questions.

- What stories of suffering catch your attention? Why?

- What can your family do to help?

- What stories give you hope?

- How can your family be a sign of Christian witness in the world?

## Pray Together

**Compassionate God, there is so much suffering in the world.**

**Help us to**

_____

_____

**We ask this in the name of Jesus. Amen.**

**NOW WHAT?**
Bring this page back to class ☐     Keep this page at home ☐

## Signs of Celebration?

Look carefully at the picture.

What signs of celebration do you see in the picture?

## Because *We Believe*

A sign stands for or tells us something. It can be something we see or something we do. An event or a person can also be a sign.

The Church has seven celebrations that are special signs of God's love and presence. We call these special signs *sacraments*. Jesus shares God's life with us in the sacraments.

Baptism, Confirmation, and Eucharist are the sacraments of Christian initiation. Through them we celebrate our membership in the Church.

Penance and Reconciliation and the Anointing of the Sick are sacraments of healing. They are two ways we celebrate Jesus' healing power.

Matrimony and Holy Orders are sacraments of service. Those who receive these sacraments are strengthened to serve God and the Church through a particular vocation.

All seven sacraments are signs of God's presence in our lives. But they are different from all other signs. Sacraments truly bring about what they represent. For example, in Baptism we not only celebrate being children of God, we actually become children of God. In Reconciliation we not only celebrate that God forgives, we actually receive God's forgiveness.

Through the sacraments we grow in trusting and believing in God who is present in every part of our lives. The gift of grace, God's own life within us, helps us to live our faith each day.

How do we show we believe this?

> "I am the vine, you are the branches."
>
> John 15:5

The sacraments are the most important celebrations of the Church.

"Sacraments confer the grace that they signify. . . . in them Christ himself is at work." *(Catechism of the Catholic Church, 1127)*

## With Your Class

Draw a picture of one of the following. Explain how it is used in the celebration of one or more of the seven sacraments. Share your responses with the rest of the class.

| | | |
|---|---|---|
| altar | wedding rings | Easter candle |
| crucifix | bread and wine | oil of the sick |
| stole | baptismal font | chrism |

## With Your Family

Read page 235 together. Talk about the meaning of signs and the importance of the seven sacraments in the Church.

Talk about a favorite holiday or family celebration. Here are some points for discussion:

- What does your favorite holiday or family celebration mean? Why do you celebrate it?

- How do you celebrate it? What customs do you use? Where did they come from?

- What do you use to celebrate it? What things—such as food, decorations, special objects, or colors—are part of the celebration? Why do you use them?

- What signs of God's presence do you see in your family celebrations?

## Pray Together

Thank you, Jesus,
for the signs of your love
in the life of our family.
Amen.

NOW WHAT?
Bring this page back to Class ☐     Keep this page at Home ☐

# SHARING FAITH
## in Class and at Home

### Sticking Together

Things changed in the Novak family the day Mom broke her leg. There had been a big snowstorm, and she slipped on the ice in the driveway. Dad called everyone together for a family meeting to decide how to help Mom through the time it would take for her leg to mend.

During this time, whenever the family sat down to dinner together, someone always remembered to pray that Mom's leg would heal quickly. One night the eldest brother, Todd, talked about how important it was to keep the sidewalk by the house clear and free from ice. "We don't want another accident," he said. Two of his sisters, Jessie and Laura, offered to help Todd with this chore.

Every member of the Novak family pitched in to help. Friends from the parish stopped by to bring dishes of food and just to visit with the family. Sister Anne also came to visit. She and Mom had been friends since they were both little girls. "My, my, Carol, you have one 'helping family' here!" Sister Anne laughed. "That's what families do," Mom replied happily. "They stick together."

### Think It Over

- How did the family stick together?
- How did the family show they cared about other people in their community?
- How did the parish help the family?

"Serve one another in love."
Galatians 5:13

### Because *We Believe*

The story of the Novaks points out certain characteristics of a family that "sticks together."

The Church has certain characteristics too. The Church is one, holy, catholic, and apostolic. These four characteristics are the *marks* of the church.

The Church is *one*. All of its members believe in the one Lord, Jesus Christ.

The Church is *holy*. God shared his holiness with all people by sending his Son to us. Throughout our lives God and the Church call us to holiness through prayer and sharing our love with others.

The word *catholic* means "universal." The Church is made up of people from all over the world. We are united by our love for Christ and our common call to holiness.

The Church is *apostolic*. Its faith and leadership are based on that of the apostles. Jesus chose the apostles to care for and lead the community of believers. Today, the pope and bishops carry out the apostles' mission, and all baptized Catholics share in this work.

How do we show we believe this?

The Church family works for justice and peace throughout the world.

## With Your Class

Think of your favorite songs. Make a classroom list of these songs. Now answer the following questions.

- What are these songs about?

- Do such songs help promote justice and peace in the world? Why or why not?

- What can your class do to promote or change the songs' messages?

Make up your own song or poem that promotes justice and peace.

## With Your Family

Read page 237 together. Talk about the marks of the Church and what it means to be a member of the Christian community.

Read the quote at the right from the *Cathechism of the Catholic Church.*

What marks your family as the "domestic church"? Answer these questions together.

- Think of a time when your family had to stick together. How did you stay united? What sort of strength do you find in being together?

- Think of a time when your family needed God's help and guidance. How do the members of your family pray?

- Think of a time when your family reached out to someone in need. What difference did it make to your family and to the person?

- To what parish does your family belong? How does the parish help your family grow as disciples? How does your family help the parish?

"The Christian home is the place where children receive the first proclamation of the faith. For this reason the family home is rightly called 'the domestic church,' a community of grace and prayer, a school of human virtues and of Christian charity."
*(Catechism of the Catholic Church, 1666)*

# Pray Together

In good times and in bad,
in sickness and in health,
we belong to each other
as we belong to you, God ever faithful.
By morning and by night
may your name be on our lips,
a blessing to all our days:
so may kindness and patience be ever among us,
a hunger for justice,
and songs of thankfulness in all we do.
We ask this through Christ our Lord.
Amen.

*(Catholic Household Blessings and Prayers)*

NOW WHAT? Bring this page back to Class ☐     Keep this page at Home ☐

**Write True or False for the following sentences. Then change the false sentences to make them true.**

1. _____ There are three marks of the Church. It is one, holy, and catholic.

_____

2. _____ Deacons are the successors of the apostles who are ordained to continue the apostle's mission of leadership and service in the Church.

_____

3. _____ The saints are models for living a life of virtue.

_____

4. _____ The love between a husband and wife is a sign of God's love for all his people and of Christ's love for his Church.

_____

5. _____ Laypeople are all the baptized members of the Church who share in the mission to bring the good news of Christ to the world.

_____

6. _____ In the sacrament of Matrimony the bride and groom are the celebrants. Jesus acts through them and through their promise to always love and be true to each other.

_____

7. _____ The laying on of hands and prayer of consecration are the main parts of the sacrament of Matrimony.

_____

8. _____ Love is the greatest of all virtues; it is the goal of our lives as Christians.

_____

**Write the letter that best defines each term.**

9. _____ catholic

10. _____ Holy Orders

11. _____ stewards of creation

12. _____ fidelity

13. _____ priesthood of the faithful

14. _____ religious

15. _____ virtue

16. _____ faith

**a.** women and men who belong to communities of service to God and the Church

**b.** Christ's priestly mission in which all those who are baptized share

**c.** the virtue that enables us to believe in God and all the Church teaches us, it helps us to believe all that God has told us about himself and all that he has done

**d.** the sacrament in which men are ordained to serve the Church as deacons, priests, and bishops

**e.** those who take care of everything God has given them

**f.** a good habit that helps us to act according to God's love for us

**g.** universal, worldwide, open to all people

**h.** faithfulness to a person and to duties, obligations, and promises; in marriage the loyalty and the willingness to be true to each other always

**i.** the promise to live simply as Jesus did

**Answer the questions.**

17–18. Friendships prepare us for future vocations. What would you tell a good friend who asks you to tell him or her about all the possible vocations?

19–20. As a fifth grader, how can you show that you have been called to live as a disciple of Jesus?

**Across**

2. To be _____ is to be blessed with holy oil.

4. The call to holiness that all Christians share is our _____ vocation.

5. _____, Confirmation, and the Eucharist are the sacraments of Christian initiation.

8. The mission of the Church is to share the good _____ of Christ and to spread the Kingdom of God.

9. A sacrament is an effective sign given to us by Jesus through which we share in God's _____.

10. The _____ is all those who believe in Jesus Christ, have been baptized in him, and follow his teachings.

**Down**

1. In Baptism the bishop, priest, or deacon who celebrates the sacrament for and with the community is the _____.

2. The bishops of the Church are the successors to the _____.

3. Some men are ordained as _____ to assist the bishops in works of service to the Church.

6. _____ is another word for Christ that means "anointed one."

7. Sanctifying _____ is the gift of sharing in God's life that we receive in the sacrament.

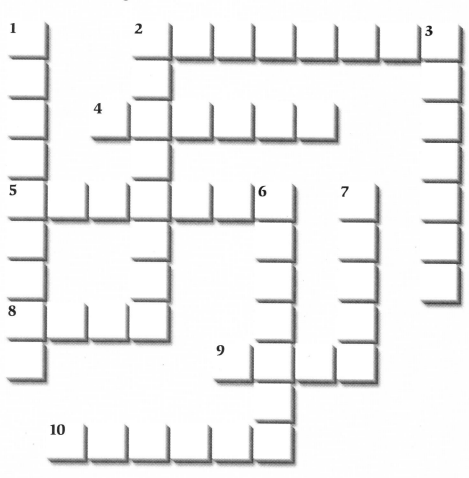

**Using the clues, unscramble the letters to make words. Then write the words in the spaces and the circles.**

1. In this sacrament we receive the gift of the Holy Spirit in a special way. TIMANOCFIRON

__ __ __ __ __ __ Ⓞ __ __ __ __ __

2. In the _____ Jesus becomes truly present under the appearances of bread and wine. SURATEICH

__ __ Ⓞ __ __ Ⓞ __ __ __

3. This feast celebrates the coming of the Holy Spirit. COTTENEPS

__ __ __ __ __ __ __ __ Ⓞ

4. At this part of the eucharistic prayer the bread and wine become Christ's Body and Blood. NOITANOCCRES

__ __ __ __ __ __ __ __ Ⓞ __ __ Ⓞ

5. Jesus celebrated this Jewish feast with the apostles on the night before he died. VERASOPS

__ __ __ Ⓞ __ __ __ __

6. At Mass, during the _____ of the Word, we listen and respond to God's word. GUILTRY

Ⓞ __ __ __ __ __ __

7. Among the gifts of the Holy Spirit are _____, understanding, courage, and reverence. DOMSIW

__ __ Ⓞ __ __ __

8. _____, kindness, humility, and self-control are some of the fruits of the Holy Spirit. ATENPICE

__ __ __ __ Ⓞ __ __ __

9. The Eucharist is a memorial, a meal, and a _____. CRAISICEF

__ Ⓞ __ __ __ __ __ __

10. In _____ we open our minds and heart to God. YERRAP

__ __ Ⓞ __ __ __

**Write the circled letters here.**

Ⓞ Ⓞ Ⓞ Ⓞ Ⓞ Ⓞ Ⓞ Ⓞ Ⓞ Ⓞ

**Then unscramble these letters to find the word that completes this sentence.**

__ __ __ __ __ __ __ __ __ __ __ __ are blessings, actions, and objects that help us respond to God's grace.

ALTERNATIVE ASSESSMENT

**Use the spaces below to design three prayer cards.**

**1.** The first will be a card to give to someone who is about to celebrate Reconciliation.

**2.** The second will be a card to give to someone who is caring for someone who is elderly or sick.

**3.** The third will be a card dedicated to Mary, honoring her under one of her titles or on one of her feast days.

**You may use pictures, symbols, prayers, or any combination of words and images that you think best conveys the message of each card.**

(front of card 1)

(front of card 2)

(front of card 3)

(back of card 1)

(back of card 2)

(back of card 3)

**In the spaces below write four brief prayers asking God to bless those called to love and serve him in different vocations.**

**In each prayer mention one or more specific ways in which someone in that particular vocation is called to love and serve God and the Church.**

- Ask God to bless someone called to serve him as a single person living in the world.

_____

_____

_____

_____

- Ask God to bless someone called to serve him in the sacrament of Matrimony.

_____

_____

_____

_____

- Ask God to bless someone called to serve him as a member of a religious community.

_____

_____

_____

_____

- Ask God to bless someone called to serve him in the sacrament of Holy Orders.

_____

_____

_____

_____

# Prayers and Practices

## Table of Contents

# Sign of the Cross

In the name of the Father,
and of the Son,
and of the Holy Spirit. Amen.

# Glory to the Father

Glory to the Father, and to the Son,
    and to the Holy Spirit:
as it was in the beginning,
    is now, and will be for ever. Amen.

# Our Father

Our Father, who art in heaven,
hallowed be thy name;
thy kingdom come;
thy will be done on earth
    as it is in heaven.
Give us this day our daily bread;
and forgive us our trespasses
as we forgive those
    who trespass against us;
and lead us not into temptation,
but deliver us from evil. Amen.

# Gloria

Glory to God in the highest,
    and peace to his people on earth.

Lord God, heavenly King,
almighty God and Father,
    we worship you, we give you thanks,
    we praise you for your glory.

Lord Jesus Christ, only Son of the Father,
Lord God, Lamb of God,
you take away the sin of the world:
    have mercy on us;
you are seated at the right hand of the Father:
    receive our prayer.
For you alone are the Holy One,
you alone are the Lord,
you alone are the Most High,
    Jesus Christ,
    with the Holy Spirit,
    in the glory of God the Father. Amen.

# Morning Offering

O Jesus, I offer you all my prayers, works,
and sufferings of this day for all the
intentions of your most Sacred Heart. Amen.

# Evening Prayer

Dear God, before I sleep
I want to thank you for this day,
so full of your kindness and your joy.
I close my eyes to rest
safe in your loving care.

## Nicene Creed

We believe in one God,
  the Father, the Almighty,
  maker of heaven and earth,
  of all that is seen and unseen.

We believe in one Lord, Jesus Christ,
  the only Son of God,
  eternally begotten of the Father,
  God from God, Light from Light,
  true God from true God,
  begotten, not made, one in Being
    with the Father.
  Through him all things were made.
  For us men and for our salvation
    he came down from heaven:
  by the power of the Holy Spirit
    he was born of the Virgin Mary,
      and became man.

For our sake he was crucified
    under Pontius Pilate;
  he suffered, died, and was buried.
  On the third day he rose again
    in fulfillment of the Scriptures;
  he ascended into heaven
    and is seated at the right hand
      of the Father.
  He will come again in glory to judge
    the living and the dead,
    and his kingdom will have no end.

We believe in the Holy Spirit, the Lord,
    the giver of life,
  who proceeds from the Father and the Son.
  With the Father and the Son he is
    worshiped and glorified.
  He has spoken through the Prophets.
We believe in one holy catholic
    and apostolic Church.
  We acknowledge one baptism for the
    forgiveness of sins.
  We look for the resurrection of the dead,
    and the life of the world to come.
  Amen.

## Apostles' Creed

I believe in God, the Father almighty,
  creator of heaven and earth.
I believe in Jesus Christ,
    his only Son, our Lord.
  He was conceived by the power
    of the Holy Spirit
    and born of the Virgin Mary.
He suffered under Pontius Pilate,
  was crucified, died, and was buried.
He descended to the dead.
On the third day he rose again.
He ascended into heaven,
    and is seated at the right hand
      of the Father.
He will come again to judge
  the living and the dead.

I believe in the Holy Spirit,
  the holy catholic Church,
  the communion of saints,
  the forgiveness of sins,
  the resurrection of the body,
  and the life everlasting. Amen.

# Hail Mary

Hail Mary, full of grace,
the Lord is with you!
Blessed are you among women,
and blessed is the fruit
   of your womb, Jesus.
Holy Mary, Mother of God,
pray for us sinners,
now and at the hour of our death.
Amen.

# Memorare

Remember, most loving Virgin Mary,
never was it heard
that anyone who turned to you for help
was left unaided.

Inspired by this confidence,
though burdened by my sins,
I run to your protection
for you are my mother.
Mother of the Word of God,
do not despise my world of pleading
but be merciful and hear my prayer.
Amen.

# The Canticle of Mary, the Magnificat

"My soul proclaims the greatness of the Lord;
   my spirit rejoices in God my savior.
For he has looked upon his handmaid's lowliness;
   behold, from now on will all ages call me
      blessed.
The Mighty One has done great things for me,
   and holy is his name.
His mercy is from age to age
   to those who fear him.
He has shown might with his arm,
   dispersed the arrogant of mind and heart.
He has thrown down the rulers from their thrones
   but lifted up the lowly.
The hungry he has filled with good things;
   the rich he has sent away empty.
He has helped Israel his servant,
   remembering his mercy,
according to his promise to our fathers,
   to Abraham and to his descendants forever."

(Luke 1:46–55)

## ♫ The Canticle of Mary

My soul proclaims the greatness
of the Lord.
My spirit sings to God, my
saving God,
Who on this day above all
others favored me
And raised me up, a light for
all to see.
Through me great deeds will
God make manifest,
And all the earth will come
to call me blest.
Unbounded love and mercy
sure will I proclaim
For all who know and praise
God's holy name.
God's mighty arm, protector
of the just,
Will guard the weak and raise
them from the dust.
But mighty kings will swiftly
fall from thrones corrupt.
The strong brought low,
the lowly lifted up.

## The Angelus

The angel spoke God's message to Mary,
and she conceived of the Holy Spirit.
Hail, Mary. . . .

"I am the lowly servant of the Lord:
let it be done to me according to your word."
Hail, Mary. . . .

And the Word became flesh
and lived among us.
Hail, Mary. . . .

Pray for us, holy Mother of God,
that we may become worthy of the promises
of Christ.

Let us pray.
Lord,
fill our hearts with your grace:
once, through the message of an angel
you revealed to us the incarnation of your
Son;
now, through his suffering and death
lead us to the glory of his resurrection.

We ask this through Christ our Lord.
Amen.

# Hail, Holy Queen

Hail, holy Queen, mother of mercy,
hail, our life, our sweetness, and our hope.
To you we cry, the children of Eve;
to you we send up our sighs,
mourning and weeping in this land of exile.
Turn, then, most gracious advocate,
your eyes of mercy toward us;
lead us home at last
and show us the blessed fruit of your womb,
    Jesus:
O clement, O loving, O sweet Virgin Mary.

# Marian Feasts

Here are some of the feast days of Mary:

*January 1*—Solemnity of Mary, Mother of God

*February 11*—Our Lady of Lourdes

*March 25*—The Annunciation

*May 25*—The Visitation

*July 16*—Our Lady of Mt. Carmel

*August 15*—The Assumption

*August 22*—The Queenship of Mary

*September 8*—The Birth of Mary

*September 15*—Our Lady of Sorrows

*December 8*—Immaculate Conception of Mary

*December 12*—Our Lady of Guadalupe

# Mysteries of the Rosary

## Joyful Mysteries

The Annunciation
The Visitation
The Birth of Jesus
The Presentation of Jesus in the
    Temple
The Finding of the Child Jesus in
    the Temple

## Sorrowful Mysteries

The Agony in the Garden
The Scourging at the Pillar
The Crowning with Thorns
The Carrying of the Cross
The Crucifixion and Death of Jesus

## Glorious Mysteries

The Resurrection
The Ascension
The Descent of the Holy Spirit
    upon the Apostles
The Assumption of Mary
    into Heaven
The Coronation of Mary as
    Queen of Heaven

## The Mysteries of Light

Jesus' Baptism in the Jordan
The Miracle at the Wedding
    at Cana
Jesus Announces the Kingdom
    of God
The Transfiguration
The Institution of the Eucharist

# The Rosary

Praying the rosary creates a peaceful rhythm of prayer during which we can reflect on the mysteries of the rosary, special times in the lives of Jesus and Mary. Follow the numbered steps to pray the rosary.

**5** Pray a Glory to the Father after each set of small beads.

**End**

**6** Pray the Hail, Holy Queen to end the rosary.

**4** Pray a Hail Mary at every small bead.

**3** Pray an Our Father at every large bead.

**2** Then pray the Apostles' Creed.

**Start**

**1** Start with the Sign of the Cross.

## Act of Contrition

My God,
I am sorry for my sins with all my heart.
In choosing to do wrong
and failing to do good,
I have sinned against you
whom I should love above all things.
I firmly intend, with your help,
to do penance,
to sin no more,
and to avoid whatever leads me to sin.
Our Savior Jesus Christ
suffered and died for us.
In his name, my God, have mercy.

## Confiteor

During Mass the whole assembly confesses
that we have sinned. We often pray:

I confess to almighty God,
and to you, my brothers and sisters,
that I have sinned through my own fault
in my thoughts and in my words,
in what I have done,
and in what I have failed to do;
and I ask blessed Mary, ever virgin,
all the angels and saints,
and you, my brothers and sisters,
to pray for me to the Lord our God.

## Prayer of Saint Francis

Lord, make me an instrument of your peace:
where there is hatred, let me sow love;
where there is injury, pardon;
where there is doubt, faith;
where there is despair, hope;
where there is darkness, light;
where there is sadness, joy.

O divine Master, grant that I may not so
   much seek
to be consoled as to console,
to be understood as to understand,
to be loved as to love.
For it is in giving that we receive,
it is in pardoning that we are pardoned,
it is in dying that we are born to eternal life.
Amen.

                                      Saint Francis of Assisi

# The Ten Commandments

1. I am the LORD your God: you shall not have strange gods before me.
2. You shall not take the name of the LORD your God in vain.
3. Remember to keep the holy the LORD'S day.
4. Honor your father and your mother.
5. You shall not kill.
6. You shall not commit adultery.
7. You shall not steal.
8. You shall not bear false witness against your neighbor.
9. You shall not covet your neighbor's wife.
10. You shall not covet your neighbor's goods.

# Examination of Conscience

Quietly sit and examine your conscience. Use these questions to help you reflect on your relationship with God and others.

Do I make anyone or anything more important to me than God? Have I read from the Bible and prayed?

Do I respect God's name and the name of Jesus?

Do I participate in Mass and keep Sunday holy by what I say and do?

Do I show obedience to God by my obedience to parents, guardians, and teachers?

Have I hurt others by my words and actions? Have I helped those in need?

Do I respect myself? Do I take good care of my body and show respect to others? Do I respect the dignity of everyone I meet?

Have I been selfish or taken the belongings of others without their permission? Have I shared my belongings?

Have I been honest? Have I lied or cheated?

Do I speak, act, and dress in ways that show respect for myself and others?

Have I been happy for others when they have the things they want or need?

# Penance and Reconciliation

## Rite for Reconciliation of Several Penitents

### Introductory Rites

We gather as an assembly and sing an opening hymn. The priest greets us and prays an opening prayer.

### Celebration of the Word of God

The assembly listens to the proclamation of the word of God. This is followed by a homily. Through his word God calls his people to repentance and leads them back to him. The readings help us to reflect on the reconciliation that Jesus' life and death have made possible. They remind us of God's mercy and prepare us to judge the goodness of our thoughts and actions. Then we examine our conscience.

### Rite of Reconciliation

The assembly prays together an act of contrition to show their sorrow for sinning. We may say another prayer or sing a song, and then pray the Our Father. We ask God to forgive us as we forgive others.

I meet individually with the priest and confess my sins. The priest talks to me about loving God and others. He gives me a penance.

The priest extends his hand and gives me absolution.

After everyone has met with the priest, we join together to conclude the celebration. The assembly praises God for his mercy. The priest offers a concluding prayer of thanksgiving.

### Concluding Rite

The priest blesses us, and dismisses the assembly saying "The Lord has freed you from your sins. Go in peace." We respond "Thanks be to God."

# Rite for Reconciliation of Individual Penitents

I examine my conscience before meeting with the priest.

### Welcoming

The priest greets me and I make the sign of the cross. The priest asks me to trust in God's mercy.

### Reading of the Word of God

The priest or I may read something from the Bible.

### Confession and Penance

I confess my sins. The priest talks to me about loving God and others. He gives me a penance.

### Prayer of Penitent and Absolution

I pray an act of contrition. The priest extends his hand and gives me absolution.

### Proclamation of Praise and Dismissal

The priest says, "Give thanks to the Lord, for he is good." I respond, "His mercy endures for ever." The priest sends me out saying "The Lord has freed you from your sins. Go in peace."

# The Celebration of the Eucharist
# The Mass

## Introductory Rites

**Procession/Opening Song**  Altar servers, readers, the deacon, and the priest celebrant process forward to the altar. The assembly sings as this takes place. The priest and deacon kiss the altar and bow out of reverence.

**Greeting**  The priest and assembly make the sign of the cross, and the priest reminds us that we are in the presence of Jesus.

**Penitential Rite**  Gathered in God's presence the assembly sees its sinfulness and proclaims the mystery of God's love. We ask for God's mercy in our lives.

**Gloria**  On some Sundays we sing or say this ancient hymn. (p. 246)

**Opening Prayer**  This prayer expresses the theme of the celebration and the needs and hopes of the assembly.

## Liturgy of the Word

**First Reading**  This reading is usually from the Old Testament. We hear of God's love and mercy for his people before the time of Christ. We hear stories of hope and courage, wonder and might. We learn of God's covenant with his people and of the ways they lived his law.

**Responsorial Psalm**  After reflecting in silence as God's word enters our hearts, we thank God for the word just heard.

**Second Reading**  This reading is usually from the New Testament letters, the Acts of the Apostles, or the Book of Revelation. We hear about the first disciples, the teachings of the apostles, and the beginning of the Church.

**Gospel Acclamation**  We stand to sing the Alleluia or other words of praise. This shows we are ready to hear the good news of Jesus Christ.

**Gospel Reading**  This reading is always from the Gospel of Matthew, Mark, Luke, or John. Proclaimed by the deacon or priest, this reading is about the mission and ministry of Jesus. Jesus' words and actions speak to us today and help us know how to live as his disciples.

**Homily**  The priest or deacon talks to us about the readings. His words help us understand what God's word means to us today. We learn what it means to believe and be members of the Church. We grow closer to God and one another.

**Profession of Faith**  The whole assembly prays together the Nicene Creed (p. 247) or the Apostles' Creed (p. 247). We are stating aloud what we believe as members of the Church.

**General Intercessions**  We pray for the needs of all God's people. This is also called the prayer of the faithful.

# Liturgy of the Eucharist

**Preparation of the Gifts**   During the preparation of the gifts the altar is prepared by the deacon and the altar servers. We offer gifts. These gifts include the bread and wine and the collection for the Church and for those in need. As members of the assembly carry the bread and wine in a procession to the altar, we sing. The bread and wine are placed on the altar, and the priest asks God to bless and accept our gifts. We respond "Blessed be God for ever."

**Eucharistic Prayer**   The eucharistic prayer is truly the most important prayer of the Church. It is our greatest prayer of praise and thanksgiving. It joins us to Christ and to one another. This prayer consists of

- offering God thanksgiving and praise. We lift up our hearts to the Lord. We praise and thank God for the good work of salvation by singing "Holy, Holy, Holy."

- calling on the Holy Spirit to bless the gifts of bread and wine will be changed into the Body and Blood of Christ. We pray that we, too, will be changed into the Body of Christ on earth.

- recalling Jesus' words and actions at the Last Supper. By the power of the Holy Spirit and through the words and actions of the priest, the bread and wine become the Body and Blood of Christ. This part of the prayer is called the consecration.

- recalling Jesus' passion, death, Resurrection, and Ascension.

- remembering that the Eucharist is offered by the Church in heaven and on earth. We pray for the needs of the Church. We pray that all who receive the Body and Blood of Christ will be united.

- praising God and praying a great "Amen" in love of God: Father, Son, and Holy Spirit. We unite ourselves to this great prayer of thanksgiving which is prayed by the priest in our name and in the name of Christ.

**Communion rite**   The Communion rite is the third part of the Liturgy of the Eucharist. We pray aloud or sing the Lord's Prayer. We pray that Christ's peace be with us always. We offer one another a sign of peace to show that we are united in Christ.

We say aloud or sing the Lamb of God, asking Jesus for his mercy, forgiveness, and peace. The priest breaks apart the Host, and we are invited to share in the Eucharist. We are shown the Host and hear "The body of Christ." We are shown the cup and hear "The blood of Christ." Each person responds "Amen" and receives Holy Communion.

While people are receiving Holy Communion, we sing as one. We are working for Christian Unity. However, people who are not Catholic may not receive Holy Communion at Mass, except in special cases. After this we silently reflect on the gift of Jesus and God's presence with us. The priest then prays that the gift of Jesus will help us live as Jesus' disciples.

# Concluding Rite

**Greeting**   The priest offers the final prayer. His words serve as a farewell promise that Jesus will be with us all.

**Blessing**   The priest blesses us in the name of the Father, Son, and Holy Spirit. We make the sign of the cross as he blesses us.

**Dismissal**   The deacon or priest sends us out to love and serve God and one another.

**Closing Song**   The priest and deacon kiss the altar. They, along with others serving at the Mass, bow to the altar, and process out as we sing.

# The Beatitudes

 Matthew 5:3–10 ✦ ✦ ✦ ✦ ✦ ✦ ✦ ✦ ✦ ✦

| The Beatitudes | Living the Beatitudes |
|---|---|
| "Blessed are the poor in spirit, for theirs is the kingdom of heaven. | We are "poor in spirit" when we depend on God and make God more important than anyone or anything else in our lives. |
| Blessed are they who mourn, for they will be comforted. | We "mourn" when we are sad because of the selfish ways people treat one another. |
| Blessed are the meek, for they will inherit the land. | We are "meek" when we are patient, kind, and respectful to all people, even those who do not respect us. |
| Blessed are they who hunger and thirst for righteousness, for they will be satisfied. | We "hunger and thirst for righteousness" when we search for justice and treat everyone fairly. |
| Blessed are the merciful, for they will be shown mercy. | We are "merciful" when we forgive others and do not take revenge on those who hurt us. |
| Blessed are the clean of heart, for they will see God. | We are "clean of heart" when we are faithful to God's teachings and try to see God in all people and in all situations. |
| Blessed are the peacemakers, for they will be called children of God. | We are "peacemakers" when we treat others with love and respect and when we help others to stop fighting and make peace. |
| Blessed are they who are persecuted for the sake of righteousness, for theirs is the kingdom of heaven." | We are "persecuted for the sake of righteousness" when others disrespect us for living as disciples of Jesus and following his example. |

# Prayer for Vocation

Dear God,

You have a great and loving plan for
our world and for me.
I wish to share in that plan fully,
faithfully, and joyfully.
Help me to understand what it is you
wish me to do with my life.

How might you be calling me to live?
Help me to be attentive to the signs
that you give me about preparing
for the future.

And once I have heard and understood
your call, give me the strength and the
grace to follow it with generosity
and love.

Amen.

## Act of Faith

O God, we believe in all that Jesus has
taught us about you.
We place all our trust in you
because of your great love for us.

## Act of Hope

O God, we never give up on your love.
We have hope and will work for your
kingdom to come and for a life that lasts
forever with you in heaven.

## Act of Love

O God, we love you above all things.
Help us to love ourselves and one another
as Jesus taught us to do.

# The Orders

Bishop

The bishops are the chief teachers of the Church. They are called to make sure that the faithful receive the teachings of Jesus and the beliefs of our faith. The bishops help us to understand and live out these teachings.

The bishops are the chief leaders and pastors of the Church. They have authority in their dioceses, and together with the pope they are the pastors of the whole Church. The bishops lead their people and oversee the work of their dioceses. In the United States, the bishops meet twice a year to make decisions that effect the Church in our country.

The bishops are the chief priests in their dioceses. They make sure that the Christian faithful in the diocese have the opportunity to participate in the celebration of the sacraments, most especially the Eucharist. By providing for the liturgy of the diocese, the bishop helps all the faithful to live Christian lives and to grow in holiness.

There are two kinds of priests: diocesan priests and religious priests. Religious priests are those who belong to religious communities.

Diocesan priests are ordained to serve in a diocese. They usually serve in parishes. But diocesan priests may also serve in hospitals, schools, the military, prisons, or other institutions.

Priest

Religious priests serve wherever their communities send them. They usually take the vows of chastity, poverty, and obedience. They might be pastors of parishes, or they might be missionaries, teachers, doctors, writers, or work in any field where their service is needed. They might spend their time in prayer and work within their community. All priests are called to make prayer, most especially the Mass, the heart of their ministry. This strengthens them to help the Church grow in faith through prayer and worship.

Deacon

Deacons are called to serve the community in worship. They are called to the ministry of service in the diocese.

# Holy Orders

In the sacrament of Holy Orders, the newly ordained are presented with signs of their service and ministry in the Church.

## Signs of Service

| | |
|---|---|
| **Deacon** | He is given a stole as a sign of his ministry as deacon. It is worn across the left shoulder and fastened at the right.<br><br>He is given the Book of the Gospels as a sign of the deacon's role in preaching the good news. |
| **Priest** | His stole is rearranged as a sign of his ministry as priest. It is now worn around the neck and down over his chest.<br><br>The palms of his hands are anointed so that he can serve to make the people of God holy through the sacraments.<br><br>He is given the chalice and paten as a sign that he may now celebrate the Eucharist to offer the sacrifice of the Lord. |
| **Bishop** | His head is anointed, and he is blessed to perform his duties as bishop.<br><br>He is given a miter, a pointed hat that is a sign of his office as bishop.<br><br>He is given a ring as a sign of his faithfulness to Christ and the Church.<br><br>He is given a pastoral staff as a sign of his role as shepherd. He will care for and watch over the Church, the flock of Christ. |

# Holy Days of Obligation

Here are the holy days of obligation that the Church in the United States celebrates:

**Solemnity of Mary, Mother of God**
(January 1)

**Ascension**
(when celebrated on Thursday during the Easter season)

**Assumption of Mary**
(August 15)

**All Saints' Day**
(November 1)

**Immaculate Conception**
(December 8)

**Christmas**
(December 25)

# Forms of Prayer

These are the forms of prayer. An example of each form is given.

### Blessing

"The grace of the Lord Jesus Christ and the love of God and the fellowship of the holy Spirit be with all of you." (2 Corinthians 13:13)

### Petition

"O God, be merciful to me a sinner." (Luke 18:13)

### Intercession

"And this is my prayer: that your love may increase ever more and more in knowledge." (Philippians 1:9)

### Thanksgiving

"Father, I thank you for hearing me." (John 11:41)

### Praise

"I shall praise the LORD all my life, sing praise to my God while I live." (Psalm 146:2)

# The Precepts of the Church

The pope and bishops have established some laws to help us know and fulfill our responsibilities as members of the Church. These laws are called the precepts of the Church.

It is helpful to think of the precepts as rules or principles intended as a guide for behavior. They teach us how we should act as members of the Church. These precepts also make sure that the Church has what it needs to serve its members and to grow.

1. Celebrate Christ's Resurrection every Sunday (or Saturday evening) and on holy days of obligation by taking part in Mass and avoiding unnecessary work.

2. Lead a sacramental life. Receive Holy Communion frequently and the sacrament of Reconciliation regularly. We must receive Holy Communion at least once a year between the first Sunday of Lent and Trinity Sunday. We must celebrate Reconciliation once a year if we have committed mortal, or serious, sin.

3. Study Catholic teaching throughout life, especially in preparing for the sacraments, and continue to grow in faith.

4. Observe the marriage laws of the Church and give religious instruction and formation to one's children.

5. Contribute to the support of the Church: one's own parish community, priests, the whole Church, and the pope.

6. Do penance, including not eating meat and fasting from food on certain days.

7. Join in the missionary work of the Church.

# The Corporal and Spiritual Works of Mercy

## Corporal Works of Mercy

Feed the hungry.

Give drink to the thirsty.

Clothe the naked.

Visit the imprisoned.

Shelter the homeless.

Visit the sick.

Bury the dead.

## Spiritual Works of Mercy

Admonish the sinner.
   (Give correction to those who need it.)

Instruct the ignorant.
   (Share our knowledge with others.)

Counsel the doubtful.
   (Give advice to those who need it.)

Comfort the sorrowful.
   (Comfort those who suffer.)

Bear wrongs patiently.
   (Be patient with others.)

Forgive all injuries.
   (Forgive those who hurt us.)

Pray for the living and the dead.

Note:
The Virtues are found on pages 188-190.
The Prayer to the Holy Spirit is found on page 83.
The gifts and fruits of the Holy Spirit are found on pages 86-87.

# Catholic Social Teaching

There are seven themes of Catholic social teaching.

### Life and Dignity of the Human Person
Human life is sacred because it is a gift from God. Because we are all God's children, we all share the same human dignity. As Christians we respect all people, even those we do not know.

### Call to Family, Community, and Participation
We are all social. We need to be with others to grow. The family is the basic community. In the family we grow and learn values. As Christians we are involved in our family life and community.

### Rights and Responsibilities of the Human Person
Every person has a fundamental right to life. This includes the things we need to have a decent life: faith and family, work and education, health care and housing. We also have a responsibility to others and to society. We work to make sure the rights of all people are being protected.

### Option for the Poor and Vulnerable
We have a special obligation to help those who are poor and in need. This includes those who cannot protect themselves because of their age or their health.

### Dignity of Work and the Rights of Workers
Our work is a sign of our participation in God's work. People have the right to decent work, just wages, safe working conditions, and to participate in decisions about work.

### Solidarity of the Human Family
Solidarity is a feeling of unity. It binds members of a group together. Each of us is a member of the one human family. The human family includes people of all racial and cultural backgrounds. We all suffer when one part of the human family suffers whether they live near or far away.

### Care for God's Creation
God created us to be stewards, or caretakers, of his creation. We must care for and respect the environment. We have to protect it for future generations. When we care for creation, we show respect for God the Creator.

# Stations of the Cross

Stations of the cross focus our attention on the passion and death of Jesus.

Jesus is condemned to die.

Jesus takes up his cross.

Jesus falls the first time.

Jesus meets his mother.

Simon helps Jesus carry his cross.

Veronica wipes the face of Jesus.

Jesus falls the second time.

Jesus meets the women of Jerusalem.

Jesus falls the third time.

Jesus is stripped of his garments.

Jesus is nailed to the cross.

Jesus dies on the cross.

Jesus is taken down from the cross.

Jesus is laid in the tomb.

# Glossary

**act of contrition**  (p. 142)
a prayer that allows us to express our sorrow and promise to try not to sin again

**Annunciation**  (p. 165)
the name given to the angel's visit to Mary at which the announcement was made that she would be the mother of the Son of God

**Anointing of the Sick**  (p. 150)
the sacrament by which God's grace and comfort are given to those who are seriously ill or suffering because of their old age

**apostles**  (p. 22)
men chosen by Jesus to share in his mission in a special way

**Assumption**  (p. 165)
the belief that when Mary's work on earth was done, God brought her body and soul to live forever with the risen Christ

**Baptism**  (p. 44)
the sacrament in which we are freed from sin, become children of God, and are welcomed into the Church

**bishops**  (p. 214)
the successors of the apostles who are ordained to continue the apostles' mission of leadership and service in the Church

**Blessed Trinity**  (p. 20)
the three Persons in one God: God the Father, God the Son, and God the Holy Spirit

**catechumenate**  (p. 52)
a period of formation for Christian initiation that includes prayer and liturgy, religious instruction, and service to others

**chrism**  (p. 55)
perfumed oil blessed by the bishop

**Christian initiation**  (p. 36)
the process of becoming a member of the Church through the sacraments of Baptism, Confirmation, and Eucharist

**Church**  (p. 23)
all those who believe in Jesus Christ, have been baptized in him, and follow his teachings

**common vocation**  (p. 37)
the call to holiness and evangelization that all Christians share

**Concluding Rite**  (p. 103)
the last part of the Mass in which we are blessed and sent forth to be Christ's servants in the world and to love others as he has loved us

**Confirmation**  (p. 78)
the sacrament in which we receive the Gift of the Holy Spirit in a special way

**conscience**  (p. 140)
our ability to know the difference between good and evil, right and wrong

**consecration**  (p. 102)
the part of the eucharistic prayer when, by the power of the Holy Spirit and through the words and actions of the priest, the bread and wine become the Body and Blood of Christ

**conversion**  (p. 132)
a turning to God with all one's heart

**Corporal Works of Mercy**  (p. 31)
acts of love that help us care for the physical and material needs of others

**deacons**  (p. 214)
men who are not priests but are ordained to the work of service for the Church

**ecumenism**  (p. 222)
the work to promote unity among all Christians

**eternal life**  (p. 47)
living in happiness with God forever

**Eucharist**  (p. 92)
the sacrament of the Body and Blood of Christ, Jesus is truly present under the appearances of bread and wine

**evangelization** (p. 28)
proclaiming the good news of Christ by what we say and do

**faith** (p. 188)
the virtue that enables us to believe in God and all that the Church teaches us; it helps us to believe all that God has told us about himself and all that he has done

**fidelity** (p. 206)
faithfulness to a person and to duties, obligations, and promises; in marriage, the loyalty and the willingness to be true to each other always

**gifts of the Holy Spirit** (p. 86)
wisdom, understanding, right judgment, courage, knowledge, reverence, and wonder and awe

**holiness** (p. 37)
sharing in God's goodness and responding to his love by the way we live; our holiness comes through grace

**holy day of obligation** (p. 109)
a day we are obliged to participate in the Mass to celebrate a special event in the life of Jesus, Mary, or the saints

**Holy Orders** (p. 213)
the sacrament in which men are ordained to serve the Church as deacons, priests, and bishops

**hope** (p. 189)
the virtue that enables us to trust in God's promise to share his life with us forever; it makes us confident in God's love and care for us

**Immaculate Conception** (p. 165)
the belief that Mary was free from original sin from the moment she was conceived

**Incarnation** (p. 45)
the truth that the Son of God became man

**Introductory Rites** (p. 100)
the part of the Mass that unites us as a community. It prepares us to hear God's word and to celebrate the Eucharist

**Jesus' mission** (p. 22)
to share the life of God with all people and to save them from sin

**Kingdom of God** (p. 22)
the power of God's love active in our lives and in the world

**last judgment** (p. 30)
Jesus Christ coming at the end of time to judge all people

**laypeople** (p. 197)
all the baptized members of the Church who share in the mission to bring the good news of Christ to the world

**liturgy** (p. 29)
the official public prayer of the Church

**Liturgy of the Eucharist** (p. 102)
the part of the Mass in which the death and Resurrection of Christ are made present again. Our gifts of bread and wine become the Body and Blood of Christ, which we receive in Holy Communion

**Liturgy of the Hours** (p. 109)
public prayer of the Church made up of psalms, readings from Scripture and Church teaching, prayers and hymns, and celebrated at various times during the day

**Liturgy of the Word** (p. 101)
the part of the Mass in which we listen and respond to God's word; we profess our faith and pray for of all people in need

**love** (p. 190)
the greatest of all virtues that enables us to love God and to love our neighbor

**marks of the Church** (p. 220)
the four characteristics of the Church: one, holy, catholic, and apostolic

**marriage covenant** (p. 205)
the life-long commitment between a man and a woman to live as faithful and loving partners

**Matrimony** (p. 204)
the sacrament in which a man and woman become husband and wife and promise to be faithful to each other for the rest of their lives

**Paschal Mystery** (p. 30)
Christ's passion, death, Resurrection from the dead, and Ascension into heaven

**Passover** (p. 92)
the feast on which Jewish people remember the miraculous way that God saved them from death and slavery in ancient Egypt

**priesthood of the faithful** (p. 196)
Christ's priestly mission in which all those who are baptized share

**priests** (p. 213)
ordained ministers who serve the Christian faithful by leading, teaching, and most especially celebrating the Eucharist and other sacraments

**prophet** (p. 46)
someone who speaks on behalf of God, defends the truth, and works for justice

**real presence** (p. 94)
Jesus really and truly present in the Eucharist

**Reconciliation** (p. 134)
the sacrament by which our relationship with God and the Church is strengthened or restored and our sins are forgiven

**religious** (p. 198)
women and men who belong to communities of service to God and the Church

**sacrament** (p. 36)
an effective sign given to us by Jesus through which we share in God's life

**sacramentals** (p. 110)
blessings, actions, and objects that help us respond to God's grace received in the sacraments

**sacrifice** (p. 93)
a gift offered to God by a priest in the name of all the people

**saints** (p. 47)
followers of Christ who lived lives of holiness on earth and now share in eternal life with God in heaven

**salvation** (p. 45)
the forgiveness of sins and the restoring of friendship with God

**sanctifying grace** (p. 36)
the gift of sharing in God's life that we receive in the sacraments

**sin** (p. 134)
a thought, word, deed, or omission against God's law

**Spiritual Works of Mercy** (p. 31)
acts of love that help us care for the needs of people's hearts, minds, and souls

**stewards of creation** (p. 223)
those who take care of everything that God has given them

**virtue** (p. 188)
a good habit that helps us to act according to God's love for us

# Index

The following is a list of topics that appear in the pupil's text.
**Boldface** indicates an entire chapter or section.